Series Editors:
Alan G. Kamhi, Ph.D.
Rebecca J. McCauley, Ph.D.

Communication and Language Intervention Series

Case Studies for the
Treatment of Autism Spectrum Disorder

Communication
and Language
Intervention
Series

Case Studies
for the Treatment
of Autism Spectrum Disorder

edited by

Patricia A. Prelock, Ph.D.
Provost and Senior Vice President
Department of Communication Sciences and Disorders
University of Vermont
Burlington

and

Rebecca J. McCauley, Ph.D.
Professor
Department of Speech and Hearing Science
The Ohio State University
Columbus

·P A U L·H·
BROOKES
PUBLISHING Co.®

Baltimore • London • Sydney

Paul H. Brookes Publishing Co.
Post Office Box 10624
Baltimore, Maryland 21285-0624
USA

www.brookespublishing.com

Typeset by Progressive Publishing Service, York, Pennsylvania.
Manufactured in the United States of America by Sheridan Books, Inc., Chelsea, Michigan.

The individuals described in this book are composites or real people whose situations are masked and are based on the authors' experiences. In all instances, names and identifying details have been changed to protect confidentiality.

Library of Congress Cataloging-in-Publication Data

Names: Prelock, Patricia A., editor. | McCauley, Rebecca Joan,
   1952– editor.
Title: Case studies for the treatment of autism spectrum disorder / edited by Patricia
   A. Prelock, Ph.D., Provost and Senior Vice President, Department of
   Communication Sciences and Disorders, University of Vermont, Burlington
   and Rebecca J. McCauley, Ph.D., Professor, Department of Speech and
   Hearing Science, The Ohio State University, Columbus.
Description: Baltimore : Paul H. Brookes Publishing Co., [2021] | Series:
   Communication and language intervention series | Includes
   bibliographical references and index.
Identifiers: LCCN 2020056443 (print) | LCCN 2020056444 (ebook) |
   ISBN 9781681253961 (paperback) | ISBN 9781681254159 (epub) |
   ISBN 9781681254166 (pdf)
Subjects: LCSH: Autism spectrum disorders—Case studies.
Classification: LCC RC553.A88 C3775 2021 (print) | LCC RC553.A88 (ebook) |
   DDC 616.85/882—dc23
LC record available at https://lccn.loc.gov/2020056443
LC ebook record available at https://lccn.loc.gov/2020056444

British Library Cataloguing in Publication data are available from the British Library.

2025   2024   2023   2022   2021

   10   9   8   7   6   5   4   3   2   1

Contents

Series Preface

The purpose of the *Communication and Language Intervention Series* is to provide meaningful foundations for the application of sound intervention designs to enhance the development of communication skills across the life span. We are endeavoring to achieve this purpose by providing readers with presentations of state-of-the-art theory, research, and practice.

In selecting topics, editors, and authors, we are not attempting to limit the contents of this series to viewpoints with which we agree or that we find most promising. We are assisted in our efforts to develop the series by an editorial advisory board consisting of prominent scholars representative of the range of issues and perspectives to be incorporated in the series.

Well-conceived theory and research on development and intervention are vitally important for researchers, educators, and clinicians committed to the development of optimal approaches to communication and language intervention. The content of each volume reflects our view of the symbiotic relationship between intervention and research: Demonstrations of what may work in intervention should lead to analysis of promising discoveries and insights from developmental work that may in turn fuel further refinement by intervention researchers. We trust that the careful reader will find much that is of great value in this volume.

An inherent goal of this series is to enhance the long-term development of the field by systematically furthering the dissemination of theoretically and empirically based scholarship and research. We promise the reader an opportunity to participate in the development of this field through debates and discussions that occur throughout the pages of the *Communication and Language Intervention Series*.

Editorial Advisory Board

About the Editors

Patricia A. Prelock, Ph.D., Provost and Senior Vice-President, University of Vermont, Burlington

Dr. Prelock is Provost and Senior Vice-President, University of Vermont. Formerly, she was the dean of the College of Nursing and Health Sciences at the University of Vermont for 10 years. She is also a professor of communication sciences and disorders and professor of pediatrics in the College of Medicine at the University of Vermont. Dr. Prelock has been awarded more than $11.9 million in university, state, and federal funding as a principal investigator (PI) or co-PI to develop innovations in interdisciplinary training supporting children and youth with neurodevelopmental disabilities and their families, to facilitate training in speech-language pathology, and to support her intervention work in ASD. She has more than 195 publications and 566 peer-reviewed and invited presentations/keynotes in the areas of autism and other neurodevelopmental disabilities, collaboration, interprofessional education, leadership, and language learning disabilities.

In 2019, she was named associate editor for the *Journal of Autism and Developmental Disorders*. Dr. Prelock received the University of Vermont's Kroepsch-Maurice Excellence in Teaching Award in 2000 and was named an ASHA Fellow in 2000 and a University of Vermont Scholar in 2003. In 2011, she was named the Cecil & Ida Green Honors Professor Visiting Scholar at Texas Christian University, and in 2015 Dr. Prelock was named a Distinguished Alumna of the University of Pittsburgh. In 2016, she received the ASHA Honors of the association, and in 2017, she was named a Distinguished Alumna of Cardinal Mooney High School. Dr. Prelock also received the 2018 Jackie M. Gribbons Leadership Award from Vermont Women in Higher Education. Dr. Prelock is a board-certified specialist in child language and was named a fellow in the National Academies of Practice (NAP) in speech-language pathology in 2018. She was the 2013 president for the American Speech-Language Hearing Association.

Rebecca J. McCauley, Ph.D., Professor, The Ohio State University, Columbus

Dr. McCauley is Professor in the Department of Speech and Hearing Sciences at the Ohio State University. Her research and writing have focused on assessment and treatment of pediatric communication disorders, with a special focus on speech sound disorders, including childhood apraxia of speech. She has authored or edited seven books on these topics and coauthored a test designed to aid in the differential diagnosis of childhood apraxia of speech. Dr. McCauley is a Fellow of the American Speech-Language-Hearing Association, has received honors of that association, and has served two terms as an associate editor of the *American Journal of Speech-Language Pathology.*

About the Contributors

Ashley R. Brien, CCC-SLP, Speech Language Pathologist and Doctoral Student, The University of Vermont, Burlington

Ashley R. Brien is a speech-language pathologist in Vermont. She is pursuing her doctorate in interprofessional health sciences at the University of Vermont under the mentorship of Dr. Tiffany Hutchins and Dr. Patricia Prelock. Her research focuses on episodic memory and its relationship to theory of mind. She is currently designing interventions and treatment materials to support episodic memory and social cognition in children with ASD.

Tom Buggey, Ph.D., Retired Siskin Chair of Excellence in Early Childhood Special Education, University of Tennessee at Chattanooga

Tom Buggey began research on self-modeling at Penn State in 1992, working with preschoolers with language delays. Following the urgings of two gifted graduate assistants, together they conducted their first research with children on the autism spectrum in 1995 with very positive results. Thereafter, children with autism became the focus of his research. Dr. Buggey was recruited to serve as the Siskin Chair of Excellence in the Special Education Department at UTC in 2007. The next 7 years were devoted to research on developing language and social skills with preschool-age children with autism. In his career as a researcher, he has conducted more than a dozen studies on the use of self-modeling, all which have appeared in major journals; published several book chapters of self-modeling and other aspects of early intervention; and published the only book on self-modeling, *Seeing is Believing* (Woodbine House, 2007), which is currently being translated and published in Russia.

Erik W. Carter, Ph.D., Cornelius Vanderbilt Professor of Special Education, Vanderbilt University, Nashville, Tennessee

Erik W. Carter is Cornelius Vanderbilt Professor of Special Education at Vanderbilt University. Dr. Carter's research and writing focus on promoting inclusion and valued roles in school, work, community, and congregational settings for children and adults with intellectual disability, autism, and multiple disabilities.

Geraldine Dawson, Ph.D., Professor of Psychiatry and Behavioral Sciences, Duke University School of Medicine, Durham, North Carolina

Geraldine Dawson is the William Cleland Professor of Psychiatry and Behavioral Sciences at Duke University, director of the Duke Institute for Brain Sciences, and director of the Duke Center for Autism and Brain Development. Dawson is a licensed, practicing clinical psychologist and internationally renowned scientist whose work has focused on early detection and treatment of autism and brain development.

V. Mark Durand, Ph.D., Professor of Psychology, University of South Florida St. Petersburg

Dr. Durand is known worldwide as an authority in the area of ASD. He is professor of psychology at the University of South Florida–St. Petersburg, where he was the founding dean of Arts and Sciences and vice chancellor for Academic Affairs. He has more than 145 publications and more than a dozen books, including *Optimistic Parenting: Hope and Help for You and Your Challenging Child* and, most recently, *Autism Spectrum Disorder: A Clinical Guide for General Practitioners.*

Elizabeth A. Fuller, Ph.D., Vanderbilt University, Nashville, Tennessee

Dr. Fuller specializes in early intervention and behavioral therapy for children with autism and developmental disabilities. She received her doctorate from Vanderbilt University in early childhood special education and is a Board-Certified Behavior Analyst (BCBA). She has over ten years of experience in play and behavior therapies and in coaching parents to implement effective strategies with their children.

Sima Gerber, Ph.D., Professor, Queens College, City University of New York

Sima Gerber, Ph.D., CCC, is a professor of speech-language pathology in the Department of Linguistics and Communication Disorders of Queens College, City University of New York. She has been a speech-language pathologist for more than 40 years, specializing in the treatment of children with ASD and other developmental challenges. Dr. Gerber has presented nationally and abroad (China, Italy, the Netherlands, South Africa, Israel, Georgia) on language acquisition and developmental approaches to assessment and intervention for children with language and communication disorders. Dr. Gerber is a Fellow of the American Speech-Language-Hearing Association.

Jodi K. Heidlage, Ph.D., BCBA, Project Director, Vanderbilt University, Nashville, Tennessee

Jodi K. Heidlage is a special educator with expertise in behavioral and naturalistic interventions for children with autism and significant learning challenges. She has more than 10 years of experience providing direct services for young children with ASD and has served as a therapist and parent interventionist on several clinical trials. She currently is the project director for an early reading intervention for children with intellectual and developmental disabilities at Vanderbilt University.

Jill Howard, Ph.D., Assistant Professor, Licensed Psychologist, Duke University School of Medicine, Durham, North Carolina

Dr. Jill Howard is a licensed psychologist and assistant professor at the Duke Center for Autism and Brain Development in the Department of Psychiatry and Behavioral Sciences. She specializes in conducting comprehensive diagnostic assessments and delivering intervention services to individuals and families affected by ASD. Dr. Howard's primary research interests involve the early identification of and evidence-based treatments for ASD, as well as the development of social attention and behavior. Dr. Howard is certified as an Early Start Denver Model therapist and trainer.

Tiffany L. Hutchins, Ph.D., Associate Professor, University of Vermont, Burlington

Dr. Hutchins conducts research in social cognition and language development in autism, attention-deficit/hyperactivity disorder, hearing loss, and childhood trauma. She also teaches courses in measurement, language disorders, and psycholinguistics. Dr. Hutchins is primary author of the Theory of Mind Inventory and the Theory of Mind Atlas.

Ann Kaiser, Ph.D., Susan W. Gray Professor of Education and Human Development, Department of Special Education, Peabody College, Vanderbilt University, Nashville, Tennessee

Ann P. Kaiser is the Susan W. Gray Professor of Education and Human Development at Vanderbilt University. She is the author of more than 175 articles on early intervention for children with autism and other development communication disabilities. Her research focuses on therapist- and parent-implemented naturalistic interventions.

Connie Kasari, Ph.D., Professor of Human Development and Psychiatry, University of California Los Angeles

Dr. Kasari received her Ph.D. from the University of North Carolina at Chapel Hill and was a National Institute of Mental Health postdoctoral fellow at the Neuropsychiatric

Institute at UCLA. Since 1990, she has been on the faculty at UCLA, where she teaches both graduate and undergraduate courses and has been the primary advisor to more than 60 doctoral students. She is a founding member of the Center for Autism Research and Treatment at UCLA. Her research aims to development novel, evidence-tested interventions implemented in community settings. Recent projects include targeted treatments for early social-communication development in at-risk infants, toddlers, and preschoolers with autism and peer relationships for school-age children with autism. She leads several large multisite studies, including a network on interventions for minimally verbal school-age children with ASD, and a network that aims to decrease disparities in interventions for children with ASD who are underrepresented in research trials. She is on the science advisory board of the Autism Speaks Foundation and regularly presents to both academic and practitioner audiences locally, nationally, and internationally.

Brittany Lynn Koegel, Ph.D., Researcher, Stanford University School of Medicine, California

Brittany Lynn Koegel received her doctorate in education from University of California, Santa Barbara. She currently works doing research in Autism at Stanford University in the area of Pivotal Response Treatment. She also conducts Pivotal Response Treatment training all over the world.

Lynn Kern Koegel, Ph.D., CCC-SLP, Clinical Professor, Stanford University School of Medicine, California

Dr. Lynn Kern Koegel and her husband developed Pivotal Response Treatment, an intervention used worldwide for the treatment of ASD. She has published well over 100 articles and chapters, field manuals, and eight books, including *Overcoming Autism* and *Growing Up on the Spectrum* with parent Claire LaZebnik, published by Viking/Penguin and available in most bookstores. The Koegels have received many awards, including the first annual Children's Television Workshop Sesame Street Award for Brightening the Lives of Children, the first annual Autism Speaks award for Science and Research, and the International ABA award for enduring programmatic contributions in behavior analysis. Dr. Lynn Koegel has appeared on numerous television and radio shows discussing autism, including the Discovery Channel, and ABC's hit show *Supernanny*, working with a child with autism. The Koegels' work has also been showcased on ABC, CBS, NBC, and PBS, and they are the recipients of many state, federal, and private foundation gifts and grants for developing interventions and helping families with ASD.

Amy C. Laurent, Ph.D., OTR/L, Developmental Psychologist, Educational Consultant, Pediatric Occupational Therapist, Autism Level UP!, North Kingston, Rhode Island

Dr. Laurent specializes in the education of autistic children. Her work involves creating learning environments designed to facilitate children's active engagement at home, in schools, and throughout their communities. She is a coauthor of The SCERTS Model and frequently lectures around the globe. She is passionate about neurodiversity and helping others to honor and understand the implications of "different ways of being" in relation to navigating the physical and social world.

Stephanie Meehan, Ph.D., Clinical Assistant Professor, Schiefelbusch Speech-Language-Hearing Clinic, University of Kansas

Dr. Meehan is a clinical assistant professor at the University of Kansas. She currently leads a team of clinical practicum students, which serves clients in a local school district as well as in the Schiefelbusch Speech-Language-Hearing Clinic. She teaches the Introduction to AAC class to speech-language pathology master's students. Her primary professional interests include improving the preservice education and training in the area of augmentative and alternative communication and issues of diversity, equity, and inclusion in the field of speech-language pathology.

Lauren J. Moskowitz, Ph.D., Assistant Professor, St. John's University, Queens, New York

Lauren Moskowitz is an associate professor in the Department of Psychology at St. John's University. She earned her bachelor of science degree from Cornell University, her master's and doctorate in clinical psychology from Stony Brook University, and completed her clinical internship and postdoctoral fellowship at NYU Child Study Center. Her research focuses on behavioral assessment and intervention for problem behavior and anxiety in children with ASD and developmental disabilities, Dr. Moskowitz has coauthored several papers and book chapters; has presented at numerous international, national, and regional conferences; has taught several undergraduate and graduate courses covering ASD and developmental disabilities, applied behavior analysis, and positive behavior support, and has been on the editorial board for the *Journal of Positive Behavior Interventions* since 2013.

Elizabeth Ponder, M.A., BCBA, Clinical Supervisor, PRT Trainer, Stanford Autism Center, California

Elizabeth began her training in Pivotal Response Treatment (PRT) as a research assistant at the Koegel Autism Center while completing her bachelor of arts in psychology at the University of California, Santa Barbara. After graduating, Elizabeth expanded her knowledge and skills pertaining to ASD and PRT by working as an interventionist. In 2009, she entered the Special Education, Disabilities and Developmental Risk Studies (SPEDDR) graduate program at the University of California, Santa Barbara, with Dr. Robert Koegel as her advisor. After receiving her master's degree in 2011, she went on to become a board-certified behavior analyst (BCBA) and has continued her work with individuals on the spectrum, with a focus on parent and professional education and training.

Barry M. Prizant, Ph.D., CCC-SLP, Adjunct Professor, Brown University, Director, Childhood Communication Services, Providence, Rhode Island

Dr. Barry Prizant has 45 years' experience as a speech-language pathologist, author, researcher, and international consultant. He is an adjunct professor at Brown University and director at Childhood Communication Services, a private practice. Barry is a codeveloper of The SCERTS Model, an educational framework now being implemented in more than a dozen countries. His recent book is *Uniquely Human: A Different Way of Seeing Autism* (Simon & Schuster, 2015), which has received the Autism Society of America's Dr. Temple Grandin Award for the Outstanding Literary work in autism and is published in 16 languages.

Kathleen D. Ross, M.S., CCC-SLP, Director of University of Vermont's Speech-Language Pathology Assistant & CSD Prerequisites Programs; Lecturer; Advisor

Kathleen D. Ross, M.S., CCC-SLP, directs the University of Vermont's online speech-language pathology assistant (SLPA) program and the Communication Sciences and Disorders (CSD) prerequisite program along with being lecturer and advisor. A 35-year veteran speech-language pathologist, Kathleen specializes in early intervention (EI) and early childhood special education (ECSE). Since 1990, she manages her private practice, providing services, including telepractice throughout Vermont. Kathleen authored the text *Speech-Language Pathologists in Early Childhood Intervention* (Plural Publishing, 2018). She was a member of the writing team for Vermont's Early Learning Guidelines (2015), has written weekly education articles for local newspapers, and has published in the educational market, including with Redleaf Press, Gryphon House, and Edcon Publishers. She is a member of the Brain Injury Association of Vermont board of directors. She was involved in creating the American Speech-Language-Hearing Association's credentialing system for SLPAs, including developing a national examination to be launched in 2020. Kathleen is a member of the advisory board for the Interprofessional Education program, collaborating coursework for CSD and EI/ECSE students.

Emily Rubin, M.S., CCC-SLP, Director, Educational Outreach Program, Marcus Autism Center, Atlanta, Georgia

Emily Rubin, MS, CCC-SLP is the director of the Educational Outreach Program at the Marcus Autism Center in Atlanta, Georgia. She is a speech-language pathologist specializing in autism, Asperger syndrome, and social-emotional learning. She is a coauthor of The SCERTS Model, a criterion-referenced assessment tool and educational framework for social communication and emotional regulation. Her current work is focused on building the capacity of public-school systems to embed interpersonal and learning supports that benefit all students and young children.

Kyle Sterrett, M.A., Doctoral Candidate, University of California Los Angeles

Kyle's research interest lies in the optimization of evidence-based interventions through the understanding of their active ingredients using quantitative methods— for example, understanding of the role of speech-generating devices within efficacious interventions for language learners with autism. He has been involved as a clinician in a number of recent intervention trials, implementing interventions for children with autism and developmental delays within schools and in home settings through parent training in the JASPER intervention model.

Kristen Strong, Ph.D., Psychologist, Acacia Counseling and Wellness, Isla Vista, California

Dr. Strong is a clinical psychologist and received her doctoral degree from the University of California at Santa Barbara. She worked with Drs. Robert and Lynn Koegel and has significant experience working with individuals with ASD across the life span.

Shawnna Sundberg, M.A., Ball State University, Muncie, Indiana

Shawnna received a bachelor of arts degree in psychology from Purdue University in 2008, and a master's degree in special education with certifications in applied behavior analysis (ABA) and autism from Ball State University in 2015. Shawnna is a board-certified behavior analyst (BCBA) with more than 10 years of experience working in the mental health and ABA/verbal behavior (VB) field. Shawnna has worked as a child and adolescent home-based case manager, ABA/VB therapist, training specialist, parent-training coordinator, and behavior consultant.

Jane R. Wegner, Ph.D., Clinical Professor, Clinic Director, Schiefelbusch Speech-Language-Hearing Clinic, University of Kansas, Lawrence

Dr. Wegner is a clinical professor and director of the Schiefelbusch Speech-Language-Hearing Clinic at the University of Kansas (KU). She directs the Pardee Augmentative and Alternative Communication Resource and Research Laboratory on the Lawrence campus of KU. Dr. Wegner directed numerous personnel preparation projects funded by the U.S. Department of Education, Office of Special Education Programs, including the Communication, Autism, and Technology Project and the Augmentative Communication in the Schools Project. She has authored numerous articles and book chapters on Augmentative and Alternative Communication. Dr. Wegner is a Fellow of the American Speech-Language-Hearing Association and served on the ASHA Ad Hoc Committee on Autism Spectrum Disorders that developed the ASHA policy documents for practice with people with ASD.

Susan M. Wilczynski, Ph.D., BCBA-D, Professor, Ball State University, Muncie, Indiana

Dr. Wilczynski is the Plassman Family Distinguished Professor of Special Education and Applied Behavior Analysis and the former executive director of the National Autism Center. Dr. Wilczynski has edited or written multiple books and published scholarly works in *Behavior Analysis in Practice, Journal of Applied Behavior Analysis, Behavior Modification, Focus on Autism and Other Developmental Disabilities*, and *Psychology in the Schools*. Dr. Wilczynski is a licensed psychologist and a board-certified behavior analyst.

Acknowledgments

First, we wish to express great appreciation to the many students who have taught us that learning situated in the contexts of practical problem solving is both more enjoyable and more effective. Second, we thank our colleagues at Paul H. Brookes Publishing Company, who proposed the separate casebook as a way of extending the more limited case examples included in the first edition. Third and finally, we are indebted to the authors and the families and individuals with whom they have worked for sharing the vivid textures and tones affecting those who live with ASD.

Introduction

This casebook is a companion piece to *Treatment of Autism Spectrum Disorder: Evidence-Based Intervention Strategies for Communication & Social Interactions, Second Edition*. Thirteen case studies are provided, each aligning to at least one of the treatment chapters in the Prelock and McCauley text. Case studies play a critical role in clinical practice and richly demonstrate the critical thinking and problem solving that occurs when individual clinicians work to solve problems. In this text, we offer case studies prepared by clinical experts who share their experience and systematic approaches to assessing the needs of individual children with autism spectrum disorder (ASD) in order to determine the most appropriate approach to intervention to open up the widening possibilities associated with effective treatment. Each child with ASD who is described in the book may be based on a real individual, but with steps taken to mask their identities and those of their family members, or on a hypothetical individual based on a compilation of the authors' past experience.

DESCRIPTION OF THE CASE STUDY CHAPTERS

Each chapter is comprised of several components to develop the case study: 1) identification of the child's most significant needs, 2) assessment for communication treatment planning, 3) clinical problem solving to identify treatment goals and strategies, 4) interventions used to achieve major goals, and 5) a report on outcomes. The chapters include relevant references as well as learning activities to foster application of student learning. A brief description of the components included in each chapter is provided in the following sections.

Identification of Significant Needs

The authors introduce the child with ASD and identify the child's most significant areas of need. Birth and development history across developmental domains are described. The authors outline the child's baseline status related to communication and social skills as well as the family and community context. Specifically, a brief description of the major ways in which the child communicates, including strengths and weaknesses and opportunities for social engagement, are presented. Because the child is part of a larger family and community context, each case study features a genogram, which is a tangible, graphic representation of the family structure (Goldrick & Gerson, 1985; Prelock et al., 2003; Prelock et al., 1999). An ecomap provides a picture of the child with ASD and his or her family, identifying their professional, community, and personal supports and the energy flow among and between agencies and programs and the family (Goodluck, 1990; Prelock et al., 1999; Prelock et al., 2003).

The case studies also provide a broader profile for each child—reviewing his or her behavioral, sensory, and medical needs. Major complicating issues for the child, either related to the ASD diagnosis or to unrelated sources of challenge, are described. This section of the chapters ends with a summary of the most significant needs as perceived by the family and the child's community using the *International classification of functioning, disability and health* (ICF; World Health Organization [WHO], 2001) or the *International classification of functioning, disability and health: Children and youth version* (ICF-CY; WHO, 2007) framework, including impairments, activities, and participation.

Assessments for Communication Treatment Planning

Authors identify their approach to assessing communication challenges in several areas relevant to the particular child. Articulation, fluency, voice and resonance, receptive and expressive language, hearing, swallowing, cognitive communication (i.e., attention, memory, sequencing, problem solving, executive functioning), social aspects of communication (i.e., challenging behavior, ineffective social skills, lack of communication opportunities), and communication modalities (including oral, manual, augmentative and alternative communication techniques, and assistive technologies) are considered.

Clinical Problem Solving to Identify Treatment Goals and Strategies

A brief description of the principles the clinicians used to guide their intervention decision making is explained in this section. The authors highlight those treatment rationales and values (e.g., family centered, participant focused) and procedures (e.g., interdisciplinary team meetings, data gathering from significant communication partners) used to arrive at the treatment plan. Both opportunities and constraints in developing and implementing the plan are discussed, including modifications that may be necessary on the basis of availability of programs, facilities, and the child's overall health or family areas of challenge.

Interventions Used to Achieve Major Goals

A plan for supporting the child's overall functioning in the community, including management of the child's health, education, and communication, is outlined for each case. At least one, and sometimes multiple, communication-related interventions described in *Treatment of Autism Spectrum Disorder: Evidence-Based Intervention Strategies for Communication and Social Interactions, Second Edition* are described as the selected interventions to achieve the primary goals for each case. Any modifications to the interventions incorporated are described as relevant to the child's individual circumstances.

Outcomes

Following the description of the interventions, each chapter outlines progress the child and family have made toward meeting the primary goal established to facilitate communication. Other changes in challenging behaviors as well as developments in nontargeted areas (e.g., those managed principally by other professionals, those that were not included in major communication-related goals) are also highlighted.

Learning Activities

To support readers' application of knowledge regarding interventions designed to facilitate communication, three to five learning activities are provided at the end of each chapter. The learning activities range from proposing alternatives for examining the child's social-communication difficulties to identifying what aspect of a particular treatment might be applied to a different child with ASD. Authors have been quite creative in providing a range of activities that will challenge readers to integrate all that they have learned from *Treatment of Autism Spectrum Disorder* to a real case scenario.

SUMMARY

This book is intended to point out not just the challenges associated with ASD but the possibilities for brighter outcomes that can result from effective intervention that is planned using evidence-based practice. In particular, we hope that you will find these case study chapters helpful to you in gaining perspective on how other expert clinicians have applied their knowledge and skills to problem-solve solutions for children with ASD and their families. The case studies you will review in this casebook provide a detailed report of the characteristics, assessment, treatment, and outcomes for children with ASD who have been experienced one or more of the interventions described in *Treatment of Autism Spectrum Disorder: Evidence-Based Intervention Strategies for Communication and Social Interactions, Second Edition.*

REFERENCES

Goldrick, M., & Gerson, B. (1985). *Genograms in family assessment.* W.W. Norton.

Goodluck, C. (1990). *Utilization of genograms and ecomaps to assess American Indian families who have a member with a disability: Making visible the invisible.* Northern Arizona University.

Prelock, P. A., Beatson, J., Bitner, B., Broder, C., & Ducker, A. (2003). Interdisciplinary assessment for young children with Autism Spectrum Disorders. *Language, Speech and Hearing Services in Schools, 34*, 194–202.

Prelock, P. A., Beatson, J., Contompasis, S., & Bishop, K. K. (1999). A model for family-centered interdisciplinary practice. *Topics in Language Disorders, 19*, 36–51.

Prelock, P. A., & McCauley, R. J. (Eds.). (2021). *Treatment of autism spectrum disorder: Evidence-based intervention strategies for communication and social interaction* (2nd ed.). Paul H. Brookes Publishing Co.

World Health Organization. (2001). *International classification of functioning, disability and health.* Author.

World Health Organization. (2007). *International classification of functioning, disability and health: Children and youth version.* Author.

Finding a Voice

An Elementary Schooler With Autism Spectrum Disorder (ASD) and Down Syndrome

Stephanie Meehan and Jane R. Wegner

 Gideon

 Age 10

 Autism Spectrum Disorder and Down Syndrome

Case 1 engages with the intervention approach and strategies discussed in Chapter 4, Augmentative and Alternative Communication Strategies (Wegner, 2021) in *Treatment of Autism Spectrum Disorder, Second Edition.*

INTRODUCTION

Gideon is a 10-year-old boy with autism spectrum disorder (ASD) and Down syndrome who attends his local elementary school.

History

Gideon's mother reports that she had an unremarkable pregnancy and delivery. He was diagnosed with Down syndrome at birth. Gideon met several developmental milestones, including reaching for objects, independently holding his head up, and sitting unsupported. He first stood independently at age 3, walked unassisted at age 4, and ran at age 5. As he grew, Gideon had recurring ear infections, seasonal allergies, and influenza. Gideon had pressure equalization tubes placed at age 5 to manage recurrent ear infections. Gideon's verbal language development was delayed; he spoke his first word at 14 months. Between 12 and 16 months, Gideon quickly learned to communicate using American Sign Language and knew approximately 40 signs, but there was a significant regression in that skill around the age of 3. It was around this time that Gideon received the diagnosis of ASD.

Baseline Status

Gideon's baseline status includes his communication profile, social profile, and family and community context. Baseline status is an assessment of skills before intervention is implemented. Collecting baseline is critical to both identify the necessary features of a potential augmentative and alternative communication (AAC) device but also to develop appropriate goals. The speech-language pathologist (SLP) is interested in evaluating his expressive and receptive language skills; his cognitive skills specifically related to attention and memory; his fine and gross motor skills relevant to accessing an AAC device; any early literacy skills; and any sensory needs, specifically auditory and visual needs, that would impact his use of an AAC device. The SLP wants to find out more information about Gideon's communication partners and the environments where he spends most of his time.

Communication Profile   Gideon communicates with a few approximated signs, largely for his highly preferred items like DRINK with changes in the position and rate of the sign to indicate emphasis. He uses some vocalizations but largely communicates through bringing desired objects to his mother. Gideon sometimes expresses frustration through pushing objects or people away or escaping the situation as a result of his inability to communicate. He uses an Accent 1000 AAC device with the LAMP Words for Life user area. Gideon, now age 10, has been learning to communicate with his device since the age of 5. He most frequently communicates with his parents, peers at school, and his university clinic–based SLP. Before receiving his AAC device, Gideon and his mother used a no-tech communication book with pictures of some of his preferred items in it. Gideon was able to use the book to make choices but frequently did not choose to do so.

Social Profile   Gideon attends a local elementary school where he is included in the general education classroom with his peers. He is supported by a paraeducator the entire day. Gideon's peers are fond of him and eager to help and interact with him. It does not appear, however, that Gideon spends any time with his peers outside of the school day. Gideon most commonly interacts with his mother. They like to watch Barney videos together. Gideon enjoys his mother's singing and dancing along with the songs. Gideon claps his hands and vocalizes when they watch these videos. Gideon raises his hands as a request to clap or dance. He sometimes lightly pats his communication partner to indicate that he is having a good time. He pushes his communication partner to indicate the direction he wants him or her to move. Gideon demonstrates few other interests outside of Barney and home movies of himself.

He demonstrates interest in adults and peers by smiling and laughing at them. Gideon also waves hello and good-bye. He initiates with unfamiliar people in his environment by waving or touching and hugging them. Gideon tends to do so indiscriminately and will approach people he does not know at all. He typically terminates interactions in an unexpected way, that is, by walking away from the person.

Family and Community Context   Gideon lives at home with his mother and father. He also has a significantly older half-brother whom he interacts with sporadically. Gideon's maternal and paternal grandparents live out of state and do not visit. Gideon attends his local elementary school and is included in the general education classroom but receives special education services all day. He receives speech-language therapy, occupational therapy, physical therapy, and music therapy. The school team is supporting the goal of his using the AAC device to spontaneously express core vocabulary words in a variety of settings throughout the day. The team is also working on greeting.

Gideon occasionally swims at the local indoor pool with his mother. He is supported through the local university speech-language-hearing clinic where he receives an hour-long intervention session once per week. See the ecomap in Figure 1.1 and genogram in Figure 1.2. The ecomap and genogram demonstrate a small familial support system, which is somewhat influenced by geographical distance. Gideon's mother is a strong advocate for her son and has access to a variety of resources, as depicted by the good relationships between her and Gideon's medical team. The strained relationship between Gideon's family and the school is significant and primarily driven by a value mismatch regarding the vision for Gideon.

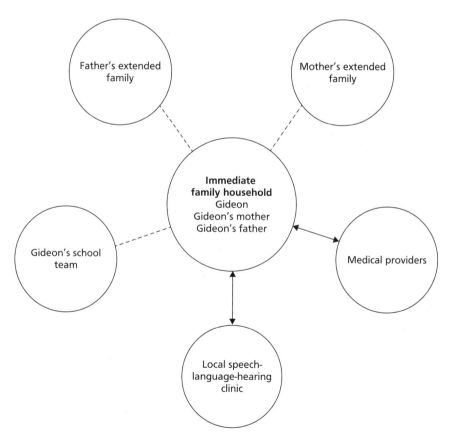

Figure 1.1.   Gideon's ecomap.

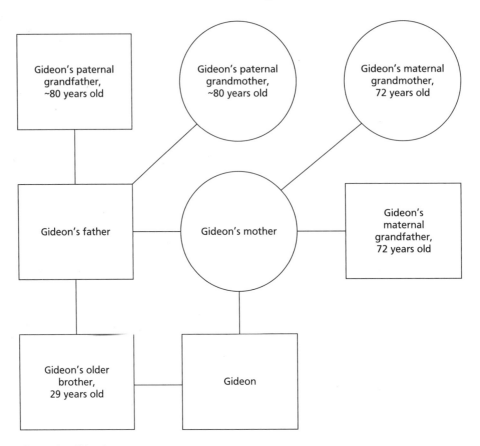

Figure 1.2. Gideon's genogram.

Broader Profile

Gideon presents with the dual diagnoses of Down syndrome and autism. Dual diagnoses complicate the process of identifying needs and treatment targets. It is not always clear what is driving how Gideon interacts with his environment. Down syndrome and autism have some overlapping characteristics, but others are more divergent. For example, children with Down syndrome are often characterized as very social, whereas children with autism may be described as less interested in social connection. In addition, Gideon demonstrates needs in his fine and gross motor skills. He easily catches colds and other infections and is heat intolerant.

Summary of Most Significant Needs

Gideon's most significant needs are related to his communication. He is unable to communicate urgent medical needs. He is often sick with the common cold, sinus infections, and so forth, and is unable to tell his mother when he feels ill. He has significant acid reflux for which he takes medication but is unable to report if the medicine is helping. In addition, he is unable to tell his communication partners that he has to go to the bathroom, which can cause accidents and an increased reliance on his care providers. Gideon's inability to communicate in meaningful ways inhibits his relationships with his peers, which, as he grows, could lead to social isolation and a reduced quality of life. In addition, Gideon can be expected to have a significantly more difficult time developing literacy skills because of his communication needs. Without intervention, his complex communication needs may impact his ability to achieve equal opportunity, self-determination, full participation, independent living, and economic self-sufficiency.

ASSESSMENTS FOR COMMUNICATION TREATMENT PLANNING

Shortly after the family moved to the area when Gideon was 6 years old, his mother requested an AAC assessment. Gideon had little functional verbal communication, and so an articulation assessment was not determined to be useful. The SLP also felt that, because of Gideon's complex communication needs and diagnoses, a standard language assessment would not be valid. Additionally, receptive and expressive language would be assessed throughout the AAC assessment.

The AAC assessment process is team based and should include all relevant stakeholders. Gideon's AAC assessment was planned on the basis of the Participation Model (Beukelman & Mirenda, 2013). The model outlines a systematic process for conducting an AAC assessment. The model also bases the intervention plan on the participation requirements of same-age peers who do not have disabilities. The Participation Model begins by identifying barriers to participation related to opportunity and access. Opportunity barriers are those that are external to the person with the disability and cannot be overcome by the person who has received the AAC device. Access barriers are related to the current capacity of the individual. During the AAC assessment, the SLP attempts to develop a profile that can be matched to specific features of various AAC systems, a strategy called *feature-matching* (Costello & Shane, 1994). To develop the profile, the clinician needs to examine four areas of potential constraints and capabilities: motor skills, cognitive/linguistic skills, literacy skills, and sensory/perceptual skills.

During the AAC assessment, Gideon was presented with several different toys and activities, including blowing bubbles, rolling a ball back and forth, crawling in and out of a toy bus, and watching Barney videos or home movies of himself. When Gideon's mother left the assessment room, Gideon waved good-bye to his mother and gave the clinician a hug.

Despite some fine motor concerns related to feeding and dressing, Gideon's mother reported that he was able to independently navigate a tablet to view videos on YouTube by using an isolated point, so there were few concerns about Gideon's ability to access the device through direct selection; as such, the team did not consider switch access and eye gaze. The SLP used the Exploration Wizard on Prentke-Romich's Accent device to identify the appropriate grid and symbol size for Gideon. Gideon was able to isolate his pointer finger to activate the buttons on the device and was able to activate the symbol up to a field of 45 buttons on a 10-inch screen.

The purpose of a cognitive/communication assessment relative to AAC is to evaluate how someone makes sense of their world and how best to support communication within this understanding (Beukelman & Mirenda, 2013). The areas of cognitive/communication development that are related to AAC include awareness, communicative intent, world knowledge, memory, symbolic representation, and metacognition. The SLP assessed Gideon's cognitive skills informally throughout the assessment process. Gideon demonstrated adequate awareness and communicative intent skills when he smiled and laughed at his SLP in response to a funny moment in a video and when he lifted his hands to clap with the SLP. Gideon made frequent eye contact with the SLP and his mother during the evaluation. He laughed and smiled at them. Gideon used a triadic eye gaze and demonstrated joint attention. Gideon presented adequate memory by remembering where specific vocabulary words were on the devices. He clearly demonstrated his world knowledge and symbolic representation during a choice-making activity when searching for a picture of Barney in a no-tech communication notebook. There were several pictures of Barney in the notebook, but Gideon searched out the specific picture that represented the video he was requesting.

At the time of evaluation, Gideon presented with highly limited expressive language aside from two to three signs, which he used to make requests for highly preferred items, like JUICE and to request MORE. He laughed and smiled to express enjoyment, waved hello and goodbye.

Gideon's mother reported that Gideon understood more than he was able to express. She also noted that Gideon retrieved objects when asked to do so, for example, his preferred toys, his tablet, or his shoes and coat. Throughout the assessment Gideon demonstrated the following receptive language skills: he attended when spoken to, recognized his name, understood one- to two-part directions, and understood simple questions.

Gideon wears glasses to correct a fairly mild/moderate vision impairment. He kept his glasses on for the length of the assessment. Gideon did not present with a hearing loss, and his mother reported no concerns about his hearing. He passed a hearing test when he was 6 years old. He responded to both the SLP's voice and the synthesized voice of the AAC device at conversational loudness.

Gideon's mother reported that he had been exposed to the Picture Exchange Communication System (PECS) and had some experience with a low-tech AAC device. Three different devices were trialed during the evaluation: the Accent 800 by the Prentke-Romich Company with Unity software, the Tobii Dynavox Maestro, and the Tobii Dynavox T10. His expressive language was assessed through observation throughout the AAC assessment and through family report. Gideon was able to learn to use the words MORE and GO on the AAC devices during the assessment and used each word a few times to communicate with the clinician.

After the assessment was finished, the team decided on the Accent device with LAMP Words for Life. This device and language system was chosen primarily because Gideon's language was still developing. The Accent device and language systems are generative and supportive of novel utterance generation. The features of LAMP Words for Life were also well matched to Gideon's needs. Unique and consistent motor planning is a primary feature of the LAMP Words for Life system (Prentke-Romich Company), and the Center for AAC and Autism (n.d.) reports that vocabulary words are learned "by repeating the consistent motor movement rather than reading a word or interpreting a picture," which enables the person using the device to communicate quickly and efficiently. The motor planning helped Gideon remember where the words were, and the simple navigation of three button hits or fewer to any given vocabulary word would help reduce Gideon's frustration and decrease his cognitive burden as he was learning language. The Accent with LAMP Words for Life also made sense to Gideon's mother, who would be the primary communication partner.

CLINICAL PROBLEM SOLVING TO IDENTIFY TREATMENT GOALS

The outcome of treatment identified in a family-centered process was that Gideon's mother wanted him to make choices and develop friendships. To achieve these outcomes, three goals were identified. The following goals were to be addressed during

1-hour individual intervention sessions at the local university clinic where Gideon's AAC assessment occurred:

1. By the end of the semester, Gideon will independently use the core vocabulary words YES, NO, STOP, HELP, LOOK, WANT, GO, I, LIKE, and LOVE within a meaningful context using his AAC device in 50% of opportunities during a 1-hour session at the clinic.

2. By the end of the semester, Gideon will use his device to independently produce utterances of two or more selections in length at least 10 times within a meaningful context during a 1-hour session at the clinic.

3. By the end of the semester, Gideon will use his device to independently communicate at least 10 total times across the semester for purposes other than requesting items/activities. The purposes may include choice making, commenting, requesting help, protesting, greetings/farewells, and so on.

Gideon's mother and the evaluator also agreed that providing training with Gideon's school team was important and vital to his success, so several training sessions were scheduled. The SLP met primarily with the paraeducators who would be supporting Gideon most frequently. The SLP and paraeducators met with and without Gideon present to practice and model appropriate teaching strategies (see description in next section) and work collaboratively to problem-solve through a variety of everyday scenarios at school. The SLP also met with Gideon's mother for an initial training session after Gideon's device was delivered and continued to support Gideon's mother as needed.

INTERVENTIONS USED TO ACHIEVE MAJOR GOALS

Gideon attends speech-language intervention once per week for 1 hour at a university speech-language-hearing clinic. His therapy follows a social-pragmatic developmental approach that centers on Gideon and his primary interests. His interests include Barney, singing, drinking juice, and watching videos of himself. Within this context, the following teaching strategies were used: aided language stimulation, expansion, verbal modeling, pause time, and prompting.

Aided Language Stimulation

Aided language stimulation (Sennott et al., 2016) is a teaching strategy in which the SLP verbalizes a word or utterance while simultaneously producing this utterance on Gideon's device. The SLP provides aided language stimulation consistently throughout each session and across activities. Aided language stimulation provides Gideon with exposure to verbal language and to the language system with which he is learning to communicate. This strategy supports Gideon's language comprehension and provides him with examples of how he can use his device to communicate for various purposes. During aided language stimulation, the communication partner does not need to model the verbal utterance verbatim; rather, the partner should communicate the intent of the message and include core vocabulary words. For example, if the SLP verbalizes, "Barney is dancing with them," he or she may simultaneously produce BARNEY IS DANCING on Gideon's device.

Expansion

Expansion (Binger et al., 2010; Bunce & Watkins, 1995) is a teaching strategy in which the SLP repeats Gideon's utterances while adding grammatical and semantic detail. The clinician can expand Gideon's utterances while using aided input. For example, if Gideon says JUICE, the SLP expands his utterance by saying, "I want juice." The SLP seeks to provide input slightly above Gideon's current language level while maintaining the intent of his production.

Verbal Modeling

Modeling (Bunce & Watkins, 1995) is a teaching strategy the SLP uses to demonstrate a target skill in order to provide an example prior to expecting Gideon to do so himself. The SLP uses modeling frequently when providing instruction on Gideon's AAC device. During modeling, the clinician provides an example of a communication skill, or the production of an utterance using the device, without additional verbal input. The SLP also uses modeling to demonstrate tasks and activities. The SLP models activity options before expecting Gideon to make a choice. For example, when presenting the activity option of coloring pictures of Barney, the SLP demonstrates the activity by briefly coloring to show Gideon what the activity choice would look like. The SLP uses modeling consistently across sessions, activities, and goals to encourage Gideon's use of his device.

Pause Time

Pause time (Kozleski, 1991; Mathis et al., 2011) is a teaching strategy in which the SLP provides time for Gideon to respond or complete a task. Pause time allows Gideon time to process, formulate a response, produce the utterance on his device, complete a desired task, or make a choice. The SLP should provide pause time consistently throughout each session and across activities. Pause time of approximately 15–20 seconds is beneficial for Gideon. However, the amount of pause time necessary may depend on the task. Pause time is an important way to encourage Gideon to use his device to communicate. Often, Gideon waits until the SLP provides a desired activity or item before indicating his interest or making any communication attempts. Pause time places just enough pressure on Gideon to encourage him to communicate independently.

Prompting

Prompting (MacDuff et al., 2001) is a teaching strategy in which the SLP encourages communication. Prompting may include verbal, visual, or physical cues. The SLP uses prompting consistently across sessions, activities, and goals to support Gideon in using his device to express himself and communicate for a variety of communication purposes. The SLP also uses prompting to support Gideon in expanding on his utterances. The SLP uses a least-to-most prompting hierarchy (Finke et al., 2017) with Gideon, which provides him with the necessary support while encouraging him to complete the task independently.

For example, the SLP might use a least-to-most prompting hierarchy to support Gideon in using his device to request juice. The prompting hierarchy would begin with an expectant pause. Gideon often produces a sign approximation for juice or reaches toward his cup. After this indication, the SLP should provide an expectant pause (looking at Gideon, waiting with raised eyebrows) to allow Gideon to use his device if he wants to. Next, the SLP provides an indirect verbal prompt (i.e., "You could tell me on here"). If Gideon does not use his device, the SLP provides an indirect nonverbal prompt by a gesture or by moving Gideon's device closer to him. If that is not successful, the SLP provides a direct verbal prompt (i.e., "I know you are signing juice, but you can tell me on here"). To end the prompting hierarchy, the SLP could opt to move to a yes/no question or model the utterance on his device. For example, the SLP could ask, "Do you want juice?" and continue the hierarchy by requesting a response (i.e., "Do you want juice? You could tell me yes or no"). If the prompting hierarchy proceeds to modeling, the SLP models a complete utterance while providing aided input, avoiding hand-over-hand support or forcing Gideon to produce the utterance. It should always be Gideon's choice to access his device. If Gideon is not interested in accessing his device, the SLP should simply model the utterance for him.

OUTCOMES

Gideon's progress on his three goals are reviewed in this section. His semester-long goals were described earlier under "Clinical Problem Solving to Identify Treatment Goals." They involved use of core vocabulary, independent production of utterances involving two or more selections, and independent use of his device for communicative functions other than requesting (e.g., commenting, choice making).

Goal 1: Core Vocabulary Use

Throughout the semester, Gideon made progress toward his first goal, utilizing some of the target core vocabulary words, including *no, yes, want,* and *I*. Over the course of the semester, he produced multiple-word utterances with increasing frequency. It is also important to note Gideon made several productions that did not include the target core vocabulary words, including words like *juice, need, song, like,* and *love*. He demonstrated increased use of his device throughout the semester. Gideon received instruction on this goal primarily through modeling, aided input, and prompting. The SLP provided language input during the activities that she and Gideon were participating in. For example, while watching Barney videos, the SLP paused the video in order to model *stop* and *go*. When the video was paused, it presented the opportunity for Gideon to make a request and the SLP to model the use of the word *want*.

Occasionally, when Gideon made a request using a one-word utterance, the SLP utilized yes/no questions in order to clarify what he wanted. For example, Gideon drank juice during his sessions; when Gideon said JUICE on his device, the SLP asked, "Do you want more juice?" After asking the question, she provided pause time to allow him to respond. If no response was provided, she rephrased the question by asking, "Do you want more juice? You could tell me yes or no," while modeling on his device. This allowed the SLP to model the use of *yes* and *no* and helped Gideon understand that just because he says JUICE, it does not mean he is requesting more. In order to obtain the desired object, the SLP encouraged Gideon to be more specific in his requests.

Goal 2: Increased Utterance Length

In addition to the target core vocabulary words, the SLP provided input on many other words on Gideon's device. This input also pertained to the activities she and Gideon completed as well as Gideon's interests. Although she did not understand all of Gideon's utterances, or they did not relate to the immediate context, it was apparent that Gideon demonstrated communicative intent during these productions. In the utterances that were very long, Gideon continually selected items on his device in a way that indicated he might be unsure of where the words were positioned and he was searching for the vocabulary he would like to communicate. The SLP noticed that Gideon was very persistent, and it seemed as if he was searching for something. In addition, the SLP noted instances throughout the semester in which Gideon may have selected buttons that were not the intended selections. For example, in one instance, Gideon said GET on his device. Based on the activity that Gideon was engaged in (playing chase with his mother or the clinician in the hallway), the SLP suspected that Gideon was trying to select GO on his device. The folder for *get* and *go* are next to each other the homepage of the device. Verbs are always located in the same folder, so *get* and *go* were both in the top-left quadrant of the screen. After opening the folder, Gideon immediately selected the verb on the page. Through this automaticity, Gideon demonstrated his developing motor plan for the device. A motor plan is the memory of the sequence necessary to make productions on the device, which is central to the LAMP Words for Life system. Gideon's motor plan and motivation to communicate supported him in increasing his expressive vocabulary and proficiency with his device.

Goal 3: Increased Use of the Device for Communicative Functions Other Than Requesting

Although Gideon did not communicate with the exact frequency stated in the established goal related to increased use of the device, he did increase use of his device for purposes other than requesting throughout the semester. Gideon used his device to communicate for the purposes of choice making, commenting, and protesting. The SLP targeted this goal through modeling and aided input during activities that pertained to Gideon's interests. The SLP modeled greetings and farewells during arrival and departure from the therapy room. During his sessions, the SLP also provided Gideon with activity options. All of the activities pertained to Gideon's interest in Barney. These activities provided Gideon with the opportunity to communicate to make choices. In addition, the SLP modeled the use of his device for choice-making and rejecting purposes. If Gideon was not interested in the alternative activities, the SLP presented the opportunity to watch more Barney. While watching Barney, the SLP modeled the use of Gideon's device for commenting. She commented on various aspects of the video (e.g., "They are dancing."). She also commented on Gideon's reactions and emotions (e.g., "You are happy. You like Barney.") and shared her own opinions (e.g., "I like this song"). The SLP often paused the Barney videos during Gideon's sessions in order to support Gideon in attending to the models. When Gideon was engaged in watching the videos, he did not attend to this language input. In addition, this interruption of the preferred activity provided Gideon with the opportunity to use his device to make requests.

Occasionally, the SLP incorporated props while she and Gideon were watching Barney videos. For example, during one session, she brought paper hats and recycled instruments. These props related to the content of the video that they were watching. The SLP introduced and utilized the props alongside the video. During this activity, she modeled the use of Gideon's device for a variety of communication purposes. For example, when the SLP put the hat on Gideon's head, he threw it on the floor. This presented the opportunity to model the use of his device in order to protest. In addition, while using the props, the SLP rewound the video in order to incorporate the props more than once. This increased exposure to the activity and core vocabulary.

These activities as well as those described previously in which Gideon was asked to confirm that he was drinking juice rather than just using JUICE to request it are examples of the activities designed to encourage Gideon to use his device to communicate. The objectives of such activities is that, as Gideon receives input and instruction on using his device to communicate for purposes other than requesting, he will increase the number and frequency of these productions. The ability to communicate for a wider variety of purposes will support Gideon in advocating for himself and communicating across environments.

Currently, Gideon uses approximately 30 different words on his AAC device spontaneously and/or after prompting. At the beginning of the semester he was using only two to three words spontaneously. He primarily uses his AAC device to request preferred items or activities, but on occasion, he comments using the word *awesome*. Gideon selects two buttons to create a two-word utterance only occasionally and usually with verbal prompting.

Gideon's goals have evolved in the last 5 years. The target vocabulary words have changed on the basis of Gideon's acquisition of each word and his mother's priorities. Most recently, the goals have evolved to include a specific number of models for the SLP to use. In 2016, Sennott and colleagues published a systematic review of the effects of AAC modeling on the language development of people who use AAC. Modeling was found to influence growth in semantics, syntax pragmatics, and morphology. By intentionally targeting the AAC modeling that the SLP was doing, the team can better track Gideon's progress relative to the direct input from the clinician. The team is using the data-logging feature on the device to support increased use of the device by measuring the number of words modeled during his sessions.

Learning Activities

1. What additional evaluation instruments can be used to identify treatment goals and track progress over time for children with ASD who are likely to benefit from an AAC device?

2. Discuss what adjustments might be made to the assessment plan if a child exhibits limited fine motor skills.

3. Given Gideon's age and year in school, how would his goals change if the primary service provider was the school-based SLP? Why?

4. With a colleague, discuss how an AAC device can be used across settings. What training would be important for family members to have to ensure effective use of the AAC device in the home?

REFERENCES

Beukelman, D. R., & Mirenda, P. (2013). *Augmentative and alternative communication: Supporting children and adults with complex communication needs* (4th ed.). Paul H. Brookes Publishing Co.

Binger, C., Kent-Walsh, J., Ewing, C., & Taylor, S. (2010). Teaching educational assistants to facilitate the multisymbolic message productions of young students who require augmentative and alternative communication. *American Journal of Speech-Language Pathology, 19*, 108–120.

Bunce, B. H., & Watkins, R. V. (1995). Language intervention in a preschool classroom: Implementing a language-focused curriculum. In M. L. Rice & K. A. Wilcox (Eds.), *Building a language-focused curriculum for the preschool classroom: Vol 1. A foundation for lifelong communication* (pp. 39–71). Paul H. Brookes Publishing Co.

Center for AAC and Autism. (n.d.). *What is LAMP?* Retrieved January 24, 2021 from https://aacandautism.com/lamp

Costello, J., & Shane, H. (1994, November). *Augmentative communication assessment and the feature matching process.* Mini seminar presented at the Annual Convention of American Speech-Language-Hearing Association, New Orleans, LA.

Finke, E. H., Davis, J. M., Benedict, M., Gaga, L., Kelly, J., Palumbo, L., Peart, T., & Waters, S. (2017). Effects of least to most prompting procedure on multisymbol message production in children with autism spectrum disorder who use augmentative and alternative communication. *American Journal of Speech-Language Pathology, 1*(26), 81–98. https://doi.org/10.1044/2016_AJSLP-14-0187

Kozleski, E. (1991). Expectant delay procedure for teaching requests. *AAC: Augmentative and Alternative Communication, 7*(1), 11–19.

MacDuff, G. S., Krantz, P. J., & McClannahan, L. E. (2001). Prompts and prompt-fading strategies for people with autism. In C. Maurice, G. Green, & R. M. Foxx (Eds.), *Making a difference: Behavioral intervention for autism* (pp. 37–50). PRO-ED.

Mathis, H., Sutherland, D., & McAuliffe, M. (2011). The effect of pause time upon the communicative interactions of young people who use augmentative and alternative communication. *International Journal of Speech-Language Pathology, 13*(5), 411–421.

Sennott, S., Light, J., & McNaughton, D. (2016). AAC modeling intervention research review. *Research and Practices for Persons with Severe Disabilities, 41*(2), 101–115.

Wegner, J. R. (2021). Augmentative alternative communication strategies: Manual signs, picture communication, and speech-generating devices. In P. A. Prelock & R. J. McCauley (Eds.), *Treatment of autism spectrum disorder: Evidence-based intervention strategies for communication & social interactions* (2nd ed., pp. 81–108). Paul H. Brookes Publishing Co.

CASE 2

Promoting Early Social Communication Skills

A Preschooler With ASD

Jill Howard and Geraldine Dawson

 Maddie

 Age 3

 Autism Spectrum Disorder

> **Case 2 engages with the intervention approach and
> strategies discussed in Chapter 5, The Early Start Denver
> Model (ESDM): Promoting Social Communication in Young
> Children With ASD (Howard & Dawson, 2021) in *Treatment
> of Autism Spectrum Disorder, Second Edition*.**

INTRODUCTION

Maddie is a 3-year-old girl with a recent diagnosis of autism spectrum disorder (ASD). In terms of birth and early history, Maddie was born at 37 weeks' gestation via vaginal delivery, weighing 7 pounds at birth. Her mother experienced hyperemesis gravidarum (i.e., severe nausea and vomiting) during her pregnancy for which she took the prescription medication ondansetron. Medical providers noted no complications immediately following Maddie's birth.

Concerns regarding delays in Maddie's speech development first emerged when she was approximately 15 months old. Although between 11 and 14 months, Maddie used approximately five single words to communicate; at 15 months of age, she stopped using words altogether. With regard to early motor development, Maddie met major motor milestones within typical limits, sitting independently at 7 months, crawling at 9 months, and walking at 12 months.

Currently, Maddie's expressive language skills are delayed relative to same-age peers. She has been involved in speech-language therapy for approximately 1 year and is beginning to combine words into phrases and shows a strong ability to imitate speech. She also uses a handful of basic gestures to communicate (e.g., waving, reaching, blowing a kiss, clapping when excited) but does not frequently use pointing to initiate joint attention. Although she also evidences a weakness in receptive language skills, her mother reported that she follows some two-step instructions (e.g., "pick up the ball and bring it to me"). Her response to her name is inconsistent.

Socially, Maddie generally uses inconsistent eye contact. Her family indicated that it can be difficult to engage her at times because of her "self-willed" nature, although she enjoys receiving physical affection from close family members. She shows limited interest in other children, and most of her opportunities to interact with other children occur within the context of her developmental preschool classroom. Maddie tolerates being around peers but generally does not initiate interactions. When given a choice, Maddie's preference typically is to play alone at a distance away from rather than nearby other children.

With regard to family and community context, Maddie is an only child whose father stays home with her while her mother works. Maddie's mother has completed an associate's degree, and her father has completed high school. Financial stressors are present intermittently; when Maddie enters kindergarten, her father plans to return to work to alleviate some of this concern. Maddie's family lives in a small town, and they report that their church community is a great source of support. Maddie's paternal grandparents live within an hour's drive and assist with childcare from time to time; her maternal grandparents are no longer living. Other extended family (e.g., maternal aunt, uncle, cousin) live out of the area and rarely visit. Figure 2.1 shows a family genogram of Maddie's immediate and extended family.

In addition to speech-language therapy, Maddie receives occupational therapy and part-time developmental preschool services. Her family recently became connected with the Early Start Denver Model (ESDM) parent-implemented version (P-ESDM) and expressed eagerness to initiate the program (Rogers & Dawson, 2009; Rogers et al., 2012). The ESDM is an empirically tested early intervention for young children with ASD, combining an emphasis on play and relationship building with systematically validated teaching practices from applied behavior analysis (ABA); for more information, see Chapter 5 in *Treatment of Autism Spectrum Disorders, Second Edition*. The family has not yet been able to access intensive ABA services owing to limited availability in their community. Figure 2.2 is an ecomap, which displays professional and personal supports for Maddie and her family; solid lines denote strong relationships, arrows denote direction of energy flow, dotted lines denote tenuous relationships, and hatched lines denote stressful relationships.

With regard to other key aspects of Maddie's history, Maddie's medical history is unremarkable. Other than experiencing reflux as an infant, she has had no major medical difficulties, accidents, or surgeries, and she is not taking any medications. Maddie has typical vision and hearing and has no gastrointestinal concerns. Her food preferences are slightly restricted (i.e., she prefers carbohydrates), although she

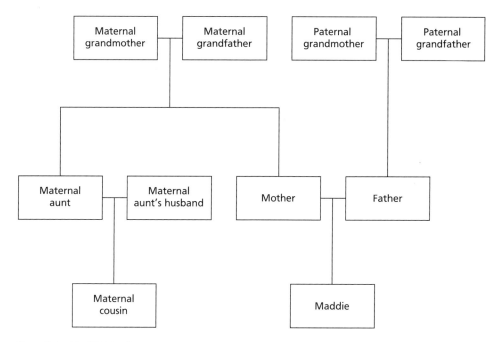

Figure 2.1. Maddie's family genogram.

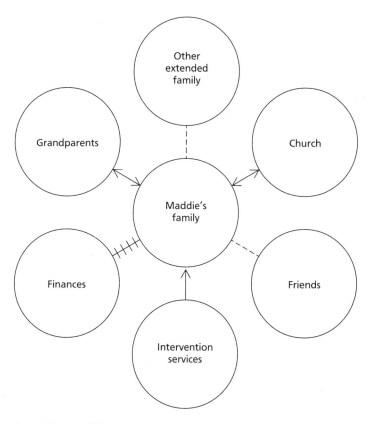

Figure 2.2. Maddie's ecomap.

eats a handful of different foods from each food group, including fruits, vegetables, and protein. Her family denied concern for staring spells or seizure activity. She has not yet participated in genetic testing. Regarding sleep, Maddie's family indicated that she wakes multiple times during the night but generally receives an adequate amount of sleep, including a 2-hour nap in the afternoon.

Maddie has particular difficulty with changes in routine and also demonstrates tantrums in loud, crowded environments. In these situations, she typically cries and has been observed to engage in mild self-injury characterized by hitting herself on the head. Maddie frequently puts nonfood objects in her mouth, which may reflect a sensory seeking behavior. Currently, Maddie's most significant needs involve her developmental delays and impairments in social communication skills. In addition, other than church participation, her family is somewhat limited in their community involvement (e.g., shopping trips, trips to the park) because of concern for Maddie's behavior should she become overwhelmed or upset, which has led to some social isolation and infrequent contact with family friends. Her parents have indicated that they would like some assistance with developing these areas of community and social participation.

ASSESSMENTS FOR COMMUNICATION TREATMENT PLANNING

Maddie completed standardized developmental testing through state early intervention services approximately 1 year prior to her family initiating ESDM parent coaching. This testing consisted of the Developmental Assessment of Young Children–Second Edition (DAYC-2; Voress & Maddox, 2013), and the Preschool Language Scales–Fifth Edition (PLS-5; Zimmerman et al., 2011). Maddie earned the following standard scores on the DAYC-2: Cognitive, 79; Adaptive, 80; and Social-Emotional, 77. All of these scores fell in the below average range. On the PLS-5, Maddie earned a Total Language Standard Score of 66 (with scores below 79 considered delayed). She received a Receptive Language Scaled Score of 3 and an Expressive Language Scaled Score of 5 (with scores of 8 to 12 considered average and scores of 6 or lower considered delayed). Based on these scores, Maddie qualified for and soon thereafter became involved with early intervention services.

Following the general developmental evaluation, which also identified potential red flags for ASD, Maddie participated in autism-specific testing that confirmed the diagnosis. On the basis of parent report of developmental history and clinical observations from the Autism Diagnostic Observation Schedule–Second Edition (ADOS-2; Lord et al., 2012), Maddie met criteria for ASD according to the *Diagnostic and Statistical Manual of Mental Disorders, Fifth Edition* (DSM-5; American Psychiatric Association, 2013).

The ADOS-2 revealed difficulties in social communication skills as well as in restrictive behaviors and repetitive interests. For example, Maddie did not respond to or initiate joint attention, made few social overtures, used the clinician's hand as a tool (rather than using more appropriate forms of communication to request that she move it), did not respond when her name was called, and rarely directed vocalizations to other people. In addition, she evidenced some sensory interests (e.g., rubbed sandpaper block on her face, peered at objects) and demonstrated finger posturing. With regard to strengths, Maddie demonstrated shared enjoyment in several activities (e.g., bubbles) and used communicative reaching to request. Her demeanor was generally positive and relaxed throughout the assessment, and she did not evidence clear signs of anxiety or overactivity.

In regard to current communicative strategies, Maddie generally requests preferred items using words or communicative reaching. However, her parents also anticipate her needs and do not require an attempt at communication before giving her what she wants. At the same time, she also uses several ineffective forms of behavior/communication, such as tantrums, to indicate that she needs a break or is overstimulated. Occasionally, she evidences other challenging behaviors such as mild self-injury.

While Maddie had not completed a formal evaluation for alternative communication techniques at the time of her entry into the P-ESDM program, her parents were aware that this evaluation might be worthwhile to pursue in the future should she not continue to progress in developing speech. Given that Maddie shows emerging multiword speech, the primary focus of her speech-language therapy is to continue developing her verbal communication skills.

CLINICAL PROBLEM SOLVING TO IDENTIFY TREATMENT GOALS

Before her family connected with the clinic for P-ESDM, Maddie had completed several developmental and diagnostic evaluations that identified some of her strengths and weaknesses and confirmed the diagnosis of ASD. These evaluations identified speech-language therapy, occupational therapy, developmental preschool, and ABA as appropriate treatments for developing Maddie's skills. Limited ABA services are available in the area where Maddie lives, but her family was recently able to connect with the clinic for P-ESDM, which incorporates ABA components. Before the P-ESDM program became available, Maddie had already been involved in speech-language therapy, occupational therapy, and developmental preschool for a number of months, and her family reported some improvement in related areas of skill. The clinic's intake process consisted of a full review of paperwork completed by Maddie's family as well as a review of available records, previous evaluations, and treatment progress reports by a clinical psychologist—all of which were used to evaluate her appropriateness for the P-ESDM program.

The first session of P-ESDM consisted of a curriculum assessment aimed at identifying treatment goals (involving both the clinician's observations and parent report) as well as a discussion with Maddie's mother regarding family priorities. ESDM delivered via caregiver coaching is by definition family centered and involves active caregiver involvement in terms of learning and practicing strategies to be used during typical daily routines at home and in the community. The ESDM treatment plan was informed by information gathered during the curriculum assessment session as well as by previous testing and progress reports that were made available to the clinician.

The discussion with Maddie's mother emphasized that Maddie's well-being and development is of utmost importance to her parents. Specifically, her parents are particularly concerned about her poor eye contact, as they feel it makes her disability more apparent to those outside the family. Her mother expressed self-consciousness related to what others might think when they see Maddie acting out in public and concerns that others might treat her daughter differently because Maddie does not interact with others as would be expected for a child her age. Although Maddie is only 3 years old, her parents already have considerable anxiety for her future and how ASD and related delays may limit her future potential. However, Maddie's treatment providers have assured them that her involvement in early intervention services is extremely positive and that her continuing progress is encouraging.

Although her parents are extremely motivated to ensure Maddie's success, there are some constraints that may shape the treatment plan. First, financial constraints have made it difficult for Maddie's parents to access services beyond what she is eligible for through state early intervention. While they have found it financially possible for her father to take some time off from full-time employment in order to take Maddie to therapy appointments and care for her during the day, he ultimately plans to return to full-time employment when she enters a full-day school program. He takes occasional night classes, as he is working toward an associate's degree, recognizing that he would be eligible for a higher rate of pay were he able to complete the degree, which would allow the family to secure more services for Maddie.

The area in which Maddie's family lives is largely lacking ABA and similar services, which means that once her family completes the 12-week program of P-ESDM, it is unlikely that they will be able to continue to benefit from comparable programs and strategies. They have looked into the possibility of moving closer to extended family living in a more metropolitan area, as they believe it may provide them with easier access to services.

Maddie's family feels fortunate that she does not experience significant medical difficulties that would complicate her treatment plan. Overall, she is physically healthy and growing as expected. Given that her grandparents occasionally assist with caregiving, Maddie's parents are able to sometimes run household errands and attend their own appointments without her having to accompany them. Maddie's grandparents are interested in learning strategies aimed at promoting her social communication skills. Maddie's mother frequently shares with them websites containing information on ASD and how to develop speech and language skills in a young child. Their understanding of autism is developing, which allows them to better understand Maddie's behavior, strengths, and weaknesses.

INTERVENTIONS USED TO ACHIEVE MAJOR GOALS

As noted, Maddie is already involved in a number of interventions aimed at improving her developmental and social communication skills. Her involvement in the community is relatively limited at this time, although as she has continued to show progress. Her parents have become more comfortable with the idea of taking Maddie to parks or playgrounds to allow her to play with other children. Occasionally, Maddie accompanies her parents on community outings, such as going to the grocery store or shopping center, although her parents try to limit these experiences, when possible, for the sake of efficiency and minimization of their own stress and frustration.

As noted, Maddie has no major needs related to the care of her physical health. Her parents consistently take her to well-child visits and follow the recommendations of their pediatrician related to minor concerns that they have had over the course of her life (e.g., ear infection, low-grade fever). Maddie's pediatrician has a good understanding of developmental disorders and a sharp awareness of potential medical comorbidities that may occur. Overall, her parents believe they have a good plan in place for managing Maddie's health needs should any concerns arise.

When Maddie turns 5 years old, she will be eligible for a full-day kindergarten program through the public school system, where she will likely continue to receive speech-language therapy and occupational therapy. She will complete an updated evaluation to determine an appropriate classroom setting for her at that time. Depending on how her skills progress over the next couple years, she may also be eligible for extended school year, which would allow her to continue to receive school-based services throughout the summer recess period.

In order to achieve primary goals of improving Maddie's social communication skills, her parents decided to initiate caregiver coaching in ESDM in addition to the speech-language therapy, occupational therapy, and developmental preschool services already in place. Please see Chapter 5 in *Treatment of Autism Spectrum Disorder, Second Edition*, for more information on what this intervention entails. Briefly, the program consists of weekly sessions attended by both the parent and child; the parent receives live coaching during parent–child activities and participates in a reflection with the coach following each activity. Each session covers one new topic (e.g., imitation, play, language), and the program builds upon itself so that the parent continues to receive coaching across the range of topics throughout the program.

For the most part, Maddie and her family were able to participate in P-ESDM as designed without need for modification. She and her mother attended sessions consistently, and her mother responded well to coaching, participated in in-session discussion, and practiced using ESDM strategies outside of the training sessions. Maddie's mother promoted her daughter's social communication and engagement by managing Maddie's attention, modulating her affect and arousal, using dyadic engagement, optimizing Maddie's motivation, and promoting multiple and varied communicative opportunities, to name a few key areas of focus.

OUTCOMES

During the warm-up portion of each session (i.e., beginning of the session when the parent engages the child in an activity without live coaching from the clinician), the clinician observes and takes fidelity data on Maddie's mother's use of ESDM strategies. On the basis of an update from Maddie's mother and observation of her skills over the course of the session, the coach also gathers data on progress toward individually tailored objectives. As such, progress is continually monitored in order to make appropriate adjustments as needed.

Maddie's mother demonstrated steadily increasing mastery of ESDM strategies over the course of the program (12 weeks with one 60-minute coaching session per week) and met criteria for mastery (defined as an average score of 80% across all strategies) between the seventh and eighth sessions of the program. In particular, she showed improved ability to introduce variation into activities, attended to Maddie's affect, and matched Maddie's level of language using the one-word-up rule (i.e., use only one additional word beyond the child's level of spontaneous language production, or mean length of utterance).

Similarly, Maddie made progress toward her objectives by advancing to next steps slowly and steadily over the course of the program. By the end of the program, she had achieved all of her objectives, reflecting progress in developmental skills across all targeted domains. Specific objectives achieved included spontaneously producing multiple words associated with a play routine (e.g., "roll," "go"; Expressive Communication), matching and sorting by size (Cognition), imitating animal sounds and other sounds (Imitation), and using gesture or words to attain adult's attention (Social Skills); see Figure 2.3 for summary of progress. Further, Maddie showed improvements in nontargeted areas (e.g., reduction in disruptive behavior).

Domain	Objective	Mastery criterion	Achieved?
Expressive communication	Spontaneously produces smultiple words associated with a play routine (e.g., *roll, go*) Matches/sorts by sizez	Produces three words or approximations for verbs	√
Cognition	Matches/sorts by size	Matches/sorts independently 80% of the time	√
Imitation	Imitates animal sounds and other sounds	Imitates within 5 seconds of your model 80% of the time	√
Social skills	Uses gesture or words to gain adult's attention	Uses either words or clear gestures five times per day	√

Figure 2.3. Summary of progress.

Although the P-ESDM program did not include interactions with peers, Maddie's mother stated that her improved confidence in her ability to support and attend to Maddie's needs made her more willing to participate in community outings such as visiting the park and playground. Consequently, Maddie began to have more opportunities to observe and engage with children with typical development. Although still limited in her initiation of social interaction, Maddie started to show brief but clear interest in other children in these settings. Overall, both Maddie and her mother evidenced clear progress over the 12-week P-ESDM program, with development observed across Maddie's social communication and interaction skills and a reduction observed in disruptive behavior. Following the conclusion of the P-ESDM program, Maddie's family will be able to continue to apply skills learned to their family routines in home and community settings.

Learning Activities

1. How might a caregiver's understanding (or lack thereof) of ASD contribute to (or detract from) potential progress in a parent-mediated intervention? In other words, what are some ways in which having a solid understanding of ASD may help a caregiver to promote progress in social communication development?

2. What other types of assessments or evaluations may be helpful in continuing to shape Maddie's treatment plan? Are there areas that have not yet received sufficient attention that may require additional focus in terms of ensuring maximal

developmental progress? If these assessments or evaluations would lead to additional types of recommended interventions, please indicate what those interventions might entail.

3. How might the P-ESDM treatment program target increased community involvement for Maddie and her family? Prior to beginning the program, her parents had elected to keep Maddie home from most outings, including trips to the grocery store and shopping mall. In addition, they generally avoided taking her to places such as the park and playground. How might this program set up the family for success in terms of involving Maddie in these activities, and what are some of the benefits of doing so?

4. Understanding that there may be financial or time constraints (or lack of community availability) that may prevent Maddie's family from increasing services at this time, what other recommendations might you have for the family in terms of continuing to increase their understanding of ASD and continuing to ensure Maddie's progress?

REFERENCES

American Psychiatric Association. (2013). *Diagnostic and statistical manual of mental disorders, fifth edition* (DSM-5). Author.

Howard, J., & Dawson, G. (2021). The Early Start Denver Model (ESDM): Promoting social communication in young children with ASD. In P. A. Prelock & R. J. McCauley (Eds.), *Treatment of autism spectrum disorder: Evidence-based intervention strategies for communication & social interactions* (2nd ed., pp. 109–132). Paul H. Brookes Publishing Co.

Lord, C., Rutter, M., DiLavore, P. C., Risi, S., Gotham, K., & Bishop, S. (2012). *Autism Diagnostic Observation Schedule, Second Edition (ADOS-2) Manual (Part I): Modules 1–4*. Western Psychological Services.

Rogers, S. J., & Dawson, G. (2009). *Early Start Denver Model Curriculum Checklist for Young Children with Autism*. Guilford Press.

Rogers, S. J., Dawson, G., & Vismara, L. A. (2012). *An early start for your child with autism: Using everyday activities to help kids connect, communicate, and learn.* Guilford Press.

Voress, J. K., & Maddox, T. (2013). *Developmental Assessment of Young Children–Second Edition (DAYC-2)*. PRO-ED.

Zimmerman, I. L., Steiner, V. G., & Pond, R. E. (2011). *Preschool Language Scales–Fifth Edition (PLS-5)*. Pearson.

Teaching Social Skills and Self-Regulation to Decrease Challenging Behavior and Improve Quality of Life

A Preschooler With ASD

Susan M. Wilczynski and Shawnna Sundberg

 Benjamin

 Age 4

 Autism Spectrum Disorder

Case 3 engages with the intervention approach and strategies discussed in Chapter 6, Discrete Trial Instruction (Kazee, Wilczynski, Martino, Sundberg, Quinn, & Mundell, 2021) in *Treatment of Autism Spectrum Disorder, Second Edition.*

INTRODUCTION

Benjamin is a 4-year, 10-month-old boy who was diagnosed with autism spectrum disorder (ASD) at 2 years, 8 months old. He lives with his family, which consists of his two fathers, an older brother, and a younger brother. He began receiving speech-language services soon after his diagnosis. Benjamin is able to speak using full sentences and primarily has difficulties with being understood by a novel listener.

Current speech-language services target articulation and pressured speech (i.e., speaking extremely rapidly with a sense of urgency that seems inappropriate to the given context). At the age of 3 years, 2 months, Benjamin began demonstrating high rates of aggression (e.g., hitting and kicking) when in non-preferred social situations. After these behaviors, Benjamin would often run away and hide (i.e., elopement) from others. Aggression and elopement created problems for the family and conflict in his preschool, which precipitated his parents' decision to place him in an applied behavior analysis (ABA) clinic 8 months after these behaviors emerged.

A detailed description of Benjamin's communication and social profiles, the family and community context, and the broader profile are presented in Table 3.1, and the interrelationships between family members and sources of support or distress are described in Figures 3.1 (genogram) and 3.2 (ecomap). A summary of his most significant needs is described here. Benjamin's anticipated transition to his local school for the fall term of kindergarten could be disrupted if he continues to demonstrate inappropriate behaviors (i.e., aggressive behaviors and elopement). Although these behaviors have occurred for only 1 year, this represents approximately 25% of Benjamin's life, which means the behaviors are rather entrenched and could further undermine his social opportunities across relevant settings (e.g., community and school).

Table 3.1. Baseline status

Profile type	Background information
Communication	Benjamin speaks in complete sentences with proper grammar usage when addressing preferred topics (e.g., specific videos, dinosaurs).
	He consistently shifts topic when a less preferred topic is initiated by others.
	He has poor articulation.
	He has pressured speech.
	He has difficulty identifying why he is upset.
Social	Benjamin runs and hides in the presence of social-communication demands in groups, difficult academic tasks, or engagement in social interactions with peers.
	Aggression (i.e., hitting, kicking, scratching, biting, hair pulling) occurs under the same conditions for an average of five times per day for 48 minutes in the applied behavior analysis (ABA) clinic and three to five times per day for 36 minutes at home.
	Aggression occurs frequently in the presence of difficult or non-preferred tasks.
Family and context (see Figure 3.1)	Benjamin lives with his parents and two siblings (ages 9 and 2).
	Family's quality of life is diminished because parents do not take Benjamin into the community due to inappropriate behaviors.
	Older brother is embarrassed to have friends visit the home.
	Family self-describes as Christian but reports not attending services due to Benjamin's inappropriate behavior.
Broader profile	Benjamin is healthy and not prescribed any medications.
	Benjamin was removed from preschool due to inappropriate behavior.
	Benjamin receives 20 hours of services at an ABA clinic and weekly speech services. Both settings include one-to-one treatment and social communication with peers. Peers in both settings have identified disabilities (autism spectrum disorder and/or communication).

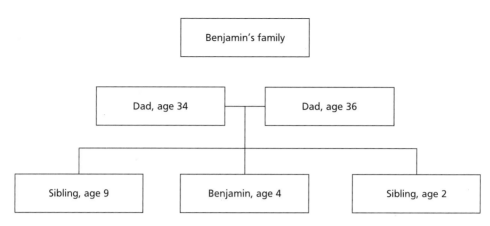

Figure 3.1.   Benjamin's genogram.

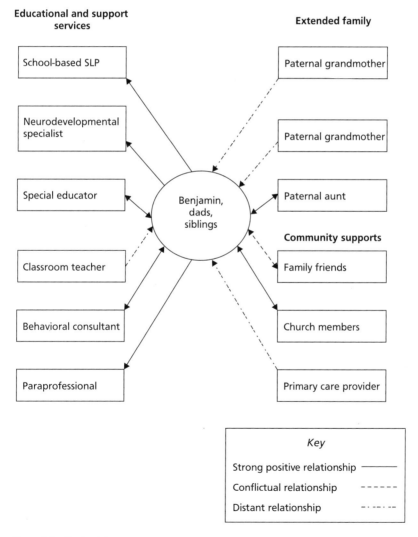

Figure 3.2.   Benjamin's ecomap.

Benjamin does not attend preschool and does not have a great deal of access to typically developing peers while at speech therapy or the ABA clinic as a result of his inappropriate behaviors. Consequently, Benjamin's opportunity to practice age-appropriate social interactions in play or other contexts is limited. His parents' goals are to be able to do more activities as a family (e.g., go to a restaurant) and to see Benjamin back in school for kindergarten.

ASSESSMENTS FOR COMMUNICATION TREATMENT PLANNING

Clinicians assessed Benjamin's receptive and expressive language, cognitive ability, the social aspects of his communication, and his communication modalities.

Receptive and Expressive Language

The behavior analyst administers and scores the Milestones, Barriers, and Transition assessments of the Verbal Behavior Milestones Assessment and Placement Program (VB-MAPP; Sundberg, 2008) to assess receptive and expressive language for children up to 48 months of age. Benjamin scores 120 on the Milestones assessment, which measures learning and language milestones and reflects the repertoire of existing communication and related skills. A typically developing peer would be expected to score 170 on the Milestones assessment. Benjamin can label pictures of more than 1,000 words but faces significant deficits in the areas of social requests, social skills, group participation, and play skills with peers. Examples of deficits include difficulty initiating and maintaining social interactions with peers, making requests for preferred items, requesting the removal from a non-preferred activity or environment, cooperative or imaginary play with peers, and group activities. Benjamin has strong receptive language skills (e.g., follows multiple-step directions, follows instructions within a group, and answers and asks questions at the same level as his same-age peers).

The Barrier assessment of the VB-MAPP is used to identify barriers that impede learning. Benjamin receives a score of 54, which indicates deficits regarding negative behaviors (e.g., tantrums, throwing things, aggression, property destruction), difficulty making requests, weak social and group skills, and articulation problems diminish his opportunities to learn life skills that optimize his long-term trajectory. The Transitions of the VB-MAPP assessment, which is designed to evaluate the skills needed for learning in a less restrictive educational setting (Sundberg, 2008), showed similar deficits in classroom routines and group skills, social behavior, and social play.

Cognitive Ability

Individuals with ASD may receive scores that underestimate their true intellectual functioning because the social-communication demands of cognitive assessments can be intense. In addition, IQ is not stable during early childhood; however, tests of cognitive functioning can predict performance in academic tasks; therefore, although results should be interpreted with caution, relevant implications are described (Kuriakose, 2014; Mayes & Calhoun, 2003). The Wechsler Preschool and Primary Scale of Intelligences–Fourth Edition (WPPSI-IV; Weschler, 2012) is administered to assess IQ and attention. Benjamin receives a below-average score of 85, with primary deficits in difficulty with attention and speed of responding.

The Developmental Neuropsychological Assessment–Second Edition (NEPSY-II; Korkman et al., 2007) is used to assess executive functioning. Benjamin scores at a borderline level, which is slightly below the level expected for his age but consistent with the results of the WPPSI-IV. His primary deficits of self-regulation and sustained attention are consistent with those implicated by the VB-MAPP, so additional supports are recommended both for the transition to school and for Benjamin's quality of life at home.

Social Aspects of Communication

The VB-MAPP also assesses social skills and challenging behaviors (Sundberg, 2008). Benjamin displays deficits across all areas of social skills in the assessment. He often demonstrates inappropriate behavior in the form of elopement and high rates of aggression when in social situations (i.e., initiating and maintaining social interactions). For example, when approached by a peer and asked to play a preferred activity, he immediately elopes. If elopement is blocked, he becomes aggressive, tries to hide, and/or destroys property. In addition, Benjamin often has difficulty expressing why he is upset. His current levels of inappropriate behavior will make transitioning to school and/or developing meaningful reciprocal social relationships difficult.

The Social Skills Improvement System (SSIS; Gresham & Elliot, 2008) is a parent-completed rating scale that assesses social skills in the home and community settings. Benjamin's social skills scores fall in the below-average range, suggesting that he possesses fewer appropriate social skills compared to same-age peers. He reportedly struggles mostly in the areas of empathy, self-control, cooperation, and engagement. Benjamin demonstrates more challenging behaviors than his typical peers and has elevated scores in externalizing behaviors and symptoms of ASD.

A functional analysis (FA) is conducted to assess which consequence (i.e., escape, attention, tangibles, homeostasis) following Benjamin's challenging behavior maintains his aggression and elopement and/or hiding (Iwata et al., 1990). Aggression is assessed because it has already led to a more restrictive environment and could prevent future educational and community-based opportunities. Elopement and hiding are assessed because they could lead to risk for injury. Although a functional analysis can identify what individuals with ASD are trying to communicate with their challenging behaviors, it does not determine whether these individuals with ASD are unaware of either the environmental conditions that trigger or maintain these behaviors.

Elopement and hiding do not occur during the FA. Aggression occurs most frequently in two different escape/avoidance conditions. First, Benjamin is presented with difficult, non-preferred tasks and could escape the tasks when he demonstrates any form of aggression. Second, Benjamin is told to enter a room in which multiple other students are present. These preschoolers often interact loudly (as is common among preschoolers). He is allowed to avoid entering the room if he hits or kicks the adult walking him into the room. When compared to all alternate conditions (e.g., obtaining attention or tangible preferred materials) for aggression, escape/avoidance is the clear function of the behavior. However, Benjamin demonstrates aggression when entering the room with other children only when the preschoolers are interacting loudly. When the preschoolers are working quietly, he enters the room on request without incident.

Communication Modalities

Benjamin speaks in full sentences, using age-appropriate sentence structure and grammar to communicate with others. However, his speech is not consistently intelligible by a novel listener due to articulation errors and pressured speech.

CLINICAL PROBLEM SOLVING TO IDENTIFY TREATMENT GOALS

Behavior analysis is steeped in an evaluation of the environmental conditions that produce or sustain behaviors, including consequences, immediate antecedents, and often, more distal conditions (e.g., being tired, hungry). In this case, *differential reinforcement* for targeting appropriate responses and *shaping* for skill improvement primarily drove treatment selection. The application of these strategies occurred within the application of other treatments (see Interventions Used to Achieve Major Goals).

Client preferences, family values, and contextual constraints/supports also drive treatment selection in ABA (Wilczynski, 2017). The behavior analyst interviews family members (e.g., parents, older sibling), reviews documentation from Benjamin's prior preschool and current ABA center, and reviews expectations for kindergarteners in Benjamin's school district. Benjamin's parents report feeling devastated when he encounters so many difficulties in preschool and want him to make the transition successfully to kindergarten. They are concerned that their older son seems embarrassed to have friends come to their home. His parents indicate they did not expect to have so many challenges with Benjamin because his language skills are so much stronger than those of other children they know who are diagnosed with ASD. They used baby sign language and speech to communicate with Benjamin until he was about 3 years old but stopped using sign because his speech skills seemed well developed to them.

One of the greatest challenges to a successful transition to kindergarten is Benjamin's demonstration of aggressive behavior 1) when given difficult tasks and 2) in the presence of a loud environment. Attendance at the ABA clinic varies from day to day. On some days, many of the children are very loud and communicate primarily using speech, but on other days, the composition of students in group activities includes primarily students who speak infrequently and are generally quiet.

The opportunity to work on age-appropriate social interactions is challenging in this setting as a result of a limited number of typically developing same-age peers. Although a few peer partners (i.e., typically developing children) attend the ABA clinic, they do not attend every day, and their parents have not given permission for the peer partners to spend time with children who can be expected to demonstrate aggressive behaviors.

INTERVENTIONS USED TO ACHIEVE MAJOR GOALS

This section discusses overall plans for Benjamin's support as well as specific communication- or social interaction–related interventions.

Overall Plans for Support

The interventions initially used to address Benjamin's goals are functional communication training (FCT), tolerance training, and peer-mediated support interventions. Prior to implementation of these interventions, the curriculum being used with

Benjamin is assessed to identify which goals are too difficult, which are in Benjamin's zone of proximal development, and which are mastered. In this way, the presentation of exceptionally difficult tasks can be removed and the appropriate level of prompting (see Chapter 6 in the accompanying textbook) could be used with skills that are emerging and attainable but cannot be completed independently at present.

Although long-term goals are for Benjamin to tolerate louder sounds across environments and to wait when faced with difficult tasks, FCT has to be implemented prior to a *toleration* or wait protocol so that Benjamin will have a strategy for communicating his need to leave a loud environment or take a break from difficult tasks. These protocols are by both the center and parents to increase generalization across settings. Collectively, these interventions should yield a smoother transition to kindergarten because Benjamin will have the ability both to make appropriate requests and to tolerate louder environments even when his requests cannot be immediately honored.

The SSIS and the VB-MAPP (Transitions assessment) results indicate that Benjamin's current social skills and play are limiting his functioning in the community and at home. For this reason, a peer-mediated support intervention is implemented with peer partners once aggression is reduced. The family is also taught to use the peer-mediated intervention with Benjamin's siblings, which also provides Benjamin's older brother the chance to help Benjamin while having friends over to their home.

Communication- or Social Interaction-Related Interventions

FCT involves teaching and providing reinforcement for an alternative response to inappropriate behavior (see Chapter 8 in the accompanying textbook). Based on previous reports, elopement and hiding historically occur after aggression in real-world contexts (e.g., preschool, home). Elopement and hiding are predicted to diminish because the behavior that precedes them (i.e., aggression) will be addressed.

Although Benjamin speaks in complete sentences under optimal conditions, he may not be able to communicate his need to escape situations that are particularly difficult (e.g., challenging tasks) or loud. Given his successful history with sign language, he is taught to use sign to request a break from difficult tasks as well as to leave a setting. However, verbal presentation of the statements "break" and "leave" are co-presented in sign. Speech is more efficient than sign, so speech is likely to occur more frequently in the future as sign decreases. However, the protocol should continue honoring the use of sign, as appropriate given the evolving treatment expectations. As he makes the transition to kindergarten, his teacher should be informed that signing for a break or to leave the room may still occur, particularly when Benjamin is distressed.

A tolerance protocol is implemented only after Benjamin responds to FCT intervention (i.e., he successfully signs and/or says he needs a break or leaves a setting). The tolerance protocol begins with teaching Benjamin to wait 1–3 seconds after he signs to leave a setting. Two or three seconds are added to the tolerance protocol each time Benjamin successfully tolerates waiting to leave the location without demonstrating aggression for three consecutive attempts. Once Benjamin can tolerate the setting for 30 seconds, postrequest wait times are increased in 10-second increments until he can patiently wait at least 2 minutes. In order to maintain Benjamin's use of the sign and/or speech to leave the area, the tolerance protocol is implemented only once every two to four requests. Once Benjamin can tolerate a 2-minute wait period, time until the request is honored is increased in 30-second increments until he reaches 5 minutes.

A peer-mediated support intervention (see Chapter 12 in the accompanying textbook) is implemented with peer partners and other children with disabilities at the ABA clinic. However, peers sometimes experience difficulty understanding Benjamin as a result of his articulation errors and pressured speech. Peers are taught to request clarification directly from Benjamin instead of asking the instructor, which is what Benjamin's peers have been doing automatically. The instructors generate a list of the words peers have the hardest time understanding. The behavior analyst consults with the staff speech-language pathologist (SLP) to identify 1) which words are developmentally appropriate to target (i.e., it was assumed that a 4-year-old cannot articulate all sounds and blends, but an expert is needed to determine which sounds should be targeted for improvement), 2) which prompts are most appropriate to use with Benjamin in the context of peer-mediated support interventions, and 3) which words should be targeted for improvement using discrete trial instruction (DTI; see Chapter 6 in the accompanying textbook).

OUTCOMES

Benjamin's aggressive behaviors decrease to zero at the ABA clinic with the introduction of FCT. He independently uses sign to request a break or to leave a setting after only three training sessions at the ABA clinic. Aggression remains stable in the home (approximately 3–5 times per day). After consultation with his parents, clinicians learned that one father (Briffon) is consistently prompting for signs, but Benjamin's other father (Sam) is prompting only for words because he fears Benjamin will start using only sign to communicate. Clinicians show him the data from school, which demonstrates that requesting with sign is now being replaced with verbal requests almost two thirds of the time. Benjamin's aggressive behavior reduces significantly at home following a brief retraining for both parents.

Although aggression is reduced to zero levels, Benjamin continues to occasionally run and hide when presented with unfamiliar social situations. His parents are taught to practice going to places in the community for very short periods of time (a few seconds) when they can both be in attendance and hold his hand. If he tolerates the environment for short periods of time, they will return to their car and ask Benjamin, "Would you like to go back inside or would you like to go home?" Gradually, the amount of time he is expected to remain in the novel environment without running away is increased, and both fathers no longer have to be present for community outings.

The peer-mediated support intervention increases Benjamin's responses to peer bids for interactions and play. Benjamin responds to peer bids for interactions only slightly below the level demonstrated by the peer partners, which bodes well for a transition to kindergarten. Although he responds to bids when peers provide play-organizing statements (e.g., "Do you want to play cars with me?") involving Benjamin's preferred toys, he simply looks at peers briefly when they ask him to play with less preferred toys and then he returns to his own activity. Unfortunately, the peer-mediated support intervention does not increase Benjamin's social initiations. Given the importance of play-based learning in the early years of development, further intervention is necessary to facilitate a smooth transition to kindergarten.

Both responding to bids to play with less preferred toys and social initiations are targeted for intervention with DTI owing to a lack of responding during peer-mediated interventions. An assessment is conducted to determine whether Benjamin knows how to play with the less preferred toys that are frequently used by peer partners. Clinicians identify a skill deficit (i.e., he does not know how to use the toy) for three of the items but a performance deficit (i.e., he knows how to play but does not do so) with four other less preferred items. Benjamin is taught to use the three toys that were unfamiliar to him. Clinicians collect data, and his responses to social bids to play with these toys immediately increase with peer partners. Clinicians offer Benjamin a choice for the four items that are less preferred. Specifically, they say, "Do you want to play with this [less preferred toy] and then this [highly preferred toy], or would you rather do some school work [mastered preacademic tasks]?" Benjamin begins playing with two of the less preferred toys briefly. Clinicians gradually increase the length of time Benjamin is required to play with the toy until he will play with it for 30 seconds. At this point, clinicians observe Benjamin respond to bids to play with these items during peer-mediated support interventions. With respect to the two very non-preferred toys identified during the assessment, DTI is used to teach him to say, "Not right now, thanks," when he is presented with these toys. His instructors then generalize this skill to the peer-mediated support intervention time. Specifically, he is prompted during interactions with peers to respond appropriately to bids to play with toys that are very non-preferred.

Social initiations are targeted during DTI because of a complete absence of social initiations during peer-mediated interventions. Two adults at the ABA clinic initially work with Benjamin to increase social initiations involving play activities. One adult serves as the instructor, and the other plays the role of a child who is sitting by himself. The antecedent condition of a child sitting by himself is pointed out to Benjamin, and he is then prompted to say, "Want to play with this [Benjamin's preferred toy] with me?"

The tolerance protocol is implemented at the ABA clinic, and Benjamin is able to tolerate waiting in a loud environment for 5 minutes. The protocol is then terminated, but his response to expectations to wait to leave the area is monitored. Aggression does not reemerge, even when a request is occasionally not honored, and he often has to wait 5 or more minutes before leaving the area.

The FCT protocol is faded (i.e., gradually reduced) in the home once Benjamin is independently requesting "break" or "leave." Although it takes 6 months, the family is eventually able to go out to dinner at one of Benjamin's preferred fast-food restaurants. Benjamin's parents are currently working with the school district to identify which school Benjamin will attend in the fall. The behavior analyst, in collaboration with the SLP, plans to develop a school- and classroom-specific protocol to aid his transition. The parents have agreed to have the behavior analyst and SLP consult with the school during the fall semester.

Learning Activities

1. What role should behavior analysts play in supporting language development in children with ASD? How could you work more collaboratively with the behavior analyst to address Benjamin's case? What strategies have you effectively used to collaborate with behavior analysts in the past?

2. If a family was unable to implement a peer-mediated intervention or was uncomfortable with doing so, what alternatives could be considered? How could the treatment be modified, or what alternative intervention might be more compatible for the family?

3. After reviewing the ASHA code of ethics and the Roles and Responsibilities documents, determine whether a functional analysis could present an ethical challenge for SLPs. What alternative assessments might be used before a functional analysis is completed?

4. How would you approach the behavior analyst to discuss each professional's role?

REFERENCES

Gresham, F., & Elliot, S. M. (2008). *Social Skills Improvement System (SSIS) Rating Scales.* Pearson.

Iwata, B. A., Vollmer, T. R., & Zarcone, J. R. (1990). The experimental (functional) analysis of behavior disorders: Methodology, applications, and limitations. In A. C. Repp & N. N. Singh (Eds.), *Perspectives on the use of nonaversive and aversive interventions for persons with developmental disabilities* (pp. 301–330). Sycamore Publishing Co.

Kazee, A., Wilczynski, S. M., Martino, M., Sundberg, S., Quinn, M., & Mundell, N. L. (2021). Discrete Trial Instruction. In P. A. Prelock & R. J. McCauley (Eds.), *Treatment of autism spectrum disorder: Evidence-based intervention strategies for communication & social interactions* (2nd ed., pp. 133–162). Paul H. Brookes Publishing Co.

Korkman, M., Kirk, U., & Kemp, S. (2007). *NEPSY-II.* Pearson.

Kuriakose, S. (2014). Concurrent validity of the WISC-IV and DAS-II in children with autism spectrum disorder. *Journal of Psychoeducational Assessment, 32*(4), 283–294. https://doi.org/10.1177/0734282913511051

Mayes, S. D., & Calhoun, S. L. (2003). Analysis of WISC-III, Stanford-Binet: IV, and academic achievement test scores in children with autism. *Journal of Autism and Developmental Disorders, 33*(3), 329–341. https://doi.org/10.1023/A:1024462719081

Sundberg, M. L. (2008). *Verbal Behavior Milestones Assessment and Placement Program: The VB-MAPP.* AVB Press.

Weschler, D. (2012). *WPPSI-IV: Wechsler Preschool and Primary Scale of Intelligence–Fourth Edition: Manual.* Pearson.

Wilczynski, S. M. (2017). *A practical guide for selecting treatments that work for people with autism.* Elsevier.

Understanding Foundational Developmental Capacities Related to Language

A Toddler With ASD

Sima Gerber

 Jane

 Age 22 Months

 Autism Spectrum Disorder

Case 4 engages with the intervention approach and strategies discussed in Chapter 7, The Developmental Individual-Difference Relationship Based (DIR) Model and Its Application to Children With ASD (Gerber, 2021) in *Treatment of Autism Spectrum Disorder, Second Edition*.

INTRODUCTION

Jane is a toddler with autism spectrum disorder (ASD) who is first seen for an assessment at 22 months and is reassessed after 8 months of language intervention, when she is 30 months.

History

Ms. C., Jane's birth mother, reports that her pregnancy with Jane was uneventful. Jane was born at 41 weeks' gestation through vaginal delivery and weighed 7 pounds,

6 ounces at birth. Because Ms. C. had a high fever during the delivery, Jane was observed for two days in the neonatal intensive care unit. Jane passed the newborn hearing screening.

Jane was seen in the emergency department at age 8 months for suspicion of the Coxsackie virus. She has had several ear infections, which have been successfully treated with antibiotics. She is described as a healthy child, with no concerns about vision, hearing, eating, drinking, and sleeping.

Jane sat unassisted at 7–8 months and walked independently at 13 months. Her first words were spoken at 10 months; however, by 18 months, the pediatrician referred the family to early intervention because of concerns about a speech and language delay. At that time, Jane was saying few words, did not acquire new words easily, did not imitate or repeat words, and had difficulty using language to express her intentions.

Initial Evaluations

Jane is first evaluated when she is 1 year, 6 months old by an early intervention team in Queens, New York. The team consists of a special educator, speech-language pathologist (SLP), and psychologist. Based on Jane's performance on the HELP Strands (Parks et al., 1984–2004), parental interview, and observations during the evaluation, clinicians estimate Jane's overall cognitive functioning to fall within the 9- to 12-month range. They observe Jane engaging in simple relational play, but she does not demonstrate symbolic play with realistic props.

Findings from the Developmental Assessment of Young Children–Second Edition (DAYC-2; Voress et al., 2012), parental input, and clinical observations indicate Jane's social-emotional skills are within the poor range. She is unable to play simple games; imitate facial expressions, actions, and sounds; or repeat activities that elicit laughter or a positive response from others. Motor and adaptive abilities are within typical limits.

The results of the Receptive-Expressive Emergent Language Test–Third Edition (REEL-3; Bzoch et al., 2003) estimate receptive language to be in the 8- to 12-month range, and expressive language falls within the 9- to 12-month range. Based on the *Clinical Practice Guideline: Quick Reference Guide—Communication Disorders* (Bureau of Early Intervention, 1999), Jane demonstrates the following clinical concerns: lack of communicative gestures, limited use of single words to convey meaning, lack of persistence in communication, and limited comprehension and production of words. Articulation and feeding are not of concern.

According to the Toddler Module of the Autism Diagnostic Observation Schedule–Second Edition (ADOS-2; Luyster et al., 2009), Jane's overall score of 15 falls within the moderate to severe range, suggesting behaviors that are consistent with autism spectrum disorder. The results of these assessments indicate that Jane meets eligibility criteria for early intervention services as per New York State Department of Health Standards and Procedures for Evaluations, Evaluation Reimbursement, and Eligibility Requirements and Determinations (http://www.health.ny.gov/publications/4219.pdf).

Family Considerations

Jane lives with her mother and father in Queens, New York, and is the only child in the family. Jane's mother is a homemaker, and her father is employed as an accountant. Jane's maternal aunt lives with the family and participates in caregiving (see Figures 4.1 and 4.2).

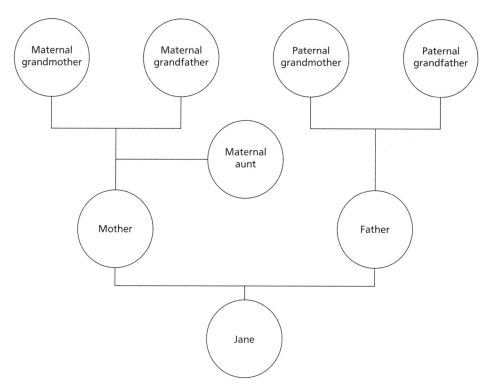

Figure 4.1. Jane's genogram.

Jane lives in a bilingual Albanian- and English-speaking home. Ms. C. began to use more English with Jane at the time of the early intervention evaluation. She reports that Jane's language skills are similar in both languages, and this is confirmed during the early intervention assessment.

ASSESSMENTS FOR COMMUNICATION TREATMENT PLANNING

Jane begins language intervention at the Queens College Speech-Language-Hearing Center when she is 22 months of age. A developmental assessment of her strengths and challenges is done through observational sampling using several developmental paradigms as a guide. Specifically, the Developmental, Individual-differences, Relationship-Based (DIR) Floortime model's functional emotional developmental levels (FEDLs; Greenspan & Wieder, 1998), a modified version of the *Diagnostic Manual for Infancy and Early Childhood* (Interdisciplinary Council on Developmental and Learning Disorders [ICDL], 2005), the Clinical Assessment of Comprehension (Miller & Paul, 1995), and Westby's (2000) Play Scale are used to assess all areas of development.

Starting with the FEDLs (see Chapter 7 of the accompanying text), the hallmark of the DIR model (Greenspan & Wieder, 1998), Jane's abilities are compromised at the first three levels relative to *shared attention and regulation, engagement and relating,* and *two-way purposeful communication.* Jane demonstrates strengths in selected contexts; however, her profile is not as robust as would be expected of a 2-year-old. During singing, Jane is animated and more engaged. She is minimally intentional during this context, periodically indicating by body movements,

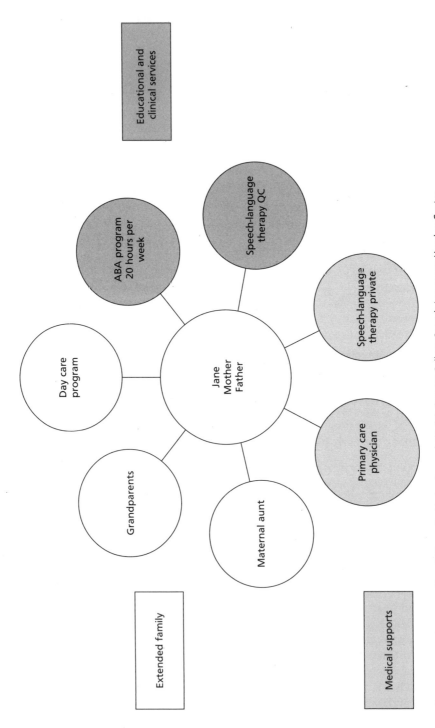

Figure 4.2. Jane's ecomap. *Key:* ABA, applied behavior analysis; QC, Queens College Speech-Language-Hearing Center.

vocalizations, or words which song she would like to sing. During singing, she displays positive affect with her partners. The level of engagement and intentional communication observed during this activity is not apparent across contexts, such as while playing with toys or during natural interactions. In those contexts, engagement and intentionality are fleeting, and shared attention is difficult to encourage. See Figure 4.3 for an assessment of her functional emotional developmental levels.

The *Interdisciplinary Council on Developmental Learning Disorders—Diagnostic Manual for Infants and Young Children* (ICDL-DMIC; ICDL, 2005) addresses many of the same areas of development as the FEDLs (Greenspan & Wieder, 1998), particularly at the first three levels (see Chapter 7 of the accompanying text). Because both of these paradigms share a perspective on foundational developmental capacities and stages of social, emotional, cognitive, and communication in typical

	1	2	3	4	5	6
Draw line through to highest level (1–6) child has reached	Not reached	With support—intermittent	With structure and scaffolding given high affect, gestural, language, sensorimotor support	Not at age-expected level, inconsistent	Age-appropriate level in certain contexts	Age-appropriate level with full range of affect states and emotional themes—consider robustness and thematic level to give this rating
Modality						
I. Shared attention and regulation						
II. Engagement and relating					3	
III. Two-way intentional communication						
IV. Complex problem solving: *Simple two- to three-step actions and presymbolic functional use of toys*						
V. Shared forms and meanings						

Figure 4.3. Assessment of functional emotional developmental levels for Jane at age 22 months and age 30 months. Key: solid arrow, Jane at 22 months; dotted arrow, Jane at 30 months. (*Source:* Greenspan & Wieder, 1998.)

development, the overlap at the early stages is predictable. In terms of the ICDL-DMIC, Level 4, First words: sharing meaning in gestures and words, typically seen in children between 12 and 18 months, Jane primarily produces some consonant + vowel combinations (e.g., /kʌ kʌ/, /tʌkʌtʌkʌ/) and the sound /m/, all of which are considered to be sound play. Jane occasionally imitates adults' productions of single words (e.g., *clap*) and produces a few words spontaneously (e.g., *cup, cat*).

Jane uses some gestures to communicate meaning and intention, for example, clapping a baby doll's hands while looking at the clinician. This signals that she wants the clinician to sing "If You're Happy and You Know It." Similarly, while her mom bounces her on a large ball, Jane puts her hands on her head when she wants the clinician to sing "Five Little Monkeys." She occasionally points to indicate objects she wants the adults to retrieve but does not point or show to share attention or make reference. See Figure 4.4 for an outline of Jane's speech-language-communication status at 22 and 30 months.

The Clinical Assessment of Language Comprehension (Miller & Paul, 1995) is used to assess Jane's developmental stage of comprehension. At the 8- to 12-month-old level of this measure, Jane understands some words in context, typically related to the songs she enjoys singing, when these forms are used with supporting gestures. She is not responsive to "Mommy," "Daddy," or to her name. She responds to some simple directions, such as "sit down please." The strategies that a child might demonstrate to support comprehension at this stage, such as looking at and object that mother looks at or acting on objects at hand, are seen infrequently.

At the next developmental level, 12–18 months, Jane understands some single words in her immediate environment (e.g., *monkey*), will on occasion retrieve an object in view when asked, and has a small receptive vocabulary of about 10 words. For the most part, Jane needs models to perform simple actions such as "kiss the baby" or "give the baby a hug." Jane's use of the strategies typically noted to enhance comprehension at her age, such as taking objects offered to her and conventional use of objects, are observed intermittently.

At the 18- to 24-month level of the Clinical Assessment of Comprehension (Miller & Paul, 1995), Jane's challenges in comprehension are apparent. She does not understand two-word combinations such as agent + action, action + object, and possessor + possession. As mentioned previously, her receptive vocabulary is fewer than 20 words, and she does not respond to words for objects that are out of view. Relative to other foundational capacities, her interaction with objects is a strength.

To summarize, at the age of 22 months, Jane's comprehension is most characteristic of behaviors expected at 8–18 months and is clearly challenged at the 18- to 24-month level.

Finally, in terms of play development, using the Westby's (2000) developmental play scale as a reference, Jane primarily exhibits presymbolic play, including exploring objects and tapping them. Relative to the presymbolic stages, Jane demonstrates some of the behaviors typical of children from 12 months to 17 months. These behaviors are characteristic of an understanding of object permanence, means-end, and object use. For example, Jane looks for objects in the room when they are named; understands in-ness, as demonstrated by her interest in putting objects in buckets; points to objects to have adults retrieve them; and explores some toys. She frequently bangs and taps objects, which is particularly worrisome to her parents, who are eager to eliminate this behavior.

Early in the semester, Jane begins imitating her mother's symbolic actions, which include bringing pretend food to her mouth, hugging a baby doll, and combing

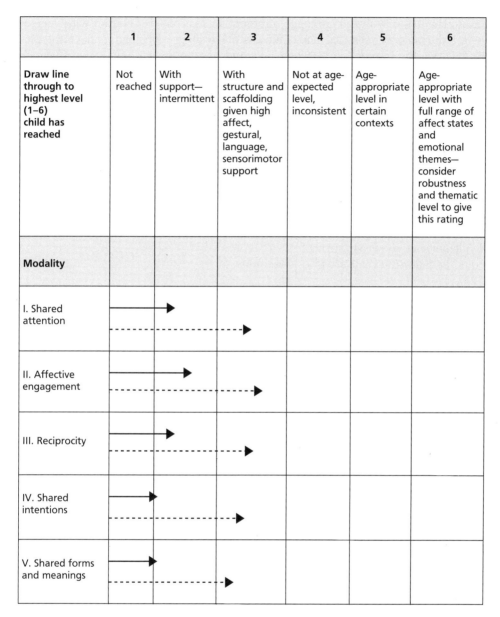

	1	2	3	4	5	6
Draw line through to highest level (1–6) child has reached	Not reached	With support— intermittent	With structure and scaffolding given high affect, gestural, language, sensorimotor support	Not at age-expected level, inconsistent	Age-appropriate level in certain contexts	Age-appropriate level with full range of affect states and emotional themes— consider robustness and thematic level to give this rating
Modality						
I. Shared attention						
II. Affective engagement						
III. Reciprocity						
IV. Shared intentions						
V. Shared forms and meanings						

Figure 4.4.   Assessment of speech-language-communication for Jane at 22 months and 30 months. *Key:* solid arrow, Jane at 22 months; dotted arrow, Jane at 30 months. (*Source:* Interdisciplinary Council on Developmental and Learning Disorders, 2005.)

the baby doll's hair. She also begins to manipulate a wider range of toys, such as opening the doors on the play kitchen and putting play figures into and out of the bus.

CLINICAL PROBLEM SOLVING TO IDENTIFY TREATMENT GOALS

Clinicians use the principles of the DIR model in combination with developmental language paradigms to determine initial goals for Jane. Based on observation of the parents' interactions with Jane, their first priority is to frame the therapy as a *parent coaching opportunity*. Clinicians ask Jane's mother, who accompanies her to the majority of the language intervention sessions, to interact with Jane at length during every session. The clinicians make suggestions and model strategies to enhance the interaction between Jane and her mother with attention to Jane's developmental level across domains.

Prior to coaching, Ms. C. attempted to address Jane's language delays by asking her to imitate words; posing who, what, and why questions during play; and holding out for words when Jane communicated nonverbally. Ms. C.'s priorities are to improve Jane's language production and to enhance her vocabulary with words a 2-year-old might know, such as colors, numbers, and opposites. Ms. C. indicates that these goals have been suggested by the applied behavior analysis (ABA) therapists.

Ms. C. is interested in how to modify her interactions with Jane to support language development and is extremely responsive to suggestions and recommendations. In many ways, once she learns more about the approach and the process being implementing, she is a natural.

The following goals are priorities for Ms. C.:

- Enhance opportunities to engage in back-and-forth interactions with Jane, related to her interests, such as sound play.

- Imitate Jane's actions and vocalizations to increase reciprocity.

- Respond to all of Jane's communicative attempts—behavioral, nonverbal, vocal, or verbal—with a pragmatically matched response.

- Follow Jane's lead relative to play choices, even when these are repetitive.

- Reduce the lexical and grammatical complexity of the language directed to Jane.

Based on the developmental observations (see Figures 4.3 and 4.4), the clinician determines that language production will not be the priority at this initial stage in therapy. This decision is similar to the one made for Mark, who is discussed in Chapter 7 of the accompanying text. Rather, the clinician focuses the therapeutic interactions on the earliest capacities of shared attention and affective engagement. From the clinician's perspective, further progress in communication and language rests on Jane's developing more robust precursory capacities, as these skills are foundational for all further language learning. Because Jane is typically regulated in terms of her emotional states, it is not necessary to address this capacity. However, the frequent tapping of toys is seen as a potential regulatory behavior, and rather than discourage it, the adults join the behavior joyfully and introduce toys where tapping would be conventional (musical instruments).

The goals for shared attention and affective engagement are framed as facilitating the following:

- Jane's participation in engaged, back-and-forth interactions with her mother and the clinicians

- Jane's joint attention with her communication partners

- Jane's engagement using a range of behaviors, actions, and conventional forms of communication

Facilitating the understanding and expression of shared intentionality is also a high priority during early therapeutic sessions. The goals for this capacity are framed as follows:

- To respond to all of Jane's behaviors as if they have communicative intent, as is typical at perlocutionary stages of development

- To facilitate Jane's response to others' communicative intent using high affect and encouraging responsiveness through modeling

The final goal generated for the first semester's therapy is in the area of shared ideas and meanings.

- To expand Jane's range of ideas and meanings during play, starting with the play schemas she prefers

It is important to note that no specific goals are set for the comprehension and production of language. However, the clinicians model language in Phases 1 and 2 (Lahey, 1988) of language, which matches Jane's actions and the actions of the adults interacting with her. Further, the adults use Jane's natural interests to enhance interpersonal interactions, whether initiated by her or engineered by the adult.

INTERVENTIONS USED TO ACHIEVE MAJOR GOALS

When working more naturalistically and developmentally, multiple intervention goals are embedded into the ongoing interaction rather than sequentially addressed by segmenting the session into modules. For example, although there are several goals for Jane's therapy, these are not designated to particular periods during the play. Rather, as opportunities arise naturally, these contexts are used to address the goals. If Jane begins to babble, for example, the clinician will approach her to get her attention and begin the sound-play game. If Jane then wanders over to a toy and begins to tap on it, the clinician will join her again and begin to sing and tap. Thus, the flow of the session follows the focus of the child's attention, and the clinician capitalizes on what the child is doing at any particular moment.

The strategy of following the child's lead is now typically recommended in most parent-centered training (Binns & Cardy, 2019; Pickles et al., 2016; Solomon et al., 2014). The approach differs considerably from adult-directed sessions in which the clinician typically introduces to the child activities chosen by the adult with the agenda of gaining the child's attention to the activity. In this latter approach, the benefits of joining the "contents of the child's mind" (Bloom & Tinker, 2001) are not capitalized on. In the DIR/developmental language approach, joining the child's ideas and making affective connections is considered a foundation for the development of meaning and thus is critical for progress in language and communication.

Although Jane is at a much earlier level of development than Mark, who is discussed in Chapter 7 of the accompanying text, intervention strategies are similar. Of course, with Jane, the nature of the interactions is at early stages of development. Interestingly, even though Mark is verbal, it is important to remember that there are many foundational capacities that are compromised, and thus the fact that comprehension and production are not goals for Mark or Jane at initial intervention stages reflects the philosophy of the approach.

It should be reiterated that although goals for comprehension and production are not prioritized, the adults present language models to Jane during therapy sessions using language that matches her actions and intentions. Simplified grammatical sentences (e.g., "Oh no, Mommy ate it") are used during interactions based on the notion that the child develops the rules of the language from hearing exemplars that are syntactically and semantically appropriate.

The key strategy derived from a DIR perspective as well as from a developmental language one is the idea of following the child's lead or, as noted previously, joining the contents of the child's mind (Bloom & Tinker, 2001). In developmental thinking, joining the child's pursuit of her interests leads to greater engagement, shared attention, and understanding and the child's more frequent expression of communicative intent. In a sense, goals are addressed where they most naturally occur, which is thought to make learning more accessible for the child. This concept is a major thread in the training done with Jane's mother, as following rather than leading her child is modeled and encouraged with the goal of affectively engaging in Jane's play scenarios. This shift in the mother's perspective is significant, as noted by the mother and observed by the clinicians.

In terms of the frequent tapping, it is obvious that both Mr. and Ms. C. become anxious and worried when Jane begins this behavior. Time is spent discussing the possible reasons Jane is tapping, such as its being a regulatory behavior, and the importance of developing a range of responses to it. Although for some children self-regulatory behaviors may be unconventional, the possibility that these behaviors serve the typical functions of managing arousal and reactivity should be considered. With this interpretation in mind, tapping would be encouraged with appropriate toys, such as musical instruments. This is an excellent choice, as Jane loves singing, and tapping can be incorporated into this typical context. At times, clinicians also encourage Ms. C. to try to make the tapping an imitative game, where she will tap, make sounds, and wait; Jane will tap, she will join, and so on. This often leads to enhanced affective interactions with Jane smiling and looking at her mom, waiting for the next round in the game. Finally, by increasing Jane's repertoire of play options, clinicians hope to increase her ideas for play and decrease her more limited option of tapping.

Clearly, a great deal of parent counseling is necessary when children demonstrate behaviors that are considered hallmarks of autism. Clinicians and educators should encourage parents to talk about why these behaviors upset them, giving the practitioner an opportunity to empathize with their feelings. Jane's tapping is a sign of autism to her parents, and supporting their feelings about the behavior and the diagnosis is an important part of the process.

OUTCOMES

The following are outcomes of Jane's language intervention during the first and second semesters.

First Semester of Language Intervention: September to January

At the end of the first semester of therapy at Queens College, Jane has made significant progress in all of the areas targeted for treatment. In addition to the clinic's services, Jane is receiving 20 hours of ABA, is receiving additional speech and language therapy, and is attending a child care center for typically developing children.

The intensity of her program undoubtedly led to the notable progress she is making. However, after meeting with her early intervention team, it is clear that the goals and strategies used in the other therapies are quite different from the ones being addressed at Queens College.

Ms. C.'s involvement in the therapeutic process and responsiveness to coaching is considered a major factor in the progress both Jane and her mother are making. Ms. C. implements the developmental approach in her interactions with Jane at home. Although Mr. C. occasionally joins the clinicians at the end of the therapy sessions, it is clear that his perspective on Jane's developmental strengths and challenges and her educational needs is different from that of the clinicians. However, Mr. C. is always interested in the clinicians' input and is key in terms of obtaining and researching additional services that Jane might receive.

In reference to Jane's progress, engagement and intentionality increase significantly, especially during selected contexts. For example, reciprocal interactions are more often initiated by Jane, are more frequent and longer in duration, and occur primarily during sound imitation games and singing. The clinician imitates Jane's vocalizations' varying loudness, pitch, and timing, and this interests Jane. These activities provide excellent opportunities to expand and encourage the goals for the first two FEDLs, as Jane's interpersonal attention and affect are most robust during these contexts.

Jane's repertoire of forms to express communicative intentionality and to keep interactions going expand, as she now uses eye gaze; gestures, such as pointing; vocalizations typical of babbling and jargon; word approximations; and recognizable words. The majority of Jane's communicative intentions serve as requests; however, within the episodes of sound play or singing, more sustained shared attention is also noted. By the end of the term, Jane's attention is often directed to the adults' activities during play rather than solely her own.

The vocalizations that Jane produces during sessions include repetitions of /kʌkʌkʌ/, /tʌkʌtʌkʌ/, /hɛhɛdʌbæ/, /ʌh tə/, and /bibibibi/. Other vocalizations include /hædɪgʌ/, /kɪkɪkɪkɪ/, and /kʌbi/. This repertoire represents progress in the complexity and diversity of Jane's sound system. Jane vocalizes frequently when singing "Five Little Monkeys" with her mother and the clinicians.

Jane's imitative and spontaneous vocabulary expand as she begins to produce /ʌk/ (duck), /kæk/ (quack), /bæbæ/ for the Barney stuffed animal, /bebi/ while holding up the pretend bottle to feed the baby, /kʌp/ during play with the cup, /sɪt/ while sitting on a chair, /hæpi/ (happy), /baɪ/ (bye), and /mʌki/ (monkey). These words were modeled during play episodes by the clinicians and Jane's mother since the beginning of the semester. It is the clinician's impression that Jane understands all of the words that she is producing.

Jane also expands her repertoire of schemas related to toys during play. She begins to use a spoon and bowl to mix, continuing when the clinician adds an object to the bowl. She expands the filling of a container play to include cups and buckets. Jane imitates the clinician's modeling of new actions, such as bringing a cup to the stuffed animal's mouth to drink. She begins to attend to toys that are new to her and enjoys figuring out how a toy works, such as how a toy dinosaur walks. Finally, she plays more independently with pop-up toys, understanding that different sections of the toy require different movements—such as pushing, turning, and sliding.

All of these observable changes in Jane's developmental profile suggest progress in a very positive direction. Although tapping continues, Jane now has more options in her play, and she does not develop any new behaviors that are worrisome to her parents. Throughout the semester, a great deal of time is spent on parent counseling, which appears quite helpful to the family. It is interesting to note here that although some of the counseling relates to behaviors that are typically associated with ASD, a great deal of the information shared with the parents relates to typical child development and how to understand Jane's development through that lens rather than through the lens of disability.

Second Semester of Language Intervention: January to June

At the beginning of the second semester, after an intersession break from the Queens College program, the clinicians observe that Jane is using words and sentences that she clearly does not have the meanings for. For example, she will use the word *open* to indicate all requests from adults. This suggests that the emphasis in other therapies might be on the production of language rather than on the foundations as outlined previously. The clinician shares this concern with Jane's parents, and a team meeting is scheduled. Both the ABA therapist and the private SLP acknowledge that they were, in fact, focusing on production, assuming that this was the best path to take. As a result of the meeting, Jane's other therapists reconsider their goals and agree to address the comprehension of language rather than the production of language.

This scenario is quite typical when the child with ASD is able to imitate and produce language easily. Clinicians must remind both parents and other practitioners of the developmental sequence of language and ask them to reduce the emphasis on talking in favor of the developmental capacities that underlie the eventual ability to talk with meaning and purpose.

Because of Jane's notable progress in the prior months, goals for comprehension and production are added to the intervention program:

Comprehension

- To pair specific Phase 1 and 2 form–content relations, such as open the door (Action) (Lahey, 1988), with Jane's actions.

Production

- To model and expand Phase 1 and 2 form–content relations (Lahey, 1988) related to Jane's spontaneous productions and actions.

As the second semester progresses (see Figures 4.3 and 4.4), Jane begins to maintain engagement throughout the majority of the session and across a range of activities. She frequently makes eye contact and references her communication partner. Periods of self-directed activities are greatly reduced.

In terms of intentionality, Jane initiates and maintains communicative interactions for the majority of the session using body language, gestures, facial expression, jargon, word approximations, and words. In the beginning of the second semester, Jane primarily names items using one-word utterances for objects in the room or in the toy closet, to express a comment, or to request. For example, Jane says "violin" to request that the clinician bring the violin into the therapy room. Toward the end of the semester, Jane begins to protest using "no" to indicate which toys she does not want to play with. She also begins to use greetings, such as "hi" and "bye," when entering and exiting the therapy room. As is often seen, if she is greeted with "Hi, Jane," she repeats this greeting, suggesting that her understanding of names is still constricted.

In terms of shared ideas and meaning, in the beginning of the semester, Jane's play schemas continue to be limited. She primarily uses the kitchen playset, feeds herself or the surrounding stuffed animals, or plays with the musical instruments and sings a variety of songs, including "Five Little Monkeys," "Jingle Bells," and "I'm a Little Teapot." As the semester progresses, the clinicians brings in playsets that Jane has not seen before. Jane begins to explore the zoo playset with intention and delight and incorporates stuffed animals into the play schema. For example, she pushes the monkey on the zoo swing or has the monkey go down the slide. When a playground playset is introduced in the session, Jane generalizes previously acquired schemas as she begins to have the monkey do similar actions on the playground. It is also noted that Jane becomes more independent in her play throughout the semester. At the outset, the clinician plays a larger role in modeling different play actions; however, more self-initiated play and less modeling are necessary toward the end of the semester. Overall, Jane's range of ideas and meanings in play increase significantly, as observed in the variety of play schemas she initiates and participates in.

In terms of comprehension, the clinicians begin to present verbal directives ("give Mommy the monkey") into the play in order to encourage contextually based understanding. Jane's responses are inconsistent, and it is difficult to determine whether she does not understand the directive or she is not engaged. Overall, Jane's comprehension of words and phrases has increased, as judged by her production of language, yet this developmental area requires ongoing assessment.

Although production is not a primary goal of therapy, it is noted that the phonological clarity of Jane's productions increases over the course of the semester, her length of utterance increases from single words to some two-word utterances, and her interpersonal use of language expands. For the most part, words are used with meaning determined from the co-occurring nonlinguistic context. In addition, Jane's coding of form–content categories (Lahey, 1988) expands. In the beginning of the second semester, Jane primarily coded existence by naming objects that she observed or wanted. As the semester progressed, Jane began to code action, locative action, state, locative state, and recurrence. Existence continued to be the most frequently coded form–content relation. A sample of the forms and form–content relations that Jane produced at the end of the semester follows:

Existence—monkeys, slide, tree, daddy
Recurrence—more, more people
Rejection—no, no
Action—open door
Locative action—sit down monkeys, go swing
Locative state—in the bus, on swing
State—want a monkey

At the time this sample is analyzed, Jane is productive in several Phase 1 categories (Existence, Locative Action, and Recurrence) and emerging in others (Action, Locative State). She also uses word combinations and syntactic utterances typical of Phase 2 with either relational + substantive or verb + object forms (e.g., "sit down monkeys"). All of these developments suggest that Jane is taking important steps in the development of a linguistic system.

Finally, it should be noted that Jane's comprehension of language continues to be a major concern. The clinicians consider that some children with Jane's profile are at risk for developing production abilities that surpass comprehension abilities. With this in mind, the clinician helps Jane's parents understand that the focus of intervention will continue to be on Jane's language understanding rather than on her language expression.

Learning Activities

1. Discuss how an aspect of the treatment might be implemented by different disciplines and what steps would be important to take to support the child's language learning success across intervention contexts.

Note: An example of supporting her learning across contexts occurred with Jane's ABA therapist and private SLP. Toward the end of Jane's first semester of therapy at Queens College, she began to use words and phrases that she did not understand, which was determined by the context in which they were used. The ABA therapist indicated that she was asking Jane to repeat words as often as possible, as she assumed this was a sound approach to teaching children language. The SLP explained that because Jane could talk, she also thought it was a good idea to have Jane ask for what she wanted (e.g., "I want _____") before giving her what she had requested nonverbally.

For children who are already enrolled in preschool programs, SLPs can make an effort to meet with the child's educational team to collaborate on language intervention strategies. Of particular concern is the interpretation by educators and clinicians of a child's behaviors as problematic. Often, these behaviors are a result of regulatory issues or language and/or communication challenges, or they represent typical emotional stages for younger children. The emphasis on expectations that align with the child's developmental stage across domains—social, emotional, cognitive, language, communication—is a high priority.

2. What assessment steps would you take to address intervention priorities for a child with delayed language development? Reflect on the solutions identified in Jane's case and whether these same solutions might work for children at different developmental levels or with different diagnoses.

Note: As is clear from the age gap between Jane (22–30 months) and Mark (5–9 years), the child discussed in Chapter 7 of the accompanying text, the framework presented has applications across chronological ages and developmental stages for children with language disorders. The principles of FEDLs and developmental language levels both emphasize the generation of intervention goals on the basis of well-documented stages of typical child development. The value of these paradigms is the focus on the core deficits experienced by children, teens, and adults with ASD— "Persistent deficits in social communication and social interaction across multiple contexts" (American Psychiatric Association, 2013, p. 51). While the DIRFloortime and developmental language models require a depth and breadth of expertise on the SLP's part, the emphasis on developmental integration speaks to the tremendous value of these approaches (Gerber, 2017).

3. Discuss the developmental benefits of prioritizing engagement and intentionality in the treatment of children with ASD.

Note: Contemporary views of interpersonal intersubjectivity, which develops during the typical child's early life, can serve as a beacon to greater understanding of the primary interpersonal challenges noted in children with ASD. These challenges affect the child's ability to develop the essence of human language, that is, the capacity to use language to interact with and relate to others. Promoting the development of interpersonal and reciprocal relatedness requires equal attention to assessing and addressing the core social deficits in autism in addition to or regardless of the child's linguistic abilities and regardless of the child's chronological age. When the broadest view of language (Bloom & Tinker, 2001), one that speaks to the integration of and dependence on cognitive, social, and emotional precursors and cocursors, is used as the assessment paradigm, intervention goals will more accurately address the roadblocks to communication experienced by children on the spectrum.

4. How can the comprehension of language be assessed in naturalistic contexts and through the child's production of language?

Note: The focus on language production or expressive language rather than on language comprehension or receptive language is problematic for those children whose ability to produce words and sentences exceeds their understanding of those forms. By using a developmental sequence such as the one provided by Miller and Paul (1995) and embedding comments and directives in natural interaction, the SLP can determine what level of comprehension the child has mastered. Further, by observing the child's use of language, the SLP will have the opportunity to assess whether the child is producing forms where meaning is compromised (e.g., using "I want _____" in incorrect contexts).

REFERENCES

American Psychiatric Association. (2013). *Diagnostic and statistical manual of mental disorders, fifth edition* (DSM-5). Author.

Binns, A., & Cardy, J. (2019). Developmental social pragmatic interventions for preschoolers with autism spectrum disorder: A systematic review. *Autism and Developmental Language Impairments, 4*, 1–18.

Bloom, L., & Tinker, E. (2001). The intentionality model and language acquisition. *Monographs of the Society for Research in Child Development, 66*(4, Serial No. 267), 1–91.

Bureau of Early Intervention. (1999). *Clinical Practice Guideline: Quick Reference Guide—Communication Disorders, Assessment and Intervention for Young Children (Age 0–3 Years).* New York State Department of Health, Publication No. 4219. http://www.health.ny.gov/publications/4219.pdf

Bzoch, R., League, R., & Brown, V. (2003). *REEL-3: Receptive-Expressive Emergent Language Test:–Third Edition: Examiner's manual.* PRO-ED.

Gerber, S. (2017). Embracing the potential of play for children on the autism spectrum: Facilitating the earliest stages of developmental integration. *Topics in Language Disorders, 37*, 229–240.

Gerber, S. (2021). Understanding foundational developmental capacities related to language: A toddler with ASD. In P. A. Prelock & R. J. McCauley (Eds.), *Treatment of autism spectrum disorder: Evidence-based intervention strategies for communication & social interactions* (2nd ed., pp. 163–192). Paul H. Brookes Publishing Co.

Greenspan, S. I., & Wieder, S. (1998). *The child with special needs: Encouraging intellectual and emotional growth.* Perseus Books.

Interdisciplinary Council on Developmental and Learning Disorders. (2005). *Diagnostic manual for infancy and early childhood: Mental health, developmental, regulatory-sensory processing, language and learning disorders*. ICDL Press.

Lahey, M. (1988). *Language disorders and language development*. Wiley.

Luyster, R., Gotham, K., Guthrie, W., Coffing, M., Petrak, R., Pierce, K., & Lord, C. (2009). The Autism Diagnostic Observation Schedule–Toddler Module: A new module of at standardized diagnostic measure for autism spectrum disorders. *Journal of Autism Developmental Disorders, 39*, 1305–1320.

Miller, J., & Paul, R. (1995). *The clinical assessment of language comprehension*. Paul H. Brookes Publishing Co.

Parks, S., Furuno, S., O'Reilly, K., Hosaka, C., Inatsuka, T., Zeisloft-Falbey, B., & Allman, T. (1984–2004). *HELP Strands (Hawaii Early Learning Profile): Ages birth–3*. Volt Corp.

Pickles, A., Le Couteur, A., Leadbitter, K., Salomone, E., Cole-Fletcher, R., Tobin, H., Gammer, I., Lowry, J., Vamvakas, G., Byford, S., Aldred, C., Slonims, V., McConachie, H., Howlin, P., Parr, J. R., Charman, T., & Green, J. (2016). Parent-mediated social communication therapy for young children with autism (PACT): Long-term follow-up of a randomised controlled trial. *Lancet, 388*, 2501–2509.

Solomon, R., Van Egeren, L., Mahoney, G., Quon-Huber, M., & Zimmerman, P. (2014). PLAY Project home consultation intervention program for young children with autism spectrum disorders: A randomized controlled trial. *Journal of Developmental and Behavioral Pediatrics, 35*(8), 475–485.

Voress, J., Maddox, T., & Hammill, D. (2012). *Developmental Assessment of Young Children–2*. Pearson.

Westby, C. (2000). A scale for assessing development of children's play. In K. Gitlin-Weiner, A. Sandgrund, & C. Schaefer (Eds.), *Play diagnosis and assessment* (2nd ed., pp. 15–58). Wiley.

Replacing Challenging Behavior With a Better Way to Communicate

A Fourth Grader With ASD

Lauren J. Moskowitz and V. Mark Durand

 Eli

 Age 9

 Autism Spectrum Disorder

Case 5 engages with the intervention approach and strategies discussed in Chapter 8, Functional Communication Training: Treating Challenging Behavior (Durand & Moskowitz, 2021) in *Treatment of Autism Spectrum Disorder, Second Edition*.

INTRODUCTION

Eli is a 9-year-old boy with autism spectrum disorder (ASD) and moderate intellectual disability (ID) who attends fourth grade at a special education school for children with ASD in New York City. Eli was diagnosed with autistic disorder (*Diagnostic and Statistical Manual of Mental Disorders, Fourth Edition, Text Revision* [DSM-IV-TR]; American Psychiatric Association [APA], 2000) at 2 years of age and later (between 5 and 6 years of age) also was diagnosed with attention-deficit/ hyperactivity disorder (ADHD). He lives at home with his parents and younger sister (Lee). Eli's parents are married and both actively participate in his treatment.

They describe him as a sweet, sensitive boy who loves to laugh. Eli communicates primarily through verbal language, although a large majority of his speech appears to be scripted, echolalic, or perseverative (e.g., "Dad pick me up?"). However, he can generate novel phrases, often following echolalic responses. For example, when his teacher told him, "Check your mailbox," Eli repeated, "I'm gonna check my mailbox. I have mail."

The primary concern for Eli's parents and teachers is his challenging behavior, specifically his physical aggression and disruptive behavior. Two years prior to coming to the clinic, Eli experienced several stressors, including the death of his grandmother, the birth of his 2-year-old sister Lee, and a change in school teachers. His aggression at school became problematic at that time, and as a result, he was moved to a different classroom with a lower student–teacher ratio. His aggression almost always targeted female classmates (Cindy and Jen, in particular) and younger students. He began taking Ritalin (methylphenidate) 30 mg at that time (when he was 7 years old) and was noticeably less hyperactive at home (according to his parents), although his challenging behavior at school continued. School staff did not believe their school was the appropriate setting for Eli.

The clinic would like to develop a comprehensive, multicomponent behavior intervention plan to target Eli's challenging behavior across both school and home. However, school is the greater concern for the parents and teachers. Because the purpose of this case is to describe the application of functional communication training (FCT; Carr & Durand, 1985), it focuses on the use of FCT in the school setting.

ASSESSMENTS FOR COMMUNICATION TREATMENT PLANNING

When a child presents with challenging behavior, prior to using FCT it is necessary to conduct a functional behavior assessment to determine why the child is exhibiting the behavior (i.e., to identify the function or purpose of the child's behavior). Understanding the purpose of the child's behavior allows clinicians to teach the child a communication response that serves the same function as the challenging behavior. As described in Chapter 8 in *Treatment of Autism Spectrum Disorder: Evidence-Based Intervention Strategies for Communication & Social Interactions, Second Edition*, a variety of methods can be used when conducting an functional behavior assessment, including indirect assessment (e.g., rating scales/questionnaires and interviews), descriptive assessment (direct observation of antecedents to the problem behavior and consequences that follow the behavior), and functional analysis (experimental manipulation of consequences or antecedents to examine its effect on problem behavior). Given that the principal does not allow a functional analysis, Eli's clinicians rely on indirect and descriptive assessment.

Questionnaires/Rating Scales

On the Functional Assessment Checklist for Teachers (FACTS; March et al., 2000), Eli's teachers identify his *strengths* as doing well as the teacher's assistant and doing all the work assigned in math. They identify Eli's *challenging behaviors* as 1) aggression (e.g., kicking, pulling hair), 2) disruptive behavior (e.g., yelling, falling to the floor and not getting up), and 3) elopement (i.e., running out of the classroom).

Eli's teachers report that these behaviors last approximately 15–30 minutes and that the intensity is rated as high on a scale of 1 to 6 (with 1 being low and 6 being high), often leading to injuries. His teachers indicate that *antecedents* that are likely to immediately evoke Eli's challenging behavior are certain curriculum areas (especially when given a difficult task) and, even more commonly, proximity to certain classmates (two girls in his class, Cindy and Jen), particularly when these girls start crying. *Setting events* that make Eli's challenging behavior more likely to occur are transitions (such as transitioning from his classroom to the lunchroom or from one classroom to another). Finally, in terms of the *consequences* that appear most likely to maintain Eli's problem behavior, his teachers report that he escapes difficult tasks and unwanted activities when he engages in such behavior and that he often obtains adult attention in the process. Strategies that teachers have used to attempt to prevent Eli's challenging behavior in the past were seating changes. Strategies they have used to respond to Eli's challenging behavior were providing him with sensory activities and/or a break from the classroom.

His teachers' responses on the Motivation Assessment Scale (MAS; Durand & Crimmins, 1992) indicate that Eli's aggression, disruptive behaviors, and elopement are primarily *escape-motivated* (e.g., occur following a command or requests to perform a difficult task) and, to a lesser extent, attention motivated (i.e., to obtain attention from his teachers). The MAS completed by his mother regarding his aggression toward his younger sister reveals a primary function of tangible, a secondary function of escape, and a possible tertiary function of attention (more information to follow).

Interviews With Teachers and Parents

During the Functional Assessment Interview (FAI; O'Neill et al., 1997), Eli's teachers report that he displayed challenging behavior earlier that morning in literacy class, math class, and on the way from math to the lunchroom. They describe that, in math class, one of Eli's classmates (Cindy) started crying, which led to Eli run out of the classroom. His teachers also report that, later on, when Eli walked into the lunchroom at 12:00 p.m., he paced back and forth. When one of the other classes entered the lunchroom, Eli ran up to two female students and attempted to kick them. Although his teachers prevented Eli from kicking the students, Eli then dropped to the floor. His teachers could not remember exactly what they said to Eli in that instant, but they believe they said something such as, "Eli, stand up, your body is not safe," or "Do you want to be in the lunchroom?" (The observers did not witness this exchange.) His teachers removed Eli from the lunchroom temporarily but then brought him back into the lunchroom and physically guided Eli over to a lunch table.

The FAI conducted with Eli's parents reveals that Eli's aggression and tantrums are more likely to happen in group settings such as classes than at home by himself, more likely to happen with teachers than with parents (likely because of increased demands with teachers), and more likely to happen when in close proximity to a younger child, particularly a girl, such as his sister Lee or two girls in his class. Eli's aggression and tantrums are also more likely to happen if he is engaging in an activity with performance demands. Eli is least likely to engage in aggression or tantrums when pacing or playing on the computer on his own. The FAI reveals that, when he exhibits aggression toward his sister, the primary function of his aggression appears to be to get a toy or item that Lee has (tangibly motivated), to keep playing with a toy, or to keep doing an activity that Lee is trying to get (e.g., to keep playing the computer on his own, also tangibly motivated), with a secondary function of escaping Lee.

Summary of Functional Assessment Results

Based on the questionnaire and interview with Eli's teachers and parents as well as multiple direct observations of the antecedents that preceded his behavior and the consequences that followed it, clinicians hypothesize that Eli's challenging behavior functions primarily to escape situations that are aversive (e.g., anxiety provoking, overwhelming, difficult), particularly transitions and classmates' crying. This hypothesis is based on the observation that the most frequent consequence following Eli's challenging behavior is that he escapes the given situation in which the behavior occurred. For example, after clinicians observe Eli throw a ball at Cindy when she starts screaming, the immediate consequence is his being taken out of the classroom (i.e., he escapes Cindy's screaming). In addition, it is possible that Eli's challenging behavior is motivated secondarily by a desire for attention. It may be that one-to-one attention in a separate room from his favorite teacher, Bea, is a particularly powerful motivator to engage in such behavior and subsequent escape from the classroom.

In terms of antecedents, proximity to specific students (e.g., Cindy, Jen), especially when these students cry, appears to be the antecedent that most often evokes Eli's challenging behavior. Transitions can serve as either antecedents or setting events for Eli in that, sometimes, transitions seem to be setting events that make Eli more likely to display challenging behavior if a certain antecedent is present during or prior to the transition, whereas, other times, the transitions appear to directly and immediately trigger Eli's behavior. For example, in the episode that clinicians observed in math class, it appears that a transition (e.g., bell ringing, students entering class) is the setting event that increases the likelihood of Eli displaying challenging behavior when triggered by a specific antecedent—in this case, Cindy's crying. Although Eli's challenging behavior is often evoked by transitions from one classroom to another, clinicians observe that he does not engage in these behaviors when making the transition from school to home (going home early with his father), presumably either because he is making the transition to a preferred situation or because teachers frequently remind him of the upcoming transition (i.e., resulting in increased predictability). Of note, the pattern of setting events and antecedents for Eli's challenging behavior appears to be similar outside of school. For example, Eli recently attended a cousin's birthday party; when told to get ready to leave, he attacked a smaller girl cousin. In this example (just as in school), it appears that the transition (leaving the party) was a setting event, and proximity to a smaller girl cousin (who perhaps was crying or has cried in the past) is the immediate antecedent to his challenging behavior.

CLINICAL PROBLEM SOLVING TO IDENTIFY TREATMENT GOALS

Eli's parents, principal, teachers, aides, and school counselor attend an interdisciplinary team meeting. They decide that FCT will be the primary intervention to address Eli's challenging behaviors. The rationale for choosing FCT is that Eli's parents want him to learn an appropriate way to communicate his wants and needs, especially to request a break from a situation that he finds anxiety producing or overwhelming or difficult. His school staff initially express concern about whether Eli can learn to ask for a break, which they think is too complex for him to learn to do spontaneously and independently (i.e., without prompting), but after much discussion, they decide that they are willing to give it a try. The team debates what specific communicative message Eli should be taught. A teacher initially suggests that, as soon as Cindy or Jen starts crying, a teacher or aide can immediately prompt Eli to ask for headphones and put headphones on, after which he can listen to music, which may drown out the sound of the other student's crying. The advantage of this approach is that it will keep him in the classroom in contrast to teaching him to ask for a break from the classroom. Clinicians think it might be better to teach Eli to ask for a break from the classroom, given that this communicative behavior will more closely match the function of Eli's challenging behavior (i.e., the reinforcer in both cases will be escaping the classroom/escaping the crying). In addition, in the real world, whereas headphones may not always be available to Eli, the opportunity to ask for a break will always be available.

INTERVENTIONS USED TO ACHIEVE MAJOR GOALS

As described in Chapter 8 in the accompanying text, Step 1 of conducting FCT is to assess the function of behavior, which is detailed in the previous section on assessment. The primary function of Eli's challenging behavior is hypothesized to be escaping from aversive situations, particularly escaping from classmates' crying as well as escaping from or avoiding transitions.

Step 2 is to select the mode of communication (e.g., verbal, signing, augmentative and alternative communication [AAC]) to be used for FCT. The team agrees on the communication modality of a visual BREAK card; Eli will be taught to give his teacher or therapist a laminated card with the word *break* written on it (as in Lalli et al., 1995). Eli is given a set number of BREAK cards, Velcroed to his desk and put in his pocket, that he can use throughout the school day. Although Eli has the ability to spontaneously produce single-word utterances, clinicians choose to use the BREAK card because 1) low-effort functional communication responses (e.g., handing over a card) are easier to use and more effective in replacing challenging behavior than are high-effort responses (e.g., verbally requesting a break), 2) the cards on his desk may serve as a visual prompt to remind Eli that he can ask for a break, and 3) using the cards will allow clinicians to gradually cut down on the number of BREAK cards available to Eli over time. Using a designated number of BREAK cards allows Eli to escape from class or from an activity but also allows the teachers to have some awareness of and therefore control over how many breaks he can take. Although the verbal response is not required for Eli to receive a break, clinicians also prompt Eli to say "break" as he hands over the BREAK card (with the eventual goal of shifting from visual BREAK cards to the more natural and portable modality of speech).

Step 3 of FCT is to arrange the environment to create teaching opportunities for Eli to use his BREAK cards. Although using the criterion environment (i.e., the environment in which clinicians want the person to communicate—in Eli's case, the classroom) as the training environment promotes generalization and maintenance, the team decides it would be best for his therapist to initially create teaching opportunities for Eli to use his BREAK card by exposing Eli to crying in a more controlled, safer environment rather than in the classroom. Given that Eli's challenging behavior in response to crying is conceptualized as a manifestation of fear or anxiety, FCT is used in conjunction with graduated exposure (also known as *systematic desensitization*), which is typically the most critical component of treating behaviors associated with fear or anxiety (Rosen et al., 2016). With graduated exposure, the child is gradually exposed to increasing proximity, intensity, or amounts of the feared stimulus or situation. Of note, regardless of whether Eli's challenging behavior in response to girls crying is due to fear/anxiety or to hyperacusis (hypersensitivity to sound), research has shown that, for children with ASD, their intolerant reaction to certain sounds (e.g., vacuum cleaner, blender, hand mixer, toilet flushing) can be modified using systematic desensitization to the point that the children eventually seem comfortable with these stimuli (Koegel et al., 2004). Thus, starting in the therapist's office, Eli is gradually exposed to the sounds and sights of crying, progressing from audio recordings of children crying at increasingly louder volumes to video recordings of children crying at increasingly louder volumes, to real-life adults (e.g., therapist, parent, teacher, confederates) crying in vivo, to confederate children crying, to videos of Cindy and Jen crying, and ultimately to Cindy and Jen actually crying in the classroom. These exposures to crying represent exposure to the actual trigger of the challenging behavior and a teaching opportunity to prompt the desired communication response (i.e., giving Eli the opportunity to learn to ask for a break from the crying).

Step 4 of FCT is to prompt communication. In illustration, as soon as the therapist starts playing the audio or video recording of people crying, Eli is taught to ask for a break by physically prompting him to hand the BREAK card to the therapist. As soon as Eli hands over the BREAK card, the therapist immediately stops the audio or video and allows him to leave the room (if he wishes) for a time-limited break. On the third trial of playing the recording of crying, Eli quickly picks up a BREAK card and hands it to the therapist independently before she has the chance to prompt him.

Clinicians discuss with Eli's teachers that it is better to prompt Eli to request a break before aggressing toward another student rather than after. However, if it is not possible either to prompt Eli to hand over his BREAK card when he is displaying precursor behaviors (before he aggresses) or to prompt him as soon as another child starts crying, then it is still considered better to prompt him to use a BREAK card after aggression before allowing him to leave the room than to abandon the use of the BREAK card. The hope is that, if he hands over the BREAK card, he will at least be leaving the room contingent upon communication rather than contingent upon aggression. If he engages in aggression, Eli's teachers are also instructed to provide him with as little attention as possible when escorting him out of the classroom.

Step 5 of FCT is to fade prompts as soon as possible so that Eli does not become prompt dependent. Although, as mentioned in Step 4, Eli initially learns to use his BREAK card independently very quickly in the contrived teaching situation of the therapist playing a recording of crying in her office, Eli nevertheless requires full physical prompting (i.e., hand-over-hand guiding him to pick up the card and hand it to the teacher) to use the BREAK card in his classroom. Prompting is then faded from a full physical prompt to partial physical prompts to gestural prompts (e.g., tapping the BREAK cards on Eli's desk, later pointing to the BREAK cards) to, finally, using only the verbal prompt "break." To facilitate maintenance and generalization, clinicians also gradually decrease the number of BREAK cards available to him over time and gradually increase the amount of time that Eli has to wait until he takes a break (thereby increasing the amount of time he is exposed to the sound of crying). This is important to do given that, in the real world, escape from another person crying (or any loud sound or aversive situation) may not always be immediately possible, so Eli ultimately needs to learn to cope with that reality.

When Eli hands his teacher a BREAK card, it is recommended that Eli's teachers bring him to a quiet, neutral area in the classroom or outside of it. The therapist suggests that teachers not bring him to the current break room in the school, given that Eli may already have an inconsistent and/or negative association with the current break room. (His teachers reported that, prior to intervention, either Eli could be brought to the break room in response to misbehavior, or Eli could choose to go to the break room. They also reported that Eli sometimes dropped to the floor on the way to the break room and was sometimes then brought to another room.) Therefore, as part of intervention, when Eli hands over his BREAK card, teachers bring him to the counselor's office for a break. When Eli is taking a break, his teachers set a timer for 5 minutes. When the timer beeps, teachers prompt Eli to return to the original setting in which he requested a break. Eli also earns tokens counting toward reinforcers for coming back from his break as soon as the timer beeps. Eventually, the break area is changed from the counselor's office to a break area in the back of the classroom (a bean bag chair set between two bookshelves) to help Eli to learn that he does not need to leave class to calm down but rather that he can calm down in class. Eli's teachers are advised that the break area should not contain highly reinforcing objects or activities for Eli (e.g., computer), only calming objects or activities.

Step 6 is to teach Eli new forms of communication and expand the settings in which requests are made. The primary function of Eli's aggression toward his younger sister is tangible (e.g., to obtain or maintain access to playing on the computer by himself, without his sister touching it), with a secondary function of escape (e.g., his challenging behavior often results in escape from his sister—that is, his sister running out of the room—allowing him to play with the computer alone). As such, clinicians teach Eli to give his sister a MY TURN card, while teaching him to take turns using the computer with his sister using a timer, as well as a PLEASE LEAVE ME ALONE card that he can give to his sister. Clinicians, in turn, teach (prompt and reinforce) his younger sister to run to a parent when given the PLEASE LEAVE ME ALONE card.

Step 7 is to modify the environment. First, clinicians create a visual schedule for Eli, given that a visual schedule is one way to reduce the unpredictability associated with transitions by informing children about the upcoming sequence of events (Dettmer et al., 2000). Even though there is a visual schedule that is posted for the entire class, given Eli's difficulty with transitions, the team decides it will help for Eli to have his own, individualized, personal schedule—a portable visual schedule Velcroed to his desk that he can carry with him from class to class.

Second, clinicians provide Eli with advanced warnings of upcoming transitions using a timer in addition to a verbal reminder and countdown (e.g., "You have 2 minutes left until we leave the Sparrow Room and walk to the lunchroom, . . . 1 minute left, . . . 10 seconds left, 10-9-8-7-6-5-4-3-2-1"; Dettmer et al., 2000). Although Eli's school staff report that they have tried using advanced warnings in the past, the direct observation during the assessment reveals that these warnings or reminders are given inconsistently. Thus, it is recommended that Eli be regularly prompted to look at the timer or clock and that, instead of being asked, "Where are you going?" as they are already making the transition (e.g., walking down the hallway), it could be more helpful to remind him of the upcoming transition *prior to* the transition occurring in order to prepare him.

Third, it is also recommended that priming be used to help increase predictability surrounding transitions. Priming is one way to preview future events so that they become more predictable (Wilde et al., 1992). It is suggested that one of Eli's parents (and/or a favorite teacher) can rehearse Eli's transitions with him repeatedly when school is not in session, such as on a weekend day or a holiday or before or after school hours. Given that the school is not in favor of this recommendation (as they cannot require staff to be there during off hours), clinicians opt to use video priming (Schreibman et al., 2000), in which an adult carries a video camera throughout the transition setting to show the environment as the child will see it when progressing through the transition (e.g., moving through the school building, exiting one classroom and entering another classroom). The video is taken as a bird's-eye view from Eli's point of view so that, when he watches the video, it will look as if he is walking through the halls at school. For example, one of the videos begins with exiting the Robin Room, showing the walk through the halls and up the stairs, entering the lunchroom, sitting at the lunch table, and ends with a reinforcer that Eli will receive upon completing the transition successfully (e.g., showing a sound machine sitting on the lunch table). Each video is viewed every night for at least a week in order to make the transition highly predictable for Eli.

OUTCOMES

School staff use tally marks to record each occurrence of Eli's functional communication response (i.e., independently handing a BREAK card to his teacher without prompting) and specify challenging behavior per day. In terms of the communication-related goal, Eli's functional communication responses increase from an average of 0 instances per day during baseline to an average of 8.8 instances per day (range 7–10) following intervention. In terms of concomitant decreases in challenging behavior, Eli's mean frequency of physical aggression decreases from an average of 5 instances per day during baseline (range 3 to 6) to 0.5 instances per day after intervention (range 0–2), a 90% mean baseline reduction in aggression. Eli's mean frequency of disruptive behavior decreases from an average of 11 instances per day during baseline (range 9–15) to 1.3 instances per day after intervention (range 0–3), an 88% mean baseline reduction in disruptive behavior. Last but not least, Eli's mean frequency of elopement decreases from an average of 6.2 instances per day during baseline (range 5–8) to 0.8 instances per day after intervention (range 0–3), an 87% mean baseline reduction in elopement. Most dramatically, at home, Eli's mother (who took data more reliably and for a longer period of time than did school staff) reports a decrease from 15 instances of aggression toward his sister per day in April to only 1 instance of aggression per week 2 in June.

Overall, clinicians find FCT to be a highly effective intervention for reducing Eli's challenging behaviors. A number of implementation issues arise with his teachers, but clinicians are able to adapt the procedures to meet their needs as well. This is an extremely important issue when working with teachers, families, and others. There are often practical obstacles to implementing behavioral interventions in real-world situations. In addition, some individuals often have cognitive obstacles (e.g., believing they are not capable of implementing the intervention or the child is not capable of changing); procedures have been developed to assist with these kinds of thoughts that can interfere with success (Durand et al., 2013). These procedures involve asking parents (Durand et al., 2013) or teachers (Steed & Durand, 2013) to identify their unhelpful self-talk surrounding difficult situations with their children/students, reflect on the effect of these negative thoughts and feelings on their behavior and their interactions with their children/students, generate alternative ways of looking at these difficult situations, and substitute unproductive self-talk with more productive or helpful self-talk.

Learning Activities

1. Based on the results of the functional behavior assessment—which consisted of questionnaires, interviews, and multiple direct observations (of antecedents, behaviors, and consequences)—clinicians hypothesized that Eli's challenging behavior functioned primarily to escape situations that were aversive (e.g., anxiety provoking, overwhelming, difficult), particularly transitions and classmates crying. Explain how the results of the functional behavior assessment informed the selection and development of the intervention.

2. Had the primary function of Eli's challenging behavior been to obtain attention from teachers (rather than to escape an aversive situation), how might the selection and development of the intervention have been modified?

3. Strategies that Eli's teachers had used to attempt to prevent his challenging behavior in the past were seating changes. Strategies they had used to respond to his behavior in the past were providing Eli with sensory activities and/or a break from the classroom. Discuss the reasons why FCT may have been more successful than these past strategies.

4. Discuss whether you think the antecedent interventions discussed in Step 7, modifying the environment (e.g., creating a visual schedule, providing an advanced warning, video priming), would have been sufficient on their own to reduce Eli's challenging behavior—without teaching Eli a functional communication response. Discuss what the advantages are (if any) of teaching a functional communication response over and above antecedent interventions alone.

5. In the ABC chart in Table 5.1, which comes from a direct observation of another child with ASD (Bobby), what is the most likely function of Bobby's challenging behavior (assuming this pattern repeats itself across more than one observation)? Given the function that you hypothesize, what functional communication response could you teach Bobby that would serve the same function as his challenging behavior?

Table 5.1. Bobby's ABC chart

Antecedent	Behavior	Consequence
Mother says, "Time to do your homework."	Bobby screams, kicks, and drops to floor.	Mother picks him up, puts him on her lap, and says, "You can sit on my lap while you do your work, honey."

REFERENCES

American Psychiatric Association. (2000). *Diagnostic and statistical manual of mental disorders, fourth edition, text revision* (DSM-IV-TR). Author.

Carr, E. G., & Durand, V. M. (1985). Reducing behavior problems through functional communication training. *Journal of Applied Behavior Analysis, 18*(2), 111–126.

Dettmer, S., Simpson R. L., Myles, B. S., & Ganz, J. B. (2000). The use of visual supports to facilitate transitions of students with autism. *Focus on Autism and Other Developmental Disabilities, 15*, 163–169.

Durand, V. M., & Crimmins, D. B. (1992). *The Motivation Assessment Scale (MAS) administration guide.* Monaco & Associates.

Durand, V. M., Hieneman, M., Clarke, S., Wang, M., & Rinaldi, M. L. (2013). Positive family intervention for severe challenging behavior I: A multisite randomized clinical trial. *Journal of Positive Behavior Interventions, 15*(3), 133–143.

Durand, V. M., & Moskowitz, L. J. (2021). Functional communication training: Treating challenging behavior. In P. A. Prelock & R. J. McCauley (Eds.), *Treatment of autism spectrum disorder: Evidence-based intervention strategies for communication & social interactions* (2nd ed., pp. 193–228). Paul H. Brookes Publishing Co.

Koegel, R. L., Openden, D., & Koegel, L. K. (2004). A systematic desensitization paradigm to treat hypersensitivity to auditory stimuli in children with autism in family contexts. *Research and Practice for Persons with Severe Disabilities, 29*, 122–134.

Lalli, J. S., Casey, S., & Kates, K. (1995). Reducing escape behavior and increasing task completion with functional communication training, extinction, and response chaining. *Journal of Applied Behavior Analysis, 28*, 261–268.

March, R. E., Horner, R. H., Lewis-Palmer, T., Brown, D., Crone, D. A., Todd, A. W., & Carr, E. (2000). *Functional Assessment Checklist for Teachers and Staff (FACTS).* University of Oregon.

O'Neill, R. E., Horner, R. H., Albin, R. W., Storey, K., Newton, J. S., & Sprague, J. R. (1997). *Functional assessment and program development for problem behavior* (2nd ed.). Brooks/Cole.

Rosen, T. E., Connell, J. E., & Kerns, C. M. (2016). A review of behavioral interventions for anxiety-related behaviors in lower-functioning individuals with autism. *Behavioral Interventions, 31*, 120–143.

Schreibman, L., Whalen, C., & Stahmer, A. C. (2000). The use of video priming to reduce disruptive transition behavior in children with autism. *Journal of Positive Behavior Interventions, 2*, 3–11.

Steed, E. A., & Durand, V. M. (2013). Optimistic teaching: Improving the capacity for teachers to reduce young children's challenging behavior. *School Mental Health, 5*, 15–24.

Wilde, L. D., Koegel, L. K., & Koegel, R. L. (1992). *Increasing success in school through priming: A training manual.* University of California.

CASE 6

Implementing the Joint Attention, Symbolic Play, Engagement, and Regulation (JASPER) Intervention

A Toddler With ASD

Connie Kasari and Kyle Sterrett

 Jason

 Age 3

 Autism Spectrum Disorder

> **Case 6 engages with the intervention approach and strategies discussed in Chapter 9, The JASPER Model for Children With Autism: Improving Play, Social Communication, and Engagement (Kasari & Sterrett, 2021) in *Treatment of Autism Spectrum Disorder, Second Edition*.**

INTRODUCTION

Jason is a 25-month-old toddler with autism spectrum disorder (ASD) who receives in-home services.

History

Jason received a diagnosis of ASD at age 25 months by a community clinical psychologist using structured observation and parent report. His parents reported an unremarkable medical history in his first year of life with no complications observed during pregnancy. Although there is some family history of developmental delays (father reported beginning to speak late, around 2 years of age), his parents did not report any family history of ASD.

His parents were initially concerned when Jason was approximately 14 months old, as they began to notice that Jason was showing limited social reciprocity when they tried to play with him and was having severe tantrums in new settings and around new people. These initial concerns lingered until his lack of functional language by age 24 months led them to seek a formal diagnosis. At this age, Jason had no functional language and communicated primarily by using others' hands as tools and through tantrum behaviors such as crying.

After receiving a formal diagnosis through a regional center, the family was able to quickly access a number of services, including speech therapy and 20 hours per week of in-home applied behavior analysis (ABA; Cooper et al., 2007) sessions. This in-home program set clear and observable goals for Jason, such as mastering (with 80% accuracy) five one-step commands relevant to daily routines across at least two contexts (e.g., community and home) and correctly sorting (80% accuracy) 10 categories of objects with at least two distractors present. They also included brief parent education sessions to inform his parents of current goals and the methods they were using to reach those goals, the primary of which was discrete trial instruction (DTI). Clinicians used no standardized or validated tests to inform his treatment targets, and nearly all of his programs were targeted at preacademic skills. Jason made rapid progress in these programs, it was believed, because he had relatively stronger visual reception skills than skills in other areas of development.

Despite the progress noted in some preacademic areas, such as matching and categorizing skills, Jason's parents were concerned that he still had little functional language or communication skills. They chose to seek services that would more directly address these developmental domains.

Baseline Status

Clinicians used standardized and validated measures to assess Jason's abilities across developmental domains. These assessments occurred over two visits and took approximately 3 hours to complete. The first set of assessments took place at the university clinic to confirm a diagnosis of ASD and to measure both his developmental quotient as well as his adaptive functioning. The second set of assessments were clinical assessments used to identify intervention targets.

Standardized Assessments   Clinicians conducted three standardized assessments to measure Jason's autism severity, developmental quotient, and adaptive functioning:

1. *Autism severity:* To confirm a diagnosis of ASD, clinicians used the Autism Diagnostic Observation Schedule–Second Edition: Toddler Version (ADOS-2; Lord et al., 2010). Jason received a rating of moderate to severe risk. Of note,

many of the behaviors identified as problems using the ADOS-2 matched the areas of concern identified by Jason's parents, including his lack of social reciprocity and presence of clear repetitive behaviors.

2. *Developmental quotient:* Clinicians used the Mullen Scales of Early Learning (MSEL; Mullen, 1995) to measure Jason's development across five domains: expressive language, receptive language, visual receptive, gross motor, and fine motor. Jason had a relatively average and even profile of gross and fine motor skills, somewhat below average visual receptive and receptive language skills, and very low expressive language scores. This profile was also consistent with what his parents reported.

3. *Adaptive functioning:* Clinicians used the Vineland Adaptive Behavior Scale parent interview (Sparrow et al., 2016) to assess Jason's adaptive skills, which were low across all domains except his adaptive communication, which was very low.

Intervention-Specific Targets   Clinicians assessed three specific intervention domains: Jason's communication, play skills, and engagement.

1. *Communication:* To assess Jason's early communication skills, clinicians used an observational assessment, the Early Social Communication Scales (ESCS; Mundy et al., 2003). The ESCS is a structured observation that provides children the opportunity to show communicative behaviors both for the function of requesting and for joint attention. Jason coordinated his looking between objects and the examiner twice but displayed no other gestures of joint attention. He reached to request a toy once. Overall, he showed little functional communication and no language.

2. *Play skills:* To assess Jason's developmental level of play, clinicians used the Structured Play Assessment (SPA; adapted from Ungerer & Sigman, 1981; Kasari et al., 2010). This assessment probes children's spontaneous and independent play. His mastered level of play was presentation combination. Along the developmental play hierarchy (Lifter et al., 1993; Ungerer & Sigman, 1981), this level of play refers to the child being able to place an object into a clearly designated spot, such as a ring on a ring stacker. He was emerging in general combination play, the next level in the play hierarchy. General combinations involve putting objects together that do not necessarily go together (e.g., stacking blocks and cups together). He showed little interest in or ability to play with pretense; that is, he did not engage in early presymbolic pretend play. Examples of presymbolic play include actions such as putting a bottle to a baby doll's mouth or putting play food onto a plate. This type of play, as well as truly symbolic play (such as giving life to dolls), in comparison to combination play, is generally more difficult for children with ASD.

3. *Engagement:* To assess Jason's engagement, clinicians used an unstructured observation of an interaction between Jason and his mother. He spent most of the interaction attempting to line up a variety of blocks and toys on the table. Each time his mother tried to play with him, he pushed her away and got upset if she touched his toys. In the 10-minute interaction, his mother made 12 attempts to take turns with Jason, and all were rejected.

Family and Community Context   Jason has no siblings and lives with his biological mother and father. His mother and father both have a college education. His mother works from home, and his father commutes about 1-hour per day to work. Jason has no other immediate family in the same city where he lives. A family genogram is presented in Figure 6.1.

Jason was enrolled in a child care setting for 2 months following his first birthday, but he had a number of behavioral challenges throughout the day, including difficulties with transitions to the child care classroom and within activities. He would cry often throughout the day and was disinterested in other children. These concerns led his mother to take over primary child care responsibilities. During this time, he was receiving speech therapy in a community clinic and was receiving ABA services in the home starting just after his second birthday.

An ecomap of the various community supports provided to Jason is presented in Figure 6.2. In the diagram, solid lines denote strong relationships, arrows denote direction of energy flow, and dotted lines denote tenuous relationships:

Broader Profile   Jason was not a particularly active child, as most of his preferred activities were sedentary in nature, such as listening to music on his tablet and lining up his favorite toys. His parents did have safety concerns, however, as he would consistently elope both in the home and when they were in the community. An additional concern from parents and a source of many behavioral challenges was Jason's very restricted diet, which consisted almost entirely of chicken nuggets and chips. Although his ABA interventionists attempted to address the eloping and food sensitivities and some progress was made, these remained active areas of concern for the family. Most daily activities—going to the store, attempted play dates, visits to the doctor's office—were complicated by Jason's rigidity and difficulty with transitions. Slight deviations from his normal routines would lead to behavioral issues, such as tantrums, flopping to the ground, and throwing toys and materials.

Summary of Most Significant Needs   Jason had a number of notable strengths prior to beginning intervention using Joint Attention, Symbolic Play, Engagement, and Regulation (JASPER), specifically his strong visual receptive abilities and receptive language. The most significant areas of need, which were the root of most other concerns for the family and educational team, were related to Jason's rigidity and lack of functional communication. These areas of need, paired with poor

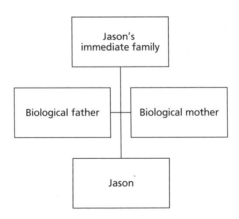

Figure 6.1.   Jason's genogram.

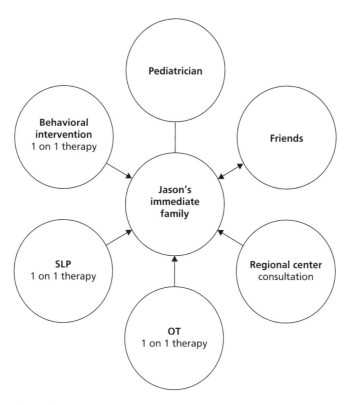

Figure 6.2. Jason's ecomap. *Key:* OT, occupational therapist; SLP, speech-language pathologist.

self-regulation skills, halted progress across other important domains, including language development.

ASSESSMENTS FOR COMMUNICATION TREATMENT PLANNING

The JASPER (Kasari et al., 2006) intervention protocols begin with a thorough assessment of Jason's development across the core social-communication domains noted previously (communication, play, and engagement). To review, Jason's targets, based on the entry assessments, are a point to request as well as a point to share for social-communication targets and the general combination play level, which involves putting objects together that do not necessarily go together (e.g., stacking blocks and cups together). Both skills are within his zone of proximal development. Clinicians also made the initial goal to establish periods of supported joint engagement and to reduce the amount of time he is engaged with objects alone throughout the session. Clinicians establish a clear behavioral plan to work through Jason's episodes of rigidity and tantrums.

CLINICAL PROBLEM SOLVING TO IDENTIFY TREATMENT GOALS AND STRATEGIES

Clinicians select the JASPER intervention because it is well suited to address Jason's core clinical areas of need. Children receiving JASPER have increased time jointly engaged in play activities with others and make gains in joint attention initiations (e.g., Kasari et al., 2010; Kasari, Lawton, et al., 2014), language (e.g., Kasari et al., 2008; Kasari, Kaiser, et al., 2014), play diversity (e.g., Kasari et al., 2010), and play level (e.g., Kasari, Lawton, et al., 2014). Beyond targeting these core deficits, clinicians determine that a sound and consistent behavioral plan that can be feasibly implemented by Jason's mother is essential to improving the behavioral problems consistently seen in the home and community. Clinicians prepared a simple visual schedule prior to the first session and gave his mother a brief psychoeducation session outlining basic behavioral principles, such as identifying the function of behaviors.

INTERVENTIONS USED TO ACHIEVE MAJOR GOALS

In his first session of JASPER with a therapist, Jason is able to put small animals on pegs, taking turns with his therapist. When he finishes putting all of the animals on pegs, the therapist models a new action, taking an animal off and putting it on a tower. Jason begins to cry. This is not what he had in mind. He finished the task and is done. It is clear that Jason does not take much pleasure in playing. His idea about toys is more about completing a task than continuing the activity. The therapist gets a sense of what Jason's mother is experiencing at home, as she talked about not being able to engage him in play and that he preferred to be left alone. When he does play, he has to do things his way, on his own terms. In other words, he cannot really play socially with another person.

Because the first session of JASPER is not very successful, adjustments need to be made, particularly around toy choice. In the second session, Jason's therapist brings in toys that are just below his mastered level of play and that do not have a clear visual cue to their completion (such as puzzles do). She has a car ramp and cars and also brings a tablet with speech-generating software (i.e., a speech-generating device [SGD]). She programmed eight pictures that say the corresponding words when pressed. The pictures represent nouns and verbs that relate to the toys and activities she prepared.

This session is much more successful. The therapist imitates Jason when he puts the car on the ramp, putting her car on the ramp behind him. She also says "car," then presses a picture of a car on the tablet, which also produces the word CAR. As they take turns with the cars going down the ramp, the therapist continues to model spoken and augmented language, expanding both her play actions (the car drives into a garage at end of ramp) and her language ("car goes down ramp"). In this session, the child imitates the therapist, pressing the button on the tablet and expanding his augmented talk to two words. He begins to initiate on the tablet, and he is regulated and happily playing. The change in toy choice along with support of visual and auditory input from the tablet help to regulate Jason so that he can learn from the interaction.

While Jason continues to develop his play and social-communication skills in the context of JASPER over many sessions, clinicians also continue to prompt his use of sounds and approximations for words. He begins to pair vocalizations along with his use of the SGD. He also uses more gestural communicative intent, pointing to request and to share events or activities during play. As his engagement within the session improves, clinicians incorporate more complex toys such as blocks throughout the sessions, and the overall length of the sessions increases from 30 minutes to nearly an hour.

OUTCOMES

The baseline levels of each outcome listed next are described with the change over the course of Jason's time in the JASPER intervention. See also Table 6.1.

Social Communication

Jason begins with very little functional communication; he does not have any spoken language, nor does he use any form of augmented or alternative communication. He is able to reach to ask for things that he wants, but his joint attention is limited to rare instances of coordinated eye contact. Through the JASPER intervention, Jason masters pointing to request and also begins to use his SGD to request toys throughout the session as well as at home within structured routines, such as mealtime, to request preferred options. Within sessions, he is able to ask for preferred choices and for help, for example, when he cannot reach the top of a tower of blocks to put the last piece on. He progresses quickly through his joint attention gesture targets, mastering point to share and showing to share across a variety of play routines. His mother also reports that he uses these gestures more often at home and in the community (e.g., at the store). He consistently uses the SGD to comment throughout play routines. For example, as he is building with blocks, he will label the structure as a BIG HOUSE. Beyond using the SGD, he is emerging in his use of one-word verbal comments. A continued goal for Jason is the integration of multiple forms of communication, such as pointing to something and labeling it at the same time.

Table 6.1. Jason's baseline levels and outcomes

Domain	Assessment	Baseline	Endpoint mastery
Joint attention gestures	Parent–child interaction and Early Social Communication Scales (ESCS; Mundy et al., 2003)	No joint attention gestures	Joint attention point and show
Requesting gestures	Parent–child interaction and ESCS	Reach to request	Point to request
Verbal communication	Parent–child interaction and ESCS	None	Two-word phrases both to comment and request
Play	Parent–child interaction and the Structured Play Assessment (adapted from Ungerer & Sigman, 1981)	Presentation combination	Conventional combination and child as agent
Engagement	Parent–child interaction and therapist session	Primarily object engaged	Primary jointly engaged
Regulation	Parent–child interaction, therapist session, and parent report	Severe tantrums and dysregulation multiple times daily during transitions	One severe tantrum per week

Play

Jason begins at the presentation combination level (puzzles, shape sorters) and often prefers simple play, such as rolling cars or dropping balls down a ramp. By the end of the intervention period, Jason masters the general combination play level and enjoys playing functionally with a wide variety of building materials. He also begins to emerge into presymbolic play, such as building a house and putting toy furniture inside. Beyond moving developmentally up the play hierarchy, Jason also plays with more diversity and flexibility with toys within his mastered level of play. For example, he initiates putting different kinds of toy foods in a cookie jar rather than just a single type, as he did at the beginning of the intervention. In addition, rather than viewing the play as a task, he begins to enjoy toy play and actively seeks out and explores new toys and activities.

Engagement

Jason spends most of his time engaged only with objects, not noticing or attending to his social partner while playing with toys. He does enjoy person engagement, such as singing songs and jumping with the therapists, but spends very little time in a jointly engaged state. By the end of his time in the JASPER program, Jason spends most of the time during sessions with therapists and with his mother in a jointly engaged state. He takes turns in the play and infuses symbols (e.g., language with his SGD) more fluidly into the engagement as well. Along with the increased time and communication with joint engagement, Jason's positive affect increases; he consistently smiles and shares enjoyment in the interactions, especially with his mother.

Regulation

Jason has very poor behavioral and emotion regulation skills and easily becomes dysregulated, specifically during transitions and when he is not allowed to play with toys the way that he likes to play with them. One clear area of improvement for Jason by the end of the JASPER program is his tolerance of transitions. The team specifically addresses transitions to and from sessions with visual schedules and transition objects, and these supports are successful in reducing his tantrums during these transition times. The behavioral plan is extended by his mother throughout the day and is successful in reducing both the frequency and intensity of his tantrums. Thus, a major source of his behavior regulation difficulty is addressed. Jason's self-regulation is also explicitly targeted, with the goal being to teach him successful coping and assistance-seeking behaviors. Because of his difficulty with verbal speech, clinicians teach Jason to identify and share his emotional state on his SGD as well as to ask for preferred activities to regulate himself, such as counting, songs, or breaks from play. Giving him access to communication strategies is successful in decreasing the number of severe behavioral tantrums from daily to once per week.

Parent Education

Initially, Jason's mother has a difficult time understanding and responding to his problem behaviors, including elopement and tantrums. In addition, she does not have many strategies to successfully engage with Jason through play and more generally in activities throughout their day. Jason's mother observes or takes part in every session. She is able to successfully engage Jason in play activities, understanding the various targets he has (e.g., increased engagement, communication and play), and is successful in learning JASPER strategies to support Jason's growth in choosing appropriate toys, imitating and expanding on his communication, establishing play routines, and programming for joint attention. She reaches the same level of fidelity required to become a certified JASPER therapist. Jason's mother is also able to successfully implement the behavioral plans developed with the team throughout the day, including supporting his transitions and teaching self-regulation. Overall, she feels empowered and happy because she is able to successfully play and engage with her son.

Learning Activities

1. When selecting targets for intervention for young children with ASD, why is it important to operate within the child's zone of proximal development? What is the impact of selecting targets that are too developmentally complex or too developmentally simple for a child?

2. Disruptive and problem behaviors stemming from emotion and regulation difficulties are often a barrier to accessing social-communication interventions. In what ways can clinicians address these behavioral challenges while still progressing on social-communication goals? Are separate programs and interventions needed, or can these goals be integrated alongside social-communication targets? In what ways are the two goals intertwined?

3. How can developmental histories and parent reports add value to the assessment process beyond traditional standardized assessments? What are the strengths and weaknesses of these two approaches to assessment of core challenges?

REFERENCES

Cooper, J. O., Heron, T. E., & Heward, W. L. (2007). *Applied behavior analysis*. Macmillan.

Kasari, C., Freeman, S., & Paparella, T. (2006). Joint attention and symbolic play in young children with autism: A randomized controlled intervention study. *Journal of Child Psychology and Psychiatry, 47*(6), 611–620.

Kasari, C., Gulsrud, A. C., Wong, C., Kwon, S., & Locke, J. (2010). Randomized controlled caregiver mediated joint engagement intervention for toddlers with autism. *Journal of Autism and Developmental Disorders, 40*(9), 1045–1056.

Kasari, C., Kaiser, A., Goods, K., Nietfeld, J., Mathy, P., Landa, R., Murphy, S., & Almirall, D. (2014). Communication interventions for minimally verbal children with autism: A sequential multiple assignment randomized trial. *Journal of the American Academy of Child & Adolescent Psychiatry, 53*(6), 635–646.

Kasari, C., Lawton, K., Shih, W., Barker, T. V., Landa, R., Lord, C., Orlich, F., King, B., Wetherby, A., & Senturk, D. (2014). Caregiver-mediated intervention for low-resourced preschoolers with autism: An RCT. *Pediatrics, 134*(1), e72–e79.

Kasari, C., Paparella, T., Freeman, S., & Jahromi, L. B. (2008). Language outcome in autism: Randomized comparison of joint attention and play interventions. *Journal of Consulting and Clinical Psychology, 76*(1), 125.

Kasari, C., & Sterrett, K. (2021). The JASPER Model for children with autism: Improving play, social-communication, and engagement. In P. A. Prelock & R. J. McCauley (Eds.), *Treatment of autism spectrum disorder: Evidence-based intervention strategies for communication & social interactions* (2nd ed., pp. 229–254). Paul H. Brookes Publishing Co.

Lifter, K., Sulzer-Azaroff, B., Anderson, S. R., & Cowdery, G. E. (1993). Teaching play activities to preschool children with disabilities: The importance of developmental considerations. *Journal of Early Intervention, 17*(2), 139–159.

Lord, C., Rutter, M., DiLavore, P. C., Risi, S., Gotham, K., & Bishop, S. (2010). *Autism Diagnostic Observation Schedule, Second Edition (ADOS-2) manual (Part I): Modules 1–4*. Western Psychological Services.

Mullen, E. M. (1995). *Mullen Scales of Early Learning* (pp. 58–64). American Guidance Service.

Mundy, P., Delgado, C., Block, J., Venezia, M., Hogan, A., & Seibert, J. (2003). *Early Social Communication Scales (ESCS)*. University of Miami.

Sparrow, S. S., Cicchetti, D. V., & Saulnier, C. A. (2016). *Vineland Adaptive Behavior Scales, (Vineland-3)*. Psychological Corporation.

Ungerer, J. A., & Sigman, M. (1981). Symbolic play and language comprehension in autistic children. *Journal of the American Academy of Child Psychiatry, 20*(2), 318–337.

Using Enhanced Milieu Teaching With an Emerging Verbal Communicator

A Young Child With ASD

Ann Kaiser, Elizabeth A. Fuller, and Jodi K. Heidlage

 Sierra

 Age 34 months

 Autism Spectrum Disorder

Case 7 engages with the intervention approach and strategies discussed in Chapter 10, Enhanced Milieu Teaching (Kaiser, Fuller, & Heidlage, 2021) in *Treatment of Autism Spectrum Disorder, Second Edition.*

INTRODUCTION

Sierra is a 34-month-old child diagnosed with autism spectrum disorder (ASD). She is an emerging verbal communicator.

History

Sierra was recently diagnosed with ASD, at the age of 30 months. She had a normal birth and health history in infancy, with no major hospitalizations or health concerns. Sierra is the second child and has an older brother, Daniel, who is currently 5 years old and typical for his age. Sierra was approximately 18 months old when her mother, Becky, first became concerned about her because she realized that Sierra seemed somewhat different than she remembered Daniel being at that age. She was not yet talking and seemed to prefer to remain distant from others in social situations. When Becky brought this up with her pediatrician, her pediatrician did not feel concerned because Sierra's motor development seemed advanced. However, when Sierra had her second birthday and her language continued to lag far behind her that of peers, Becky and the pediatrician agreed that further assessment was needed. Sierra had a full assessment by a developmental pediatrician and received a diagnosis of ASD.

Baseline Status

Communication Profile   Becky reported that Sierra had approximately 10 consistent word approximations that she used primarily for requesting. She rarely makes eye contact when she requests and has limited gesture use. Becky reported that Sierra sometimes points to request, but Sierra was not observed to point, show, or give to comment or give an item to request during an evaluation observation. Sierra often communicated her needs by taking Becky's hand and leading her to what she wanted. Sierra frequently imitated adult speech and often used script phrases from her favorite television shows.

Social Profile   Becky reported that she found it hard to play with Sierra. Sierra preferred to play alone with her dolls and dollhouse, sometimes lining them up and engaging in what Becky described as "pretend play," using scripts that she had heard in television shows. Sierra would express frustration if Becky tried to join in and play with the same dolls that Sierra was using. Becky said that when she tried to interact with Sierra while she was playing, Sierra sometimes would get up and leave the area. Becky did report that Sierra loved to play outside and would let her brother push her on the swing or take her down the slide.

Family and Community Context   Sierra lives in a small house with her brother, her mother, and her father, Ray. Their home is located in a modest suburban neighborhood approximately 10 miles from the city center. Their immediate neighborhood has an elementary school that includes inclusive preschool classrooms and a small playground. Many families with preschool and school-age children live in the neighborhood. Becky works from home during the day as a medical records technician. While Becky works, Sierra's maternal grandmother cares for her. Sierra's brother, Daniel, attends school during the day, so Sierra and her grandmother spend most of their time one-to-one. Sierra's aunt (Becky's younger sister) occasionally cares for Sierra and Daniel when her parents go out to dinner or other activity. Sierra's family, including her grandparents, have close ties to their church. They attend services twice each week, and Sierra participates in a children's nursery class held concurrently with these services. Many of the family's closest friends attend the same church.

   Once each week, a developmental therapist from early intervention (EI) services comes to the house to work with Sierra. Sierra's grandmother participates in these sessions instead of Becky or Ray because the sessions occur during their workdays. Sierra has been seen by her pediatrician, a developmental specialist, and a speech-language pathologist (SLP). The SLP consults with the EI developmental therapist but does not see Sierra regularly. Figure 7.1 shows a genogram of Sierra's family, and Figure 7.2 is an ecomap of the family in their environment.

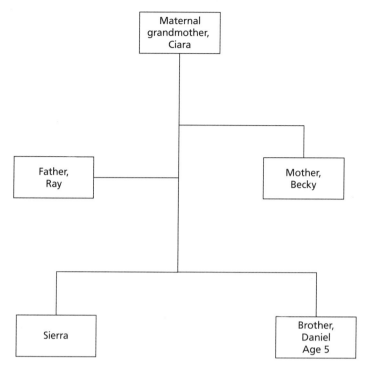

Figure 7.1. A genogram of Sierra's family.

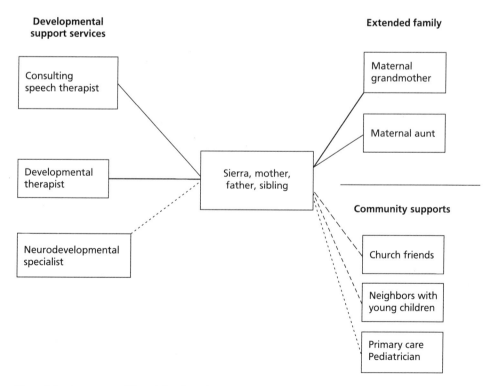

Figure 7.2. An ecomap of Sierra's family environment.

Broader Profile

Becky and Ray describe Sierra as a generally happy child. She loves playing outdoors and she loves bath time. She also is a good eater and has no specific food sensitivities, which Becky says is a relief for her. The family also feels fortunate that Sierra does not have any other medical needs. Although Becky and Ray describe Sierra as happy and generally an easy child, they have expressed concerns for the future. As Sierra gets older, she seems to have an increasingly hard time expressing her wants and needs. She does not respond when people other than her close family talk to her, and she becomes frustrated frequently. She sometimes has tantrums when she is in public with Becky, Ray, or her grandmother. She cries or runs away when other children want to join her play at the park or during play dates. Although these behaviors are not overly concerning at the moment, given Sierra's age, Becky worries that they will be more problematic when Sierra is in preschool next year. Becky also is concerned because Sierra spends a lot of time with her grandmother, who is less able than Becky and Ray to address Sierra's behaviors when she is having tantrums and who does not always understand what Sierra is trying to communicate.

Summary of Most Significant Needs

Becky and Ray's top priority is to help Sierra develop communication. They believe that developing more spoken language and effective use of gestures to indicate her wants and needs will reduce the recently emerging challenging behaviors they are seeing. Becky would love to be able to play and engage more with Sierra and for Sierra to play with her brother, other children at the church nursery, and ultimately her classmates when she starts preschool at age 3.

ASSESSMENTS FOR COMMUNICATION TREATMENT PLANNING

Receptive and Expressive Language

Several measures were conducted to inform the focus of the EMT intervention. Sierra's assessment results are provided in Table 7.1. The Preschool Language Scale–Fifth Edition (PLS-5; Zimmerman et al., 2011), a standardized assessment of global language, was used to measure Sierra's receptive and expressive language skills. Given that children with ASD are often able to perform better on standardized tests of language that rely heavily on question asking, a naturalistic language sample

Table 7.1. Pre- and postintervention results for Sierra

Assessment	Baseline results	Intervention results
Arizona 3	69.5	75
PLS-5, Auditory	50	58
PLS-5, Expressive	61	69
Language sample MLU	1.04	1.36
Language sample spontaneous utterances	15	34
Language sample word diversity	7	21
MCDI-2, Diversity	15	58

Source: Fudala (2000), Zimmerman, Steiner & Pond (2011), Fenson et al. (2007). *Key:* Arizona 3, Arizona Articulation Proficiency Scale, third revision. MCDI-2, MacArthur-Bates Communicative Development Inventories–Second Edition; MLU, mean length of utterance; PLS-5, Preschool Language Scale–Fifth Edition.

was also conducted to assess Sierra's language and communication abilities in a less structured context. This assessment provided Sierra with more opportunities to initiate communication, and it evaluated the number of different words that she used to communicate as well as her mean length of utterance (MLU). Finally, to understand her range of communication across contexts and to provide broader information about her vocabulary knowledge across a range of communication contexts, the MacArthur-Bates Communication Development Inventories–Second Edition (MCDI-2; Fenson et al., 2007), a parent-reported vocabulary measure, was completed by Sierra's mother.

Sierra's score on the PLS-5 was more than 1.5 standard deviations below the mean. Her score for the auditory comprehension subscale of the PLS was higher than her score for the expressive subscale score. She was able to produce several nouns and verbs when the instructor presented pictures and asked her to label them. She communicated using mostly gestures and a few single words ("more," "help") during this assessment. Her MLU during the 20-minute language sample was 1.15, and she produced 15 spontaneous words and 7 different words. She produced 25 different words (e.g., more, eat, kitty, go, no) per parent report on the MCDI-2.

Social Aspects of Communication

The Routines-Based Interview (McWilliam et al., 2009) was conducted with Becky prior to intervention to identify home routines that could be used to teach language during intervention sessions. During this interview, the therapist asked Becky what the routine typically looked like, how Sierra was currently communicating in the routine, and any additional information that Becky could provide about the routine. Becky reported that Sierra was generally happy when engaging in preferred routines, including bath time, meals, and outdoor play, but that she would cry and throw herself on the ground during transitions to nonpreferred routines (e.g., bedtime, getting in the car seat). Becky said that Sierra communicated infrequently and primarily used gestures and a few single words during these routines. After gathering this information, the therapist talked to Becky about prioritizing routines that were enjoyable for both Becky and Sierra as the focus for language teaching at home (outdoor play, snack, bath time). The therapist explained to Becky that the focus for intervention would be on promoting engagement within these routines so that Sierra would be motivated to communicate. She also explained that teaching during times that Sierra was highly engaged would minimize the likelihood of challenging behavior occurring but that they would problem-solve strategies for preventing and responding to challenging behaviors if these behaviors occurred after they began intervention.

Articulation

The Arizona Articulation Proficiency Scale-Third Edition (Arizona-3; Fudala, 2000) was used to capture Sierra's ability to produce speech sounds. Her level of articulatory impairment was scored as moderate on the AAPS, indicating that her speech intelligibility might make it difficult for unfamiliar others to understand her.

Communication Modalities

Although Sierra's level of articulatory impairment was moderate, she was intelligible to her mom, dad, and grandmother. The therapist asked Becky if Sierra currently used any augmentative and alternative communication (AAC) modalities. Becky said that her SLP had tried to teach Sierra to exchange pictures to communicate early in therapy but that Sierra had not seemed very interested, and it was hard to keep up with all of the pictures. Because Sierra was able to produce consistent verbal approximations and did not have an existing AAC communication system, spoken language was prioritized as the focus of intervention. For a child with an AAC modality, or who is not able to produce consistent approximations, the intervention could have been adapted so that language modeling, prompts, and time delays are conducted using the child's modality.

CLINICAL PROBLEM SOLVING TO IDENTIFY TREATMENT GOALS AND STRATEGIES

Sierra's family decided to participate in a parent-implemented EMT intervention because they felt the goal of the EMT intervention aligned with their goal of developing Sierra's everyday functional communication. Given the assessments described previously, it was determined that Sierra was a good fit for the intervention study for two reasons. First, Sierra was an early verbal communicator. EMT has shown to be effective for this population. Second, the goals of the EMT intervention aligned with the goals of the family. The therapist was able to schedule two intervention sessions per week, one in the clinic and one at home. Becky felt this was a feasible schedule and that she could manage it with her work schedule. The real intervention takes place between these two sessions, when Becky implements the strategies in daily routines. Becky felt that this model was low cost in terms of her time commitment but potentially had high payoff in that she could implement it daily. Because Sierra spends a lot of time with her grandmother, the family and therapist agreed that the grandmother would attend sessions when it was feasible, particularly the home sessions that focused on daily routines. Handouts would be provided for Ray and the grandmother so that they could support Becky in implementing EMT across the day.

The theoretical basis of EMT fits well with Sierra and her family. The social interactionist perspective directly supports Becky's goal of increasing her dyadic communication with Sierra, and the developmental and behavioral foundations will help Becky meet Sierra at her current developmental level, build on her existing skills by reinforcing positive communication, and support positive behavior interactions.

This Naturalistic Developmental Behavioral Intervention will also work within the bounds of Sierra's family. Although Becky was the primary caregiver coached for the purpose of the intervention study, Sierra's grandmother and father participated in some training sessions, and Becky shared handouts from workshops and individualized tip sheets with them. Furthermore, Sierra's brother, Daniel, participated in some sessions and learned some of the simple intervention strategies (e.g., respond when Sierra communicates, say a word for her to use when she is frustrated) during the home-based sessions.

The primary goal of EMT is to increase the frequency of spontaneous, functional communication across everyday contexts and partners. For Sierra, functional communication is both verbal and gestural. Sierra has shown that although she can produce words and gestures, including pointing, reaching, and eye contact, she uses these skills infrequently. The secondary goals of intervention are to increase her diversity of utterances and the complexity of her communication. For Sierra, this means diversifying her vocabulary and gesture repertoire and combining words or gestures plus words. These goals fit well with Becky and Ray's goals for Sierra.

Following Sierra's initial assessments, the therapist used the data to determine that Sierra's initial targets would be at the one-word level. She communicated infrequently and had a small repertoire of words, most of which were nouns. The therapist explained to Becky her goal of increasing Sierra's vocabulary to 50–75 words, with at least 10 different verbs, before moving this target to two words.

INTERVENTIONS USED TO ACHIEVE MAJOR GOALS

Preintervention

Before the therapy sessions began with Sierra, the therapist and Becky met one-to-one. This session was a workshop during which the therapist explained the initial core strategies of EMT (environmental arrangement, responsive interaction, and specific language modeling). The remaining core skills would be taught during two future workshops once Becky is fluent in using the initial EMT skills. In the first workshop, specific examples were provided on the basis of Sierra's language during the pre-baseline language sample. During this session, Becky and the therapist identified Sierra's preferred toys and activities. Preferred activities are the best place to begin a quality dyadic interaction. They discussed avoiding dolls at first because Sierra's play with dolls was a somewhat rigid ritual, and she was unable to participate with a partner while playing with them. Rather, they chose toys that were easy to manipulate, including blocks and cars, and a few toys for simple pretend play, such as play food and puppets. The therapist and Becky talked about how to use each of these toys to build a play routine, with repeatable steps and turn-taking, onto which they could map language. They generated a list of words and sentences to model while playing with these toys and focused on identifying action words (verbs) for the routines with each toy set.

Sessions With Sierra and Becky

Each session followed the Teach-Model-Coach-Review framework. In the first clinic session, the therapist defined the EMT strategies that would be the focus of that session and gave examples of what they would look like (the teaching element of the framework). For the first session, the therapist chose responsive interaction strategies and modeled them with Sierra while Becky watched. The therapist used environmental arrangement to help Sierra engage in a play routine.

Once she and Sierra were playing with each other in a simple routine (e.g., stacking blocks), she provided examples of the key strategy to Becky (e.g., "When she reached for the block that was out of her reach, I responded by labeling it and handing it to her"). The therapist played for 5–10 minutes (modeling the EMT strategies). During this time, she used all six core EMT strategies with Sierra, but she verbally highlighted only the strategies she wanted Becky to learn during this first session. During this session, Sierra was particularly interested in blocks, and both the therapist and Sierra sat on the floor with the blocks between them (environmental arrangement). Together, they took turns while building a tower. Sierra added a block to the tower, and then the therapist added a block to the tower while using simple language such as "block" and "We're building a tower" (specific language modeling). She responded to all of Sierra's gestures, which mostly included reaching for blocks, and her vocalizations (responsive interaction). When Sierra said, "Block," the therapist said, "The block goes on!" (language expansion). When the therapist offered a choice by holding up a car and a block, Sierra pointed to the car (time delay). The therapist expanded her gesture by adding a word ("car") and gave her the car. She then incorporated the car into their tower-building routine, which provided new opportunities to model target vocabulary ("road," "crash"). When Sierra clearly indicated that she wanted a small bus by reaching for the bus in the therapist's hand, the therapist used a milieu teaching prompt ("Say 'bus'"). Sierra responded by saying the word bus, which the therapist was able to respond to by giving her the requested toy and expanding her utterance ("You want the bus"). Later in the session, she used a less supportive prompt when Sierra reached for the bus again by asking a choice question without visual support ("Do you want the car or the bus?"), and Sierra again responded by saying "bus," indicating that she was beginning to use the newly taught vocabulary.

Coaching Becky

Once Sierra could play in a simple routine (e.g., stacking blocks) and the therapist had modeled and highlighted the key strategy a few times for Becky, she invited Becky to play with Sierra. While Becky was playing, the therapist helped maintain the interaction by handing Becky toys, cleaning up the environment, and suggesting when to use key strategies (coaching). Coaching support was faded over time as Becky became more fluent in the intervention. The therapist also provided frequent positive feedback to Becky and linked her behavior to Sierra's communication (e.g., "That was a great way to notice and respond to her point," "When you said 'ball,' she imitated you"). At the end on the session, the therapist talked with Becky about how she felt using the EMT strategy and addressed Becky's questions. Together, they made a plan for Becky to use the strategies in the home (review). The following day, the therapist went to the home. She and Becky followed the same Teach-Model-Coach-Review framework to implement the newly practiced EMT strategies in play and home routines. Training continued until Becky mastered the first set of EMT strategies. The therapist then presented a workshop on the second set of strategies, language expansions, and repeated the same sequence of coaching in the clinic and at home. The final workshop covered time delays and milieu prompting. Each workshop included video examples of the therapist using EMT strategies with Sierra. Between workshops, there were about 12 sessions, although the therapist had flexibility to schedule to meet the specific needs of the family.

Over the course of the 36 sessions, the therapist continued to introduce the EMT strategies as well as new vocabulary and short phrases. She faded her support as Becky became more fluent with the EMT strategies. The goal of the parent-implemented intervention was for Becky to be an effective language teacher for Sierra; the training was designed to increase her confidence and competence. A major focus of the training was on planning how Becky would use the strategies across routines at home between sessions. At the beginning of each session, the therapist checked in with Becky on how the intervention was going at home, and together they problem-solved any issues that came up.

During the 36 sessions, Becky became fluent with the six core EMT strategies and used these strategies in a variety of home routines. These routines included bath time, outside, two different art activities, snack time, helping with the laundry, dressing, and two community outings (the grocery store and the library). Sierra's father, grandmother, and brother participated in various routines. Sierra learned to play with a variety of toys. Although she still displayed scripting behaviors with certain toys, she was able to play cooperatively with her mother using a variety of agents, including dolls.

OUTCOMES

Sierra made consistent progress in her language, communication, and related skills throughout intervention. At the beginning of intervention, Sierra infrequently imitated words spoken by her mother or the therapist. After 10 sessions, verbal imitation began emerging. By session 15, Sierra was verbally imitating both Becky and the therapist when prompted and sometimes spontaneously. Becky noticed that Sierra was imitating more frequently throughout the day. Her dad and grandmother also reported she was imitating more frequently with them.

At the beginning of the intervention, Sierra's engagement in routines was inconsistent. Sierra would typically stay engaged for 2–3 minutes but would soon lose interest and wander away. The therapist coached Becky to use environmental arrangement strategies to help keep Sierra in the area (handing her a preferred towel for hand washing, providing choices during snack time, helping her pour bubbles into the bath water). She also helped Becky notice when Sierra was becoming disinterested in the routine. The therapist taught Becky to respond to Sierra's behavioral cues and to reengage Sierra using strategies such as handing her materials or modeling something new Sierra could do with the materials. The therapist also coached Becky to use positive affect and physical attention (tickles, hugs, etc.) when Sierra was engaged in the routine to help motivate to her stay in the interaction. Over time, Sierra was able to engage in these routines for longer periods of time and with less scaffolding from the adult as she learned how to independently navigate the steps of the routine and as the routines became reinforcing for her.

At the beginning of the intervention, Sierra's communication was at a relatively low rate. As Becky became more responsive to Sierra's attempts to communicate, these attempts increased. The therapist also taught Becky to use simple time delay strategies (e.g., offer a choice of preferred materials) when Sierra was engaged in a routine to increase the rate of her communication initiations. Initially, Sierra would whine rather than point or say a word when preferred items were offered. Over time, she learned that communication (point, verbalize) was more powerful than whining. Her rate of communication increased and her challenging behavior decreased. With practice, Becky showed tremendous growth in her use EMT strategies throughout the intervention. Both the frequency and fidelity of her use of strategies improved, and she became more fluent in integrating strategies into everyday interactions. The therapist faded her coaching across intervention sessions. By the end of the intervention, Becky used all of the strategies with accuracy and with little support. Becky reported that she felt confident using the strategies with Sierra throughout their daily routines.

Postintervention

At the end of the intervention, Sierra's language and communication were reassessed. In addition to making consistent changes in her communication in play sessions with her mother, she showed modest changes on standardized assessments as well as in the language sample. Her communication frequency, complexity, and diversity improved from pre- to postintervention. Although some of these changes could be attributed to development, the relatively short period of time spent in intervention and the overall pattern of results suggest that the intervention had a positive impact on Sierra's development. Posttest assessments indicated a change in Sierra's global language score for both the auditory and expressive subscales of the PLS-5. Her MLU changed from 1.04 to 1.36, she gained 14 new words on the MCDI-2, and her rate of communication more than doubled in the 20-minute language sample (from 15 to 34 spontaneous utterances). In addition, her speech articulation impairment, while still moderate, was categorized as intelligible speech with careful listening (see Table 7.1 for summary). At the exit meeting, Becky reported that she had the skills to continue supporting Sierra's language across the day using the EMT strategies. She also commented that Sierra's speech was becoming more intelligible and that other people had commented on how much more she was initiating communication.

Learning Activities

1. Define and provide examples of key EMT strategies. Discuss when you would use each strategy during an intervention session.

2. Develop a simple play routine (e.g., build a house with blocks, put people in the house, crash the house). Use this routine to practice each EMT strategy separately with a partner. Problem-solve and make adjustments as needed. Then practice using the strategies together.

3. Think of the language and communication profile of two different children with ASD. How are they alike? How are they different? How would you make treatment decisions differently on the basis of each child's characteristics? What EMT strategies might you prioritize? What types of targets would you use? Will you incorporate AAC modalities?

4. How might you adapt EMT strategies to train siblings? Which strategies might be easiest for a sibling to implement? How would you teach them to implement these strategies?

REFERENCES

Fenson, L., Marchman, V. A., Thal, D., Dale, P. S., Reznick, J. S., & Bates, E. (2007). *The MacArthur-Bates Communicative Development Inventories, Second Edition: User's guide and technical manual*. Paul H. Brookes Publishing Co.

Fudala, J. B. (2000). *Arizona 3: Arizona Articulation Proficiency Scale, third revision*. Western Psychological Services.

Kaiser, A. P., Fuller, E. A., & Heidlage, J. K. (2021). Enhanced Milieu Teaching. In P. A. Prelock & R. J. McCauley (Eds.), *Treatment of autism spectrum disorder: Evidence-based intervention strategies for communication & social interactions* (2nd ed., pp. 225–286). Paul H. Brookes Publishing Co.

McWilliam, R. A., Casey, A. M., & Sims, J. (2009). The routines-based interview: A method for gathering information and assessing needs. *Infants & Young Children, 22*(3), 224–233.

Zimmerman, I. L., Steiner, V. G., & Pond, R. E. (2011). *Preschool Language Scales–Fifth Edition*. Psychological Corporation.

CASE 8

Coaching in Early Childhood Intervention

A Toddler With ASD

Kathleen D. Ross

 Gretta

 Age 22 months

- - - - - - - - - - - - - -

Case 8 engages with the intervention approach and strategies discussed in Chapter 11, Early Social Interaction (Woods, Wetherby, Delehanty, Kashinath, & Holland, 2021) in *Treatment of Autism Spectrum Disorder, Second Edition.*

INTRODUCTION

Gretta was 22 months old when her primary health care provider referred her to an early intervention program associated with Part C of the Individuals with Disabilities Education Act (IDEA). The health care provider noted communication concerns, especially related to an absence of babbling and no words heard during her well-child visit. Within 45 days of the initial referral (U.S. Department of Education [DOE], n.d.), Gretta was referred to a speech-language pathologist (SLP).

History

Through an interview with the SLP, Gretta's mother, Katherine, described her pregnancy as stressful; she was often tired because she worked 12-hour days and did not eat during those long days. Katherine suffered from high blood pressure and digestive issues from 7 weeks gestation until her child's birth. In spite of these

79

pregnancy challenges, however, Gretta's birth was unremarkable. She was born at full term weighing 8 pounds, 13 ounces and passed the newborn hearing screening. She was healthy during her first years, though she experienced two or three known ear infections, but her hearing was not assessed since birth. Gretta started walking at 13 months, which is age appropriate. She had a good appetite, eating a variety of foods, including different textures, but she occasionally gagged on both solid foods and fluids.

According to Katherine's recollection, there were times Gretta was nonresponsive when others spoke to her. However, Katherine felt her daughter was talkative at home, saying that at times she heard her daughter babble: *yeh yeh, dada, wuh wuh wuh,* and she occasionally said *ball, dada, mama* (a noted difference from the primary health care provider's observations). Katherine further reported that Gretta accompanied her vocalizations with gestures, such as pointing. Katherine stated that there were times when she did not understand "anything Gretta said" and that "others outside the family did not understand her either." When not understood, Gretta reportedly engaged in tantrums.

The initial evaluation was performed by an early interventionist and SLP, who gathered information during a home visit and a week later at a local playgroup. The service coordinator accompanied the early interventionist and SLP during the home visit. The Hawaii Early Learning Profile (HELP) Strands, Ages 0–3, a comprehensive assessment tool for 0- to 48-month-old children (Warshaw, 2013), was utilized to assess Gretta's areas of development beyond communication skills, which were evaluated via specific communication assessments. The results of her all-domain assessment follow.

Cognitive/Problem-Solving Skills: 6-Month Delay

Gretta showed some curiosity for the world around her but reacted inconsistently. She failed to turn a book right-side up when it was handed to her upside down and did not match objects to pictures or categorize three different shapes in matching piles. She inconsistently problem-solved independently. For example, after multiple unsuccessful attempts to make a key work in a lock on a shape sorter's door, she resorted to placing the blocks only into the already opened door, giving up on the lock and key. She repeatedly filled the sorter with blocks, then dumped them out for 10 minutes, never trying to push them into the sorter's shape holes. A week later, at her playgroup, she explored a shape sorter with an unfamiliar adult. When that adult suggested that Gretta try to place a block on her own into the shape hole, she complied. She then used the adult's hand like a tool to dump the blocks out.

Notably, during the observed playgroup, a boy approached Gretta and tossed chalk into the basket she held. She immediately imitated his actions. After watching an early interventionist pretend to feed a bottle to a doll, Gretta also imitated feeding the doll later during the observation visit. The SLP shared a dinosaur with Gretta and pretended to feed it a ball. Gretta watched this action a couple of times, then accepted the ball from the SLP and imitated feeding. After a minute or so, the SLP switched to feeding a block to the dinosaur. Gretta watched, but did not imitate, indicating some inflexibility to change. Symbolic play was not evident; that is, Gretta did not pretend with arbitrary objects and instead required access to actual objects to complete a task (e.g., a phone to talk into).

Fine Motor Development: Mostly Age-Appropriate Skills

After demonstration, Gretta dropped a small pebble into a narrow-necked bottle. However, she would not stack cups during the home visit when that was modeled for her but attempted this action a week later at her playgroup.

Gross Motor Development: Age-Appropriate Skills

Gretta did not imitate jumping in place. She climbed up and down stairs several times but would not jump off of the bottom stair after several demonstrations. She fearlessly climbed on top of very low monkey bars with minimal adult guidance.

Social-Emotional Development: Age-Appropriate Skills

From her mother's report, Gretta displays clinginess and whining at times but does not attempt to comfort others who are in distress. She has expressed affection, jealousy, and frustration. Gretta is independent and explores places away from her parents. Occasionally, she asserts ownership of desired items when her peers attempt to claim them, but much of the time, she just walks away. She is not yet using her name to refer to herself.

Self-Help Skills: Many Age-Appropriate Skills With Others Emerging

Gretta independently opened the refrigerator at her home and pulled out applesauce and a juice box but needed help opening both cartons; independently asking for help is an emerging skill. She is not yet potty-trained, which is age appropriate.

Baseline Status

At 24-months of age, Gretta's communication skills, including pragmatics, were assessed using the Rossetti Infant–Toddler Language Scale (Rossetti, 2005). The SLP gathered information through parent report, direct elicitation and/or observation during a home visit, then a week later at a playgroup Gretta attended. Because parents are typically with their children for the majority of time during their early years, they are acknowledged as expert informants of their child's life experiences; that is, parents are valued partners in the assessment process. Gretta's mother observed the service providers and participated during data-gathering activities (Prelock et al., 2003).

Communication Profile   Gretta approaches an adult, whines, and waits until she receives what she wants, such as something to eat or drink. She hands objects, such as a bag of pretzels, to an adult and waits with anticipation for about 1 minute before walking away unrewarded. She stands in front of an adult, whines, and raises her arms to be picked up. On occasion, she glances at her mother when her name is called and inconsistently acknowledges when others call her name. She does not consistently respond by looking, turning, or answering others' vocalizations. Eye contact and smiling are intermittent. At times, she responds vocally to the vocalizations of others. Although she was relatively quiet during the initial assessment visits, there was evidence of reduplicated babble over time.

The SCERTS® Model (Prizant et al., 2014) revealed that Gretta was either in the Social Partner or Language Partner Stage of Social Communication (SC). There were a few contradictory findings in the assessment; for example, Katherine reported she had heard three words while others had heard only limited babble. Gretta also lacked joint attention, communicative reciprocity (back and forth), and pretend play. She displayed both strengths and weaknesses in her Emotional Regulation (ER). Although she was observed to express some emotions (e.g., anger, pleasure), her self-regulation was limited, and she was not consistently available for learning.

Social Profile   At the home visit, Gretta greeted the service coordinator and SLP by screeching and shying away, but when the unfamiliar early interventionist arrived within 5 minutes, she immediately approached her and tried to climb into her lap, indicating little stranger anxiety that might be expected at this age. She inconsistently acknowledges the presence of others in her vicinity unless they reach for her possessions. Gretta's interactions with other children are limited, though she attends weekly playgroups. She sometimes watches her peers' activities from a distance; more often she attends to only objects directly in front of her at the moment. At times, she focuses intently on an activity, seemingly unaware of her surroundings. Occasionally, she gets into the face of a child and stares intensely into the child's eyes. She sometimes tugs with other children over mutually desired toys.

Family and Community Context   Gretta lives with her mother, father, and 3-year-old brother in a one-family household. They reside in a rural town with a population of approximately 1,730, mostly white (+/–98%; U.S. Census Bureau, 2012). Both parents are professionals, but her mother has chosen to stay at home during her children's early years. Figure 8.1 is a genogram of Gretta's family (Goldrick & Gerson, 1985; Prelock et al., 1999; Prelock et al., 2003).

As long as health and weather (e.g., snowstorms) are not barriers, Gretta attends weekly playgroups with her brother and mother. They often meet the SLP and early interventionist for services at the playgroups. Monthly visits are established with the service coordinator for parent support. Figure 8.2 displays Gretta's personal relationships with professional and community connections and supports (Goldrick & Gerson, 1985; Prelock et al., 1999; Prelock et al., 2003). Strong relationships are represented with solid arrows denoting bidirectionality of energy flow, and

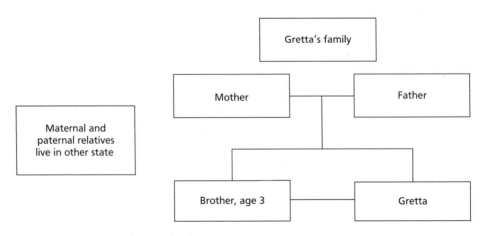

Figure 8.1.   A genogram of Gretta's family.

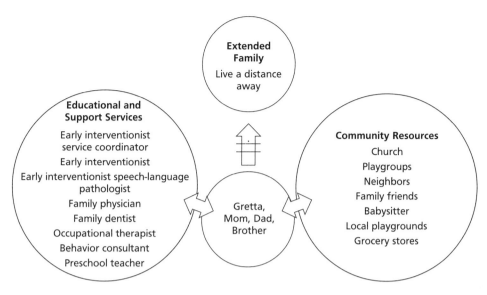

Figure 8.2. An ecomap of Gretta's family environment.

the crossed-over arrow denotes tenuous relationships due to distance and strained extended family relationships.

Broader Profile

Gretta presented as a healthy 24-month-old little girl with no medical or other comorbid diagnoses at the time of the early intervention referral. During the initial assessment process, she displayed inconsistent interest in objects, activities, and people in her surroundings. The early interventionist and SC questioned her hearing acuity because of Gretta's inconsistent response to sounds around her.

Based on the *International Classification of Functioning, Disability and Health-Children and Youth* (ICF-CY; World Health Organization [WHO], 2007), environmental areas of concern were identified for Gretta and her family. Support and relationships within the immediate family (WHO, 2007) were observed to be moderately strained. Gretta's 3-year-old brother continually sought and was rewarded with attention from his mother when the three of them were in the home, which often left Gretta doing her own thing and unengaged with others. Her brother struggled with independent play unless it was with a tablet or a video, but his mother attempted to limit technology use. Otherwise, he at times became destructive to gain his mother's attention. Gretta paid little notice to her brother, neither to his vocalizations nor to his actions. Even when he would get close to her, she did not outwardly acknowledge his presence. Gretta's father was not present during any of the visits; it was reported that he worked long hours. Katherine seemed overwhelmed during initial visits, seemingly unsure of what to do to make everyone in her family content. At the playgroups, she often spent time with other parents while the early interventionist and SLP followed Gretta around the room, engaging her in the activities she chose and keeping her safe. Interestingly, Katherine was at times noted to help other children in the playgroup more quickly than attending to the needs of her own children.

Summary of Most Significant Needs

Through the development of an individualized family service plan by her interdisciplinary team, Gretta's most significant needs were identified to be developing functional communication, including increasing circles of communication or back-and-forth interactions with others; meaningful pointing; and increasing her sound repertoire to transition to more meaningful words.

ASSESSMENTS FOR COMMUNICATION TREATMENT PLANNING

The SLP completed comprehensive assessment procedures to get a complete picture of Gretta's communication skills and inform treatment planning accordingly.

Speech Production

As part of the assessment procedure, the SLP gathered an informal speech sample. An inventory of the sounds Gretta produced included various age-appropriate vowels and consonants /j, w, h, d, t, n, k, g/; age-appropriate consonants not evidenced were /m, b, p/ (Crowe & McLeod, 2020). High-pitched screeching and whining seemed to be her primary modes of oral communication. She combined various sounds into babble, including mostly reduplicated babble (same sound repeated: *dee dee dee, doo doo doo*) with occasional variegated babble (*doh uggie, it-sih*). Gretta was often heard vocalizing *tikkuh tikkuh*, which could be classified as both reduplicated and variegated babble. Her vocal quality was clear with appropriate loudness for the circumstances; that is, screeching was more loudly produced than babbling. Informal assessment of swallowing during snack with crackers and juice was unremarkable, although as previously noted, Katherine voiced concerns with Gretta inconsistently gagging on both solid foods and liquids. Because Gretta inconsistently responded when spoken to, the early intervention team questioned her hearing and recommended a complete hearing assessment.

Language Comprehension

Functioning at 9 to 12 months (12–15 months' delay; Rossetti, 2005), Gretta identified one body part (her belly), when six is more typical at age 24 months. She briefly played the social game of peekaboo, showing comprehension of the gestures and sequencing of the tasks in the game and displaying appropriate anticipation. This indicated her developing knowledge of object permanence. Gretta maintained attention to pictures in books but did not point to pictures upon request. She rarely looked at a person who said her name but responded to the one-step command of "give me," though not to other one-step directions.

Language Expression

Functioning at 9 to 12 months (12–15 months' delay; Rossetti, 2005), from Katherine's report, Gretta said *dada* meaningfully and very occasionally *mama* along with one to two other words, but these words were not heard by the SLP. She did not ask for more, either through sign or orally, nor did she imitate words she overheard in conversations. She varied her pitch, showing emotion through her voice (e.g., pleasure, anger) and increased her volume to gain attention with others. When she wanted to shift to a new activity, she vocalized a desire for change. She did not yet babble long strings of sounds, with four syllables being her typical limit.

Social-Play Aspects of Communication

Several aspects of social communication and play were assessed, including interaction/attachment and pragmatics (Rossetti, 2005). Gretta's interaction and attachment skills revealed that she plays away from her parents' sides but does not consistently show caution with strangers, which should be present at 24 months of age. Her developing pragmatics skills revealed that several age-appropriate skills were not evident. For example, pointing was not observed, even though her mother reported Gretta pointed to indicate awareness and gain joint attention. At times, she imitated others. She did not yet say no to protest but occasionally engaged in tantrums to get her needs met. During play activities, Gretta imitated feeding a doll, placed objects inside containers, and demonstrated an emerging ability to roll a ball back and forth with an adult. These play skills indicate a 6- to 9-month delay (Rossetti, 2005).

Communication Modalities

Gretta indicated when she wanted to be picked up by raising her arms. In her home, she reportedly led a caregiver to a desired object and shook her head no. Occasionally, she used the early interventionist's hand as a tool, such as to place a block into a container. She gestured for help if adults did not immediately step in (Warshaw, 2013). Otherwise, she used vocalizations, not words, to get her needs met.

CLINICAL PROBLEM SOLVING TO IDENTIFY TREATMENT GOALS AND STRATEGIES

Early intervention support services within IDEA's Part C program focus on providing comprehensive, culturally appropriate, multidisciplinary services to all eligible children (DOE, n.d.). Services are provided within natural environments, where families are coached and supported to embed intervention activities within daily routines. Familiar materials within that natural environment are considered best for therapeutic purposes. The Part C philosophy revolves around promoting an individualized developmental approach for intervention that initiates from and continually focuses on the child's and family's strengths (Beatson, 2006, 2008; Beatson & Prelock, 2002; Prelock, 2006; Prelock et al., 2003; Ross, 2018; Woods & Wetherby, 2003). In Part C, treatment goals are written as family-focused, comprehensible, measurable tasks. Philosophically and practically, the parent is coached to become the primary service provider with support from early intervention team professionals.

Because Gretta presented with significantly limited babbling, words, and gesturing and no two-word spontaneous phrases to this point in her life (Woods & Wetherby, 2003), the following communication-related treatment goals were developed by the early intervention team that included her parents:

Goal 1: Gretta will increase her circles of communication to interact positively and functionally with peers and others.

Objective a: Parents will follow the lead of Gretta's actions during focused play activities within the home or playgroup five times during the week for 1 month by [specified date].

Objective b: Parents will gain Gretta's joint attention to a mutually interesting task during focused play activities within the home or playgroup five times during the week for 1 month by [specified date].

Objective c: Parents will extend Gretta's play actions during focused play activities within the home or playgroup five times during the week for 1 month by [specified date].

Objective d: Parents will guide Gretta to interact with one familiar peer at a playgroup during a focused play activity one time per week for 1 month by [specified date].

Goal 2: Gretta will point to objects, people, or places of interest to gain joint attention and get her needs and wants met (Korkmaz, 2011).

Objective a: During play activities, Gretta will successfully follow the point of another person to a body part, nearby object, or person three of five trials for 1 month by [specified date].

Objective b: During play activities, Gretta will accurately point to three different body parts on herself or another person upon request three of five trials for 1 month by [specified date].

Objective c: During play activities, Gretta will accurately point to an object or person at a distance within a room three of five trials for 1 month by [specified date].

Objective d: During daily routines, Gretta will make a choice by pointing to desired item from two presented items three of five trials for 1 month by [specified date].

Goal 3: Gretta will increase her expressive repertoire to include meaningful sound or word exchanges with others.

Objective a: Parents will imitate the facial expressions and sounds of Gretta during focused periods three times per day for 1 month by [specified date].

Objective b: Gretta will initiate playful exchanges of facial expressions and sounds with others during focused periods three times per day for 1 month by [specified date].

Objective c: Gretta will maintain back-and-forth gesture and/or sound production with her parent for three exchanges per playtime for 1 month by [specified date].

Objective d: Gretta will accurately imitate an altered sound production as modeled by her parent three times per day for 1 month by [specified date].

Objective e: Gretta will accurately imitate an appropriate, functional one-syllable label for an object, person, or action three times per day for 1 month by [specified date].

The SLP provided weekly visits, and the early interventionist provided twice monthly visits. The service coordinator provided monthly parent support services.

INTERVENTIONS USED TO ACHIEVE MAJOR GOALS

To engage in relationship building and positive communication development with Gretta and her family, several intervention modes were utilized to achieve the treatment goals, including Floortime, applied behavior analysis (ABA), a modified version of Pivotal Response Treatment (PRT), milieu teaching strategy, and perhaps most important, coaching parents.

In utilizing the Floortime method (Gerber, 2021; Greenspan & Wieder, 1998; Ross, 2018), there are two primary steps: 1) following the child's lead, then joining into his or her play as appropriate to sustain the child's engagement; and 2) thoughtfully restructuring to advance the steps. First, a potential play partner engages in careful observation of the child, noting his or her interests. Next, the partner carefully joins into the child's play, imitating actions and narrating what is happening for both players. The objective is to interact, be fully engaged, and meet the child at his or her level. Enjoyment is key. When perseveration or unwanted behavior occurs, the adult playfully and sensitively obstructs those behaviors, manipulating the play to something more appropriate, which creates positive steps in social-emotional development (Gerber, 2021; Greenspan & Wieder, 1998; Ross, 2018).

ABA (Kazee et al., 2021) is a frequently used approach for young children with autism, as it is focused on motivating an individual to continue behaviors that are rewarding to that individual while stopping behaviors that do not necessarily benefit the individual. Through prompting and shaping negative behaviors, the intervention team supports development of new functional behaviors as communications. Prompts are faded from continual rewards to sporadic prompting and rewarding and eventually to no prompts and intrinsic rewards as new functional communications are established (Meadan et al., 2016).

Through a modified version of Pivotal Response Treatment (Koegel et al., 2021), the intervention team incorporated documented motivators by using familiar desired objects. The team encouraged responses to various cues via natural rewards and consequences within the natural settings. Then the team guided the child to self-regulation and independent use of her new positive communications (Autism Speaks, n.d.; Koegel et al., 2021).

Milieu teaching strategies (Kaiser & Heidlage, 2021) guide parents and caregivers toward logical communications that fit into the daily routines. For example, while engaged in ball play with a child, a mother might provide a model of a relevant word (e.g., "ball"). If the child responds by repeating "ball," the child is given the ball and play continues. If not, a mand model is presented whereby the mother asks, "What do you want?" then pauses, allowing for processing time to formulate a response. If there is no response, the mother repeats the request, continuing to display the ball. She pauses again, then presents the ball to the child whether there was a response or not (Christensen-Sandfort & Whinnery, 2013). This situation presents a choice to the child via the request of "What do you want?" Choices empower children to get what they want, promoting development of a positive sense of self-concept. An essential ingredient of milieu teaching strategies is that the child's communication/play partner needs to be an astute observer, watching for what motivates the child and when he or she may be attempting to communicate through any means. Milieu teaching is representative of incidental teaching, or teaching in the moment.

Coaching is one of the main philosophies of the Part C early intervention program. The early intervention team recognizes that parents come to the process with various preconceived ideas about their child and child development but that each parent is unique in their learning style. Adults display varying preferences and motivations for learning (Woods et al., 2021). The early intervention team learns about the child from the parents while the parents learn how to foster their child's

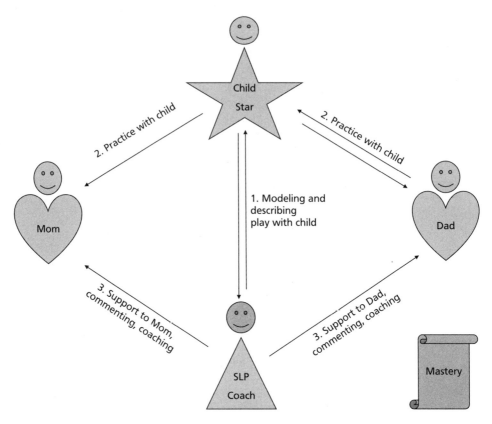

Figure 8.3. Coaching parents: modeling, describing, practicing, and commenting. (From Ross, K. D. [2018]. *Speech-language pathologists in early childhood intervention.* Plural Publishing).

development from the early intervention team, creating bidirectional information sharing (Woods et al., 2021; Woods et al., 2011). Parents are supported in their efforts to engage positively with their children via direct modeling, then side-by-side delivery to promote new skills, forming a partnership between early intervention team members and the parents (Dunst & Trivette, 2009). Eventually, when parents reach a level of comfort and confidence, service providers back away but still observe from a distance as the parent and child engage in playful and routine activities independently. Recognizing that the adult learning process is an integral part of best practices in coaching parents, the team helps them to recognize that their child's learning occurs within daily routines throughout the day in their homes and communities (Woods et al., 2021). The early intervention team guides parents to understand that they can best champion their child's development. Figure 8.3 illustrates how this coaching process unfolds.

OUTCOMES

Data were collected through ongoing assessment during each visit with Gretta in her home and at her playgroup. Parent report of new or recurring positive or challenging behaviors was continuously recorded, and observations and language samples were documented, analyzed, and shared with parents on a visit-by-visit basis. Gretta's mother shared videos and photographs of Gretta's achievements between visits through email. Program development resulted from the discussions and the ongoing assessment conclusions. Monthly collaborative team meetings kept transdisciplinary members in sync for program planning (Woods et al., 2021).

During visits, communication opportunities were utilized in the moment during daily routines. For example, when Gretta went to the refrigerator and grabbed a juice box, the team coached her mother to place desired foods on higher shelves so that the opportunity for Gretta to communicate her wants would be enhanced. If she climbed on the door, which was what her mother said she would do, the team designed a better system, via ABA approaches, to increase positive communication opportunities. Over several visits, the team shaped Gretta's need to sign MORE in order to gain her juice box.

With Floortime as the primary therapeutic method, as well as coaching Katherine, inconsistent functional communications both orally and gesturally began after 2 months of intervention. The SLP shared an informal training video about the Floortime method for adult learning purposes. Through initiated utterances, but more often via repetition, Gretta occasionally labeled (e.g., *up, there*); requested (e.g., *done, look*); negated (e.g., *no, don't*); greeted (e.g., *hello*, repeated into a toy phone), and commented (e.g., *yah!*) while clapping at her achievement. The team's goal was to increase Gretta's communication opportunities and reinforce more consistent use of recognized words through strategically playful Floortime supported with ABA methods. Gesturally, toward the end of her time in Part C early intervention programming, she waved good-bye and followed the SLP's point to look out the window, and during the final months of early intervention, her father reported Gretta was pointing to pictures in books.

After 5 months of early intervention services, and owing to the red flags that were evident, such as Gretta's lack of response to her name and her inconsistent reciprocity with others (Woods et al., 2021), a referral to the local child development center was scheduled to gather more detailed information specifically related to autism spectrum disorder (ASD) concerns. From this evaluation, it was determined that Gretta displayed the characteristics of ASD, and she therefore received a diagnosis at about 30 months of age. From this child development program, Gretta's mother received an informative book about the ABA method. A healthy discussion occurred with Katherine, who asked the SLP questions about how to integrate this ABA method into the Floortime activities that she had already observed as successful for her daughter. The SLP explained that the two were quite interconnected with the ultimate goal in both programs being to shape negative behaviors into functional communications.

From this ASD diagnosis, early intervention services were increased to twice weekly SLP visits and once weekly early interventionist visits; the service coordinator continued to visit once a month. This schedule totaled 3 hours weekly for early intervention support, significantly less than the recommended 25 hours per week (Woods et al., 2021). Because of the rural community in which the family resided, satisfying best practice recommendations was not feasible. Additional resources were provided to Katherine through website links such as Florida State University's Baby Navigator (https://babynavigator.com) and Autism Navigator (https://autismnavigator.com), sites that offer tools and courses for families and interventionists (Wood et al., 2021). Per her mother's request, the idea of placing Gretta into an intensive ABA-specific preschool for full-time programming was discussed with the early intervention team. The decision was made collaboratively, by team members from the IDEA Part C and Part B programs, that upon transition to early childhood special education services, Gretta would receive two full days in an intensive behavior intervention program combined with three half days in an inclusive school-based preschool. This preschool programming would better fulfill the 25 hours of intensive intervention recommended by the National Research Council (Lord & McGee, 2001).

Gretta's inflexibilities to change continued throughout her time in early intervention. She followed the same sequence of activity explorations each time she attended the playgroup, and this inflexibility was carried over to the summer preschool program she attended for a couple of months prior to her transition out of early intervention. Emerging skills were noted in pretend play, especially around use of a toy phone and speaking into it with a nearby conversational partner, but no symbolic play was evidenced.

While attending the playgroup, Gretta engaged in limited interactions with other children for very short periods of time. Katherine observed that Gretta's interactions with other children were nearly nonexistent at the playgroup, allowing her to begin to accept the diagnosis of ASD. She chatted with other parents developing a support network (Woods et al., 2021). She arranged play dates with one same-aged child so that Gretta would have an opportunity to learn playful exchanges in a non-distractive environment, her home. On one occasion at the summer Part B preschool program, she interactively built block towers with another child, allowing him to build on her tower, and she added to his tower. The ultimate goal of consistently initiating social interactions was not achieved when she transitioned out of early intervention. However, Gretta's circles of communication were developing with her mother because Katherine was noted to be more comfortable following the lead of her daughter's play. Interactions with her brother, however, continued to be strained. The early intervention team did note that Gretta was becoming more aware of the existence of others around her as potential play and communication partners. She was beginning to build relationships.

As Gretta transitioned to IDEA's Part B early childhood special education program, she continued to show significant delays in communication, socialization, and cognition. Her fine and gross motor and self-help skills continued to be age appropriate.

Learning Activities

1. Record a video of a parent and his or her toddler with suspected ASD.

    i.   How would you use this video to support the parent to build more functional interactions with the child?

    ii. What elements of early social communication would you focus on to enable the parent to benefit from this video analysis?

    iii. What ideas might you present to the parent that show particular promise based on the child's motivators and early communication attempts?

    iv. How will you consider cultural differences in your planning for intervention with the family?

    v.   Consider using the resources available at the First Words Project (https://firstwordsproject.com) and Baby Navigator (https://babynavigator.com) to support this parent and his or her toddler.

2. Write out how you might explain ABA therapy and the Floortime method to parents unfamiliar with these intervention methods and show how these practices interconnect.

    i. How might both methods be used successfully with toddlers diagnosed with autism?

    ii. How will you discourage parents' resistance to attempting one or the other therapy methods?

    iii. What other intervention methods might be appropriate in early intervention for young children with ASD, and why?

3. Increasingly, telepractice services are used to offer speech-language therapy. How might you use this delivery approach strategically to coach parents and work with toddlers in early intervention? How might you be creative in including in these sessions more family members, such as siblings or grandparents, who may not be technologically savvy?

4. Explain how you will gather data through ongoing assessment. How will you explain to parents the importance of maintaining this data and their role in this process? Develop a documentation sheet for parents to keep track of important outcomes established in the goals you have set to be achieved during daily routines.

5. Role-play explaining to a parent the diagnostic process for ASD.

    i. What practical barriers do you see to a quick diagnosis?

    ii. Explain who will be part of the early intervention team and the benefits of a transdisciplinary team to address the needs of families receiving an early diagnosis of ASD for their child.

    iii. Explain to the parents and perhaps other family members how and why they are an integral part of the assessment and intervention process.

REFERENCES

Autism Speaks. (n.d.). *Pivotal Response Treatment*. Retrieved September 12, 2020, from https://www.autismspeaks.org/pivotal-response-treatment-prt-0

Beatson, J. (2006). Preparing speech-language pathologists as family-centered practitioners in assessment and program planning for children with autism spectrum disorder. *Seminars in Speech and Language, 27*, 1–9.

Beatson, J. E. (2008). Walk a mile in their shoes: Implementing family-centered care in serving children and families affected by autism spectrum disorder. *Topics in Language Disorders, 28*, 307–320.

Beatson, J. E., & Prelock, P. A. (2002). The Vermont Rural Autism Project: Sharing experiences, shifting attitudes. *Focus on Autism & Other Developmental Disabilities, 17*(1), 48–54.

Christensen-Sandfort, R. J., & Whinnery, S. B. (2013). Impact of milieu teaching on communication skills of young children with autism spectrum disorder. *Topics in Early Childhood Special Education, 32*(4), 211–222.

Crowe, K., & McLeod, S. (2020). Children's English consonant acquisition in the United States: A review. *American Journal of Speech-Language Pathology, 29*(4), 2155–2169. https://doi.org/10.1044/2020_AJSLP-19-00168

Dunst, C. J., & Trivette, C. M. (2009). Let's be PALS: An evidence-based approach to professional development. *Infants and Young Children, 22*(2), 164–176.

Gerber, S. (2021). The Developmental, Individual-difference, Relationship-Based (DIR) model and its application to children with ASD. In P. A. Prelock & R. J. McCauley (Eds.), *Treatment of autism spectrum disorder: Evidence-based intervention strategies for communication and social interaction* (2nd ed., pp. 163–192). Paul H. Brookes Publishing Co.

Goldrick, M., & Gerson, B. (1985). *Genograms in family assessment*. W.W. Norton.

Greenspan, S. J., & Wieder, S. (1998). *The child with special needs*. Perseus Books Group.

Kaiser, A. P., Fuller, E. A., & Heidlage, J. K. (2021). Enhanced Milieu Teaching. In P. Prelock & R. McCauley (Eds.), *Treatment of autism spectrum disorder: Evidence-based intervention strategies for communication and social interaction* (2nd. ed., pp. 255–286). Paul H. Brookes.

Kazee, A., Wiczynski, S. M., Martino, M., Sundberg, S., Quinn, M., & Mundell, N. (2021). Discreet trial instruction. In P. Prelock & R. McCauley (Eds.), *Treatment of autism spectrum disorder: Evidence-based intervention strategies for communication and social interaction* (2nd ed., pp. 133–162). Paul H. Brookes Publishing Co.

Koegel, L. K., Strong, K., & Ponder, E. (2021). Pivotal response treatment. In P. A. Prelock & R. McCauley (Eds.), *Treatment of autism spectrum disorder: Evidence-based intervention strategies for communication and social interaction* (2nd ed., pp. 353–380). Paul H. Brookes Publishing Co.

Korkmaz, B. (2011). Theory of mind and neurodevelopmental disorders of childhood. *Pediatric Research, 69*(5), 101–108.

Lord, C., & McGee, J. P. (Eds.). (2001). *Educating children with autism*. Committee on Educational Interventions for Children with Autism, Commission on Behavioral and Social Sciences and Education, National Research Council.

Meadan, H., Ayvazo, S., & Ostrosky, M. M. (2016). The ABCs of challenging behavior: Understanding basic concepts. *Young Exceptional Children, 19*(1), 3–15.

Prelock, P. A. (2006). *Communication assessment and intervention in autism spectrum disorders*. PRO-ED.

Prelock, P. A., Beatson, J., Bitner, B., Broder, C., & Ducker, A. (2003). Interdisciplinary assessment for young children with autism spectrum disorders. *Language, Speech and Hearing Services in Schools, 34*, 194–202.

Prelock, P. A., Beatson, J., Contompasis, S., & Bishop, K. K. (1999). A model for family-centered interdisciplinary practice. *Topics in Language Disorders, 19*, 36–51.

Prizant, B., Wetherby, A., Rubin, E., Laurent, A., & Rydell, P. (2007). *The SCERTS® Model*. Paul H. Brookes Publishing Co.

Ross, K. D. (2018). *Speech-language pathologists in early childhood intervention: Working with infants, toddlers, families, and other care providers*. Plural Publishing.

Rossetti, L. (2005). *The Rossetti Infant-Toddler Language Scale*. LinguiSystems.

U.S. Census Bureau. (2012). *2010 Census of Population & Housing, Summary Population & Housing Characteristics*, CPH-1-47. U.S. Government Printing Office.

U.S. Department of Education. (n.d.). *Individuals with Disabilities Education Act (IDEA): Section 303.310. Post-referral timeline (45 days)*. Retrieved September 21, 2020, from https://sites.ed.gov/idea/regs/c/d/303.310

Warshaw, S. P. (2013). *Hawaii Early Learning Profile (HELP) Strands, Ages 0–3*. VORT Corp.

Woods, J. J., & Wetherby, A. M. (2003). Early identification of and intervention for infants and toddlers who are at risk for autism spectrum disorder. *Language, Speech, and Hearing Services in Schools, 34*(3), 180–193.

Woods, J. J., Wetherby, A., Delehanty, A., Kashinath, S., & Holland, R. D. (2021). Early social interaction. In P. Prelock & R. McCauley (Eds.), *Treatment of autism spectrum disorder: Evidence-based intervention strategies for communication and social interaction* (2nd ed., pp. 287–314). Paul H. Brookes Publishing Co.

Woods, J. J., Wilcox, M. J., Friedman, M., & Murch, T. (2011). Collaborative consultation in natural environments: Strategies to enhance family-centered supports and services. *Language, Speech and Hearing Services in Schools, 42*(3), 379–392.

World Health Organization. (2007). *International classification of functioning, disability and health: Children and youth version.* Author.

CASE **9**

Supporting Relationships and Learning in Secondary School

A Teenager With ASD and Intellectual Disability

Erik W. Carter

 Mason

 Age 15

 Autism Spectrum Disorder and Intellectual Disability

> **Case 9 engages with the intervention approach and strategies discussed in Chapter 12, Peer-Mediated Support Interventions for Students With ASD (Carter, 2021) in *Treatment of Autism Spectrum Disorder, Second Edition*.**

INTRODUCTION

You are unlikely to forget Mason after your initial encounter. When asked to introduce himself, he will shuffle into your personal space, bow halfway with a quick jolt, and push out the words "Your majesty!" in a high-pitched and excited voice. And just as quickly as he approaches you, he will slip back to his desk to flip through his favorite comic books or baseball cards. Like his father, Mason is the world's greatest St. Louis Cardinals fan and watches every game he can. The rest of his time is spent enjoying his other obsessions—anime and manga.

At age 15, Mason experiences the usual excitement and challenges associated with being a freshman at Northside High School. He takes a variety of interesting classes—some in general education classrooms (i.e., contemporary issues, English, graphic design) and others in self-contained settings (i.e., functional math, life skills, career exploration). He is accompanied by a one-to-one paraprofessional—Ms. Lloyd—who has known him since sixth grade. He is also starting to think about life after high school. His first transition planning meeting was last year.

Mason's first diagnosis came shortly after his delivery—Down syndrome. His parents soon learned that he also had a cognitive impairment and some difficulties with speech. However, as he approached his second birthday, Mason still was not combining words and seemed to be regressing in some of his language and social skills. He was almost 3 years old when a diagnosis of autism spectrum disorder (ASD) was added to the growing list of his parents' concerns. His motor development was a little slower than that of his peers, but once he started walking at 18 months, he was hard to keep up with, especially on the baseball diamond.

Elementary school was a largely positive experience. Mason attended a small public school in which he spent all of his day in the same classes as his typically developing peers with the exception of occasional therapy sessions with his occupational therapist (OT) or speech-language pathologist (SLP). He developed several friendships that spilled over beyond the school day. But that all changed in middle school. He was included less often in classes, his social network narrowed, and invitations to after-school events faded. Presently, he receives special education services under the categories of intellectual disability and autism. His freshman year has been isolating and sometimes quite lonely.

Communication Profile

Mason has received speech therapy since he started kindergarten. Although language is substantially delayed, his receptive language is much stronger than his expressive language. He speaks primarily using single words or short phrases and incorporates gestures (i.e., pointing, reaching, waving). His speech is usually peppered with favorite phrases from baseball ("st-e-e-e-rike") or cartoons ("bla-a-a-st away"), along with accompanying gestures. He was recently introduced to a symbol-based augmentative and alternative communication (AAC) system loaded on his tablet (i.e., Proloquo2Go) that included approximately 250 symbols across "home" and "school" pages. However, he uses only a couple of symbols and often forgets to bring his iPad with him.

Social Profile

Mason is handsome and has a positive disposition. He is usually cheerful and often sports a modest grin (unless his treasured Cardinals have just lost). However, he frequently appears to be lost in his own thoughts and is unlikely to initiate conversations with others. It takes time for Mason to warm up to people, especially unfamiliar peers. When he does feel comfortable, his unique sense of humor shines through, and he is likely to play a trick or two on you (e.g., hiding materials, tapping your shoulder and turning away).

Nearly all of Mason's conversations at school involve his paraprofessional or special education teacher. He has few relationships with any of his peers—with or without developmental disabilities. Although a couple of peer buddies volunteer weekly in his special education class, his teachers say Mason lacks any real friendships at school. Two children (Luis and Adrian) from his church youth group are his favorite companions.

Family and Community Context

Mason is the middle child, but only by a few seconds, as his twin sister followed him. His older brother is a senior. His mother and father were married later in life and had all three of their children in their early 40s. Other extended family (see the left panel of Figure 9.1) are still alive and live within several miles. The family is involved in a local parish that has an inclusive special needs ministry. In fact, Mason occasionally volunteers by helping put up chairs after the Sunday service and, every once in a while, by leading scripture readings that have been prerecorded into his tablet. Mason's mom is involved in a monthly support group for parents of children with ASD, but she attends less frequently as she started a new job. His parents have clerical and custodial positions at a nearby community college.

Broader Profile

Mason has few medical needs at present. His vision and hearing are excellent, his weight is average, he has no gastrointestinal conditions, and he sleeps too much on weekends like any adolescent. However, when he was younger, his doctors identified some heart problems that they continue to watch closely. Mason occasionally exhibits minor challenging behaviors at school (e.g., banging, yelling, elopement). A functional behavior assessment suggests they are evoked by unexpected changes in routine and heavy scheduling of instructional demands. His perseverative interests focus on sports and Japanese comics. His health is fairly good, although he has moderate allergies. The medication he takes during the early spring and late fall can make him a bit sleepy at school.

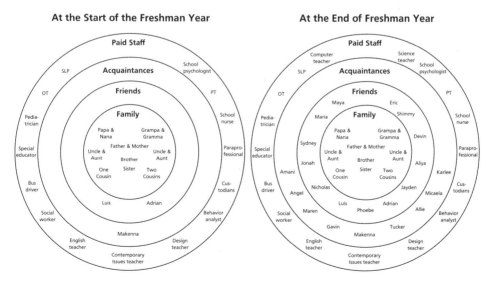

Figure 9.1. Mason's social networks—including family and friends—at the beginning (left) and end (right) of his freshman year. *Key:* OT, occupational therapist; PT, physical therapist; SLP, speech-language pathologist.

Summary of Needs

Mason's most significant needs are prioritized in his individualized education program (IEP). He has communication goals focused on using his AAC device more fluently and appropriately, increasing the reciprocity of conversations, and talking about topics that extend beyond his perseverative interests. His social goals focus on initiating conversations with peers, asking for assistance from classmates, and sharing his ideas with others. His academic goals focus on strengthening his sight word reading and learning relevant class concepts (e.g., concepts related to science, language arts). Finally, his transition goals focus on exploring extracurricular activities, identifying future career interests, and participating in activities more independently.

ASSESSMENTS FOR COMMUNICATION TREATMENT PLANNING

In preparation for intervention planning as well as for his upcoming IEP meeting, the educational team decides what new information to gather and what existing assessments from his records to review. Given the prominence of social and communication goals on Mason's IEP and his participation in inclusive courses, the team decides to conduct direct observations to examine his social and academic participation across the school day. His special education teacher, Mr. Molloy, meets with Ms. Lloyd to discuss the behaviors they will observe and the settings that will comprise their focus. They decide to sample different days within two of Mason's general education classes (i.e., contemporary issues, English) and in the cafeteria during lunch. Mr. Molloy adapts an observation form to address the following behaviors: social initiations and responses to others, communication modality (which includes use of his AAC device), academic engagement, and proximity to others (see Figure 9.2). Each observation session is divided into 1-minute intervals. They collect data on whether or not social and communication behaviors occur at *any time* during an interval (called partial interval recording) and whether he is in proximity to others or engages academically at the very end of each interval (called *momentary time sampling*). After each observation, the special education teacher or paraprofessional adds narrative notes about the quality of Mason's interactions and the contextual factors that might have influenced his behaviors.

The portrait that emerges from these multiple observations (i.e., five per setting) certainly reveals the need to rethink the prevailing models of support. In his two general education classes, Mason is always observed to be working closely with Ms. Lloyd, his paraprofessional, toward the rear of the classroom. As a result, other peers are in close proximity (within 3 feet) to Mason during only 5% of all observation intervals. Not surprisingly, he is rarely observed to interact with peers (2% of all intervals) or participate in shared work. Instead, nearly all of his interactions take place with Ms. Lloyd. He tends to respond to her using single words or gestures. In contrast, he almost never initiates interactions, and he is observed using his AAC system just twice across all of the observations (both times saying STOP when more work is presented). In addition to missed social opportunities, Mason has high levels of disengagement during instruction. He is academically engaged for an average of 42% of intervals across both classes. Ms. Lloyd has little training related to supporting access to the general curriculum and is often uncertain about how Mason should participate in ongoing class activities. A similar social pattern is seen in the

Observation Form

Student: __Mason__   Setting: __Contemporary Issues__   Date: __September 7__   Observer: __Molloy__

Min	Academic Engagement (Circle at end of interval)	Proximity to Others	Initiations to Whom?	Responses to Whom?	Communication Mode(s) Used by the Student (Circle throughout the interval)	Comments
1	EN Engaged / UN Unengaged	P Peers / A Assistant / T Teacher	P Peers / A Assistant / T Teacher	P Peers / A Assistant / T Teacher	None / Sp Speech / G Gestures / V Vocalizations / Si Signs / W Written / AAC AAC system / O Other	
2						Ignored peer's initiation
3						
4						
5						
6						
7						
8						
46						
47						
48						
49						
50						Said "stop" when asked to do more work
#	EN 17 / UN 33	P 1 / A 50 / T 0	P 0 / A 2 / T 0	P 1 / A 22 / T 0	None 27 / Sp 3 / G 18 / V 3 / Si 0 / W 0 / AAC 1 / O 0	
%	34% / 66%	2% / 100% / 0%	0% / 4% / 0%	2% / 44% / 0%	54% / 6% / 36% / 6% / 0% / 0% / 2% / 0%	

Figure 9.2. Example direct observation of Mason from Contemporary Issues class.

lunchroom. Mason sits at a table with several other students from his self-contained special education class, two paraprofessionals, and Mr. Molloy. He spends most of his lunch period flipping through his comics by himself, briefly interacting with only one other student who tried to take his dessert. In the midst of 250 other students in a crowded cafeteria, Mason is largely alone.

In addition to these observations, the team completes an adaptation of the Social Connections and Relationships Assessment (Carter et al., 2016; Kennedy & Itkonen, 1996) to determine who comprises Mason's social network. Information is sought from Mason's parents and two siblings, the paraprofessional who supports him, his general education teachers, and his special education teacher, Mr. Molloy. Each lists the names of every person with whom Mason had an extended social contact (i.e., an interaction lasting at least 15 minutes around a shared activity) in the past month since the start of the semester. For each person, the form asks 1) their name and role, 2) the approximate length of time Mason has known the person, 3) the perceived importance of the person to Mason (i.e., not very, somewhat, or very important), 4) whether the person also has a severe disability, 5) and whether or not the peer is considered a friend (i.e., someone the focus student considers to be socially important and whom they like). Other names of individuals who are part of Mason's network can be added to the bottom of the form even if a social contact has not recently occurred (e.g., family members, friends, acquaintances, and paid professionals). Mr. Molloy integrates the information into a visual picture of Mason's social network (see the left panel of Figure 9.1) and summarizes the findings for the team. Like many students with severe disabilities (Biggs & Carter, 2017), Mason's world is dominated by family members and paid staff. Only two peers—both from his church—are identified as friends, and only one peer buddy who volunteers in his special education class is considered to be an acquaintance (i.e., someone he talks to occasionally but is not considered a friend by Mason).

Finally, Mr. Molloy asks Mason's parents and general education teachers to complete aspects of the Social Skills Improvement System (SSIS) Rating Scales (Gresham & Elliott, 2008). The Social Skills scale measures behaviors presumed to promote appropriate interactions and the skills needed to manage social situations across seven subdomains (i.e., communication, cooperation, assertion, responsibility, empathy, engagement, self-control). The Problem Behavior scale measures behaviors that may interfere with one's ability to learn or engage in social behaviors across five subdomains (i.e., externalizing, bullying, hyperactivity/inattention, internalizing, and autism spectrum). Mason's percentile scores are below average on nearly all of the social skills subdomains. Skills such as joining ongoing activities, introducing oneself, taking turns, and making eye contact are all prioritized by the team. In contrast, his scores for the problem behavior subdomains are near average, with the exception of higher percentile ratings on autism spectrum.

A review of his educational records includes recent scores on the Childhood Autism Rating Scale–Second Edition (CARS-2; Schopler et al., 2010), which indicate he has mild to moderate symptoms of ASD. His Vineland Adaptive Behavior Scales–Second Edition (Vineland-2; Sparrow et al., 2005) standard scores are two standard deviations below the mean in the domains of communication (61), daily living (68), and socialization (65). Although these two norm-referenced assessments provide some insights into Mason's needs, the direct observations and rating scales are drawn upon most heavily by the team.

CLINICAL PROBLEM SOLVING TO IDENTIFY TREATMENT GOALS

Based on the information they collected and reviewed, the educational team recommends implementing peer-mediated interventions in two different settings. Mr. Molloy takes the lead, arranging peer support in the contemporary issues class and a peer network intervention during Mason's lunch period.

General Education Class

Mr. Molloy organizes an hour-long planning meeting with Ms. Lloyd, the paraprofessional, and Ms. Lambert, the contemporary issues teacher. Mr. Molloy shares a brief summary of what they learned from the assessments: The heavy reliance on support from adults instead of peers, the paucity of interactions with classmates, the near absence of initiations, and the inconsistent extent to which Mason was actively engaged in ongoing instruction. He also shares an overview of how peer support arrangements can help address some of these concerns (Carter et al., 2015). They then work collaboratively to design an individualized intervention that will support Mason in the class.

The first step involves crafting a written peer support plan. The team asks Ms. Lambert about the different instructional formats she uses in her class over the course of the semester (e.g., whole-group discussion, lectures, small-group projects, labs, independent work), the activities she uses within these formats (e.g., debates, case scenarios, worksheets, role playing), and the expectations she holds for students during these times. Next, they discuss the ways Mason can participate in each of these activities throughout the semester and the supports he will require. As an expert in special education, Mr. Molloy draws upon his knowledge of effective accommodations, adaptations, and modification. Likewise, Ms. Lloyd draws upon her intimate knowledge of Mason, having supported him across the school day over the last 4 years. Ms. Lambert shares her views on what seems feasible and beneficial based on her strong understanding of the course's curricular requirements. Next, they discuss which of those supports can be provided by peers and which are best left to school staff. All of this information is compiled into an initial written *Peer Support Plan* (Carter et al., 2016). For each of the different class activities, the plan delineates what Mason will do, how peers can provide support, and what Ms. Lloyd will do to help.

With the plan in place, they discuss which peers from the class might serve effectively in this role. They consider a variety of questions: Who already knows and interacts with Mason? Who has some interests or background in common with him? Which peers might themselves benefit from the experience? Who would be able to model appropriate social and communication skills? Which peers might Mason most like to get to know? Who could readily provide the types of support outlined on the written plan? Both Ms. Lambert and Ms. Lloyd immediately think of two students they consider ideal for this role.

Finally, the team discusses the types of data they should collect in order to refine the intervention along the way and to evaluate it at the end of the semester. They decide it would be important to continue collecting the observational data they used during the initial assessment as well as to collect data on those IEP goals that are relevant to the contemporary issues class. They also want to make sure that the two peer partners are keeping up with their own work and are affected positively by their new roles. With all of these decisions made, they are ready to launch the intervention.

Lunch

The next week, Mr. Molloy approaches the visual arts teacher, Mr. Bravo, to ask if he would be willing to facilitate a peer network for Mason for one lunch period per week. Mr. Bravo already knows Mason from his graphic design class. More important, he is a well-liked teacher and baseball coach who has connections to scores of students at the school who have one or more interests in common with Mason. Mr. Molloy shares the findings of the team's assessments, describes some of Mason's educational and transition goals (e.g., interacting with peers, exploring extracurricular activities, developing greater independence), and discusses how a group-based intervention could address these particular needs (Carter et al., 2013). Mr. Bravo has always appreciated Mason's personality and is surprised to learn just how isolated he is in the social epicenter of Northside High School—the cafeteria.

Their discussion then turns toward the goals of the intervention, the activities students can do together, and the peers who should be involved. Both teachers feel Mason will benefit from opportunities to use his AAC device more regularly, to initiate conversations, to explore his interests, and to develop new friendships. They also know they will have to select a group activity that will be motivating for Mason *and* will provide opportunities to work on these social-focused goals. Mr. Bravo suggests building the network around Mason's interest in manga. Many high school students love reading, exchanging, and talking about Japanese comics and graphic novels. Mr. Bravo can brainstorm group activities that will require Mason to ask about, comment on, or respond in relation to the shared activity. He also knows a small clique of students in his class who seem to have a real interest in this topic. With a plan in place, the next step is to recruit students and start the intervention.

INTERVENTIONS USED TO ACHIEVE MAJOR GOALS

Within a couple of weeks, both peer-mediated interventions are up and running. Each intervention approach is described more fully in Chapter 12 of *Treatment of Autism Spectrum Disorder, Second Edition.*

Peer Support Arrangement

Ms. Lambert begins by inviting Aliyah and Jayden to be peer partners in her class; both readily say yes. At the same time, Mr. Molloy trains Ms. Lloyd on how to facilitate the peer support arrangement. She learns how to prompt and reinforce peer interactions and collaborative work, to provide needed information to students, and to collect data. She also learns facilitation strategies such as highlighting commonalities, redirecting conversations, interpreting behaviors, and assigning cooperative tasks. Both peers meet with Ms. Lloyd and Mr. Molloy over two lunch periods to talk about their roles in the classroom and the guidance they will receive along the way. The orientation session addresses relevant (and nonconfidential) information about Mason, the goals of the intervention, expectations related to their roles, and guidance on the types of support they should (and should not) provide.

The next day, Ms. Lambert arranges for Mason, Aliyah, and Jayden to sit at the same table. During the first couple of weeks, Ms. Lloyd remains near the students, prompting and modeling the support strategies outlined on the plan, answering any questions from peers, and encouraging the group as they work together. Gradually, the peers take on a greater role in assisting Mason academically and socially, as they might do with any other classmate. They share materials, ask clarifying questions, encourage him to use his AAC device, talk about their shared interests, and make introductions to other classmates. They also use a visual schedule to help Mason know when there will be unexpected changes in the class schedule. Over time, Ms. Lloyd fades her direct and close support and, under the direction of Ms. Lambert, she begins assisting in other ways in the classroom. Before long, Ms. Lloyd feels confident replicating the support model in Mason's English class.

Peer Network Intervention

The first group meeting starts out a bit rocky. Although five peers agree to be part of Mason's peer network—Nicholas, Sydney, Jonas, Maya, and Maria—one shows up late and another mixes up the dates altogether. The group meets for lunch in Mr. Bravo's classroom, which is a hangout for lots of artistic kids who prefer to avoid the crowded lunchroom. Mason is especially quiet at first, clutching his latest comic book acquisition. But that quickly changes when every other student also pulls out his or her favorite manga. Mr. Bravo explains the purpose of the group and points out what is already quite clear by design—that all of the students share this particular interest in common. He invites the students to introduce themselves, mention their favorite comic series, and share how they do (and do not) like to receive help when in groups. Mr. Molloy asked Mason's mom to select some photos Mason could add to his iPad as a way of introducing himself to these new peers. Next, they all brainstorm ideas for activities they can do together throughout the semester. Mr. Bravo already pulled together ideas of interactive games, projects, and other activities built around manga. Together, they pick which of the ideas they like best and add a few of their own. All of the students bring their schedules to decide when and where their weekly meetings will be held. What was initially planned as a weekly social-focused meeting quickly turns into an everyday lunch gathering in Mr. Bravo's room. The students share their favorite comics; create manga together; and talk about other events, people, and issues that are on their minds. As the students interact around a shared activity, Mr. Bravo will make sure Mason is participating by prompting him to share ideas and ask questions, selecting or adapting activities so he can have an active and valued role, and give suggestions to peers on how to draw Mason out socially. He also keeps in contact with Mason's mom to share how the group is going.

OUTCOMES

Both interventions continue throughout the fall semester and into the spring. The team continues to collect observational data in each of the settings in which the interventions are established (see Figure 9.3). As Mason begins participating in the peer support arrangement, his proximity to peers increases substantially (from 5% to 97%), and the time he spends working directly with his paraprofessional diminishes (from 85% to 22%). Not surprisingly, his interactions with his peer partners increase, but so too do interactions with other classmates. Aliya, Jayden, Devin, and Shimmy draw other classmates into conversations and encourage Mason to share ideas, ask questions, and use his device. Overall peer interactions go from an average of 2% of intervals to 33% of intervals. The increased interaction opportunities provide a rich context for practicing new skills. Mason begins using his AAC more

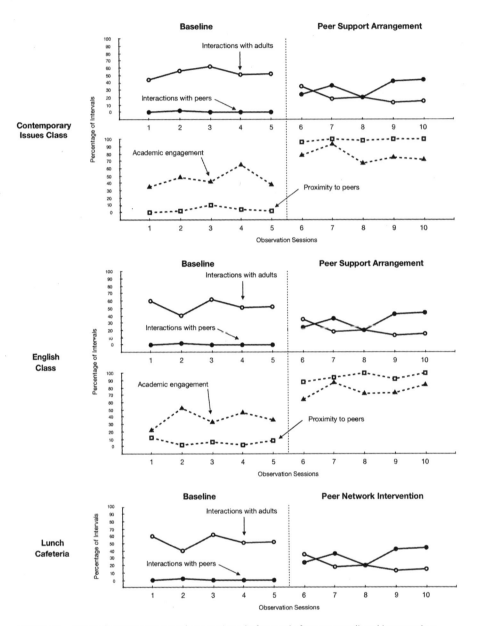

Figure 9.3. Direct observations across three settings, before and after peer-mediated interventions.

(from 1% to 21% of intervals), and his conversational initiations increases as well (from almost none to an average of eight per class period). His peers are also great at drawing him into class activities by sharing materials, asking questions, and finding creative ways for him to participate in group projects. As a result, his academic engagement increases from 42% to 86%, and Ms. Lambert notes that Mason is demonstrating a better understanding of some of the issues discussed in class. Although overall scale ratings on the SISS do not change at the end of the school year, some differences are seen on some of the individual items most closely aligned to the interventions (e.g., takes turns in conversations, responds when others start a conversation or activity, makes eye contact when talking).

The most noticeable differences are found in the number of peers with whom Mason now has personal connections. For example, he works alongside four peers in his two inclusive classrooms and meets daily with five peers in his peer network. These peer partners become a conduit for many other classmates and schoolmates to meet and get to know Mason. Reflecting on his relationships toward the end of the spring semester, his circles of friends and acquaintances have grown substantially. Whereas only three peers were named in these two circles toward the start of freshman year, 22 names are now listed (see the right panel of Figure 9.1). In addition, Jonas and Nicholas encourage Mason to join the anime club, which meets after school. Mason has even invited a few of his new friends to go to a weekend Cardinals game with him. When asked at the end of the fall whether he would like to continue participating in these peer-based interventions in the spring, Mason says yes with a smile.

The impact is not limited to just Mason. Mr. Molloy checks in with each of the peers at the midpoint of the semester. He also asks them to complete a short survey at the end of the semester asking about their relationship with Mason, the strategies they felt worked (and did not work) well, the ways they benefited from their involvement, and their recommendations for the next semester. A number of themes cut across this feedback. Peers say their attitudes about disability changed, they have a greater appreciation and understanding of diversity, they are more firmly committed to inclusion, they learned new things about themselves, and they developed new friendships. Ms. Lambert notes that Jayden, one of the peers who worked with Mason, is much more engaged and successful in class now that he has responsibilities related to supporting Mason.

Learning Activities

1. Reflect on the approaches used by the educational team to assess Mason's social-related needs and the outcomes of his peer-mediated interventions. What other approaches to assessment would you suggest the team consider? Are there other domains in which you think further assessment might be beneficial?

2. Peer-mediated interventions are often touted as having reciprocal benefits. In what ways do you anticipate peers might be affected by their ongoing involvement in these types of support models? Consider how you might respond to concerns that serving in this way might somehow detract from these peers' educational experiences.

3. Despite being identified as an evidence-based practice, peer-mediated support interventions are inconsistently implemented in elementary and secondary schools. Imagine that you were given a small block of time to present on these interventions to at school faculty meeting. How might you convince educators and school leaders that such interventions are worthwhile to pursue? What key points would you emphasize?

4. Students with ASD comprise an especially heterogenous population. A majority of these students do not have cognitive impairments or extensive support needs. What adaptations to peer-mediated support interventions might be needed for these students?

REFERENCES

Biggs, E. E., & Carter, E. W. (2017). Supporting the social lives of students with intellectual disability. In M. L. Wehmeyer & K. A. Shogren (Eds.), *Handbook of research-based practices for educating students with intellectual disability* (pp. 235–254). Routledge.

Carter, E. W. (2021). Peer-mediated support interventions for students with ASD. In P. A. Prelock & R. J. McCauley (Eds.), *Treatment of autism spectrum disorder: Evidence-based intervention strategies for communication & social interactions* (2nd ed., pp. 315–352). Paul H. Brookes Publishing Co.

Carter, E. W., Asmus, J., Moss, C. K., Amirault, K. A., Biggs, E. E., Born, T. L., Brock. M. E., Cattey, G. N., Chen, R., Cooney, M., Fesperman, E., Hochman, J. M., Huber, H. B., Lequia, J. L., Lyons, G., Moyseenko, K. A., Riesch, L. M., Shalev, R. A., Vincent, L. B., & Wier, K. (2016). Randomized evaluation of peer supports arrangements to support the inclusion of high school students with severe disabilities. *Exceptional Children, 82,* 209–233.

Carter, E. W., Asmus, J., Moss, C. K., Cooney, M., Weir, K., Hochman, J. M., Bottema-Beutel, K., & Fesperman, E. (2013). Peer network strategies to foster social connections among adolescents with and without severe disabilities. *TEACHING Exceptional Children, 46*(2), 51–59.

Carter, E. W., Moss, C. K., Asmus, J., Fesperman, E., Cooney, M., Brock, M. E., Lyons, G., Huber, H. B., & Vincent, L. B. (2015). Promoting inclusion, social relationships, and learning through peer support arrangements. *TEACHING Exceptional Children, 48*(1), 9–18.

Gresham, F., & Elliott, S. N. (2008). *Social Skills Improvement System (SSIS) Rating Scales.* Pearson.

Kennedy, C. H., & Itkonen, T. (1996). Social relationships, influential variables, and change across the lifespan. In L. Koegel, R. I. Koegel, & G. Dunlap (Eds.), *Positive behavioral support: Including people with difficult behavior in the community* (pp. 287–304). Paul H. Brookes Publishing Co.

Schopler, E., Van Bourgondien, M. E., Wellman, G. J., & Love, S. R. (2010). *Childhood Autism Rating Scale—Second edition* (CARS-2). Western Psychological Services.

Sparrow, S., Cicchetti, D., & Balla, D. (2005). *Vineland Adaptive Behavior Scales—Second edition.* Pearson.

Using Pivotal Response Treatment to Improve Social Communication and Behavior Skills

A Young Child With ASD

Lynn Kern Koegel, Brittany Lynn Koegel, Elizabeth Ponder, and Kristen Strong

 Adam

 Age 2

 Autism Spectrum Disorder

Case 10 engages with the intervention approach and strategies discussed in Chapter 13, Pivotal Response Treatment (Koegel, Strong, & Ponder, 2021) of the text *Treatment of Autism Spectrum Disorder, Second Edition*.

INTRODUCTION

Just before Adam's second birthday, his grandmother, who babysits him daily, encourages his parents to seek assistance. Although there were no complications with his birth and his parents report that he met his early motor milestones on time, Adam is not yet talking and appears to have a fixation with the ceiling fan

in their home, staring at it for hours at a time. In addition, according to his grandmother, he is more noncompliant than compliant, and Adam regularly exhibits
meltdowns when requested to engage in even simple tasks. His parents shrug
the delays and behaviors off, saying Adam is just a late talker or is frequently
under the weather, but Adam's pediatrician corroborates the grandmother's concerns and encourages his parents to seek early intervention to help speed up his
development.

His parents report a normal pregnancy and say that Adam reached his beginning developmental milestones on time or early. Adam sat up at age 4 months,
crawled at 6 months, and took his first steps at 11 months. They also report that
he was a fussy baby and was difficult to soothe. They describe him as a serious
child who smiles infrequently, is intensely focused on items, and has less interest
in engaging socially than do other infants his age. In regard to communication,
they report that he has no consistent words but on occasion has said a word at an
appropriate time, such as "ice cream." However, they cannot get him to repeat the
word when they try, nor does he consistently use any words. See Adam's ecogram
in Figure 10.1.

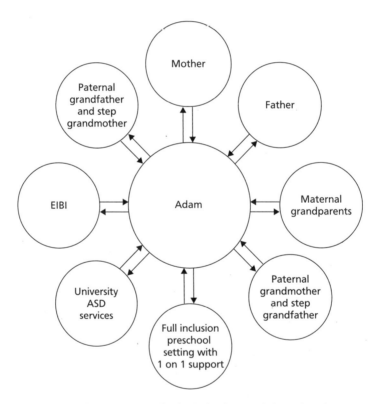

Figure 10.1. Adam's ecogram. All individuals who provided care for Adam were
trained by the Early Intensive Behavioral Intervention (EIBI) program, which
provided Pivotal Response Treatment (PRT) and was coordinated with the university.
Adam's parents received parent education (practice with feedback) sessions
several times a week. The EIBI program coordinated with Adam's preschool to assure
that he received ongoing social intervention. All programs were coordinated across
settings and providers. *Key:* ASD, autism spectrum disorder.

ASSESSMENTS FOR COMMUNICATION TREATMENT PLANNING

After gathering this information through informal family report, Adam's parents bring him to the center for assessment. Clinicians attempt an assessment using standardized tests, but Adam cannot point to any items, nor is he interested in engaging with an adult or sitting in a chair to look at test materials.

Clinicians also implement procedures for collecting a language sample. They place a variety of toys in a living room–type setting and instruct his parents to play with him and to try to get him to use words, but Adam does not say any words or make word attempts during the sample. To get a more complete picture and better understand Adam's communication and behavior, clinicians conduct observations at his home (Koegel & Koegel, 2019). Clinicians note no verbal expressive communication during any of the samples they conduct over the course of a few weeks. Adam does not make any unintelligible utterances, word attempts, or language approximations.

When Adam wants an item, clinicians observe him grab his parent's hand and place it on the desired item, such as a door handle when he wants to go outside or the refrigerator handle when he is hungry. He does not follow a point. Adam engages in limited eye contact and exhibits frequent tantrums, often lasting for 20–30 minutes. However, he is fairly competent at getting his needs met without the assistance of a parent. For example, if he wants an item that is out of reach (e.g., on a high bookshelf), he will pull a chair over and stack pillows one on top of another until he is able to reach the object. Further, he enjoys being carried by his parents and seems to have a preference for his mother and father over other people. His parents report that during the weeks of the assessment, they heard him say a few words, such as "cookie" and the name of a character on his favorite television show, *Elmo*.

After numerous observations in Adam's natural setting and the center, a variety of standardized parent questionnaires, and attempted standardized testing, clinicians provide a preliminary diagnosis of autism spectrum disorder (ASD). Adam's preliminary diagnosis is based on his lack of social communication and frequent restricted and repetitive behaviors (RRBs). Adam's immediate and extended family are supportive and fully committed to helping him in whatever way possible.

In summary, baseline measurements indicate that Adam 1) has no expressive verbal communication or word attempts that he uses regularly; 2) engages in frequent tantrums that last 10–30 minutes when denied access to a desired item or activity, during transitions (particularly from a desired to less desired activity), and when others attempt to interact with him; and 3) engages in RRBs approximately 70% of the time when not engaged in an activity (e.g., watching television, eating). In regard to strengths, he 1) enjoys looking at certain books (Disney and Sesame Street) with his mother; 2) has a few favorite toys, primarily puzzles, that he can rapidly complete; 3) exhibits preferences for certain people, particularly his parents; 4) enjoys bath time and watching repetitive motions, such as the ceiling fan; 5) can problem-solve when he wants an out-of-reach item and is able to put together a few toys when they are broken, such as ramps; and 6) enjoys physical activities with his father, including swinging, roughhousing, and being thrown up in the air. As per the center's philosophy and values, this strengths-based assessment is used to guide interventions (Cosden et al., 2006). In summary, his most significant needs involve social communication and RRBs; therefore, he is diagnosed with ASD. In addition, a frequent co-occurring behavior is regular meltdowns several times a day.

CLINICAL PROBLEM SOLVING TO IDENTIFY TREATMENT GOALS

Adam's treatment goals and strategies involve improving social communication and decreasing his challenging behaviors. Because he is nonverbal, at least when observed, and does not respond when a verbal opportunity is presented, the primary goal is to instate consistent words in his repertoire. During a goal development meeting with his parents, they express the same urgent desire to have him begin speaking. His father, with tears in his eyes, says, "If I could give him my voice and I could never talk again, I would do that." Thus, the bulk of the sessions during the beginning of his intervention program focus mainly on teaching first words.

INTERVENTIONS USED TO ACHIEVE MAJOR GOALS

Using the Pivotal Response Treatment (PRT) strategies described in Chapter 13 of the accompanying textbook, clinicians apply the concept of child choice by selecting Adam's favorite items and activities to prompt first words (Koegel & Koegel, 2019). Because clinicians incorporate desirable items and activities, Adam is motivated to engage in treatment sessions (R. L. Koegel et al., 1987). In addition, clinicians coordinate with the family and teach procedures for prompting first words in the context of parent education so that the parents can implement the treatment and incorporate intervention strategies into Adam's everyday routines (L. K. Koegel et al., 2019; Steiner et al., 2012).

PRT was developed by speech-language pathologists (SLPs) and psychologists, so it focuses on a collaborative model of communication and behavior (Koegel & Koegel, 2019). Adam's clinicians use a practice with feedback model to develop a parent–professional collaboration so that intervention can be provided consistently and seamlessly across settings throughout his waking hours (Koegel & Koegel, 2019). Using this model, clinicians 1) provide his parents with opportunities to carry over the speech intervention strategies they model and 2) provide feedback relating to their implementation (Coolican et al., 2010; Steiner et al., 2012).

Clinicians begin with requests by prompting the labels of Adam's favorite items, activities, and foods. The first step is to carefully assess Adam's interest to make sure that the selected items are important to him at the moment. A child may typically enjoy a specific toy, but if his or her attention wanders, the item may no longer be rewarding, so careful attention needs to be paid to the child's preference on an ongoing basis. To be specific, once clinicians determine the desired item or activity, they model the label of the item and provide the child with an opportunity to request the item using the word or a verbal word approximation. As soon as the child makes any attempt to verbally say the word or requests the item using the correct word, clinicians give it to him or her immediately as a natural reward (R. L. Koegel et al., 1988; R. L. Koegel & Williams, 1980). Consequently, the child learns that using verbal communication in a social manner has a positive outcome and that other behaviors that were effective in the past, such as crying and tantrums, need to be replaced with communication or good attempts at communication. Although this process is labor intensive, research shows that the best child outcomes occur with parents who provide frequent PRT opportunities with fidelity of implementation (i.e., implementing the procedures correctly). Through the practice with feedback model, most parents can effectively learn to implement the procedures (Hardan et al., 2015). However, if the intervention is not implemented properly or is implemented infrequently, children will have poorer outcomes.

For Adam, the acquisition of first words is slow, but after approximately a month, he begins to use full words with age-appropriate articulation. Once he begins using words, a rapid increase in his vocabulary occurs, and within 2 months, he can say more than 70 single words. At that point, clinicians begin teaching him to combine words. To move to this next step, clinicians generally attempt to prompt him to use two words that are already in his vocabulary. For example, if he spontaneously requests, "Ball," he is prompted to say the color, such as "Blue ball," using the colors he can label. Similarly, if he requests, "Up," he is prompted to say, "Up high," before his father throws him in the air. Adam quickly begins using word combinations.

Clinicians also note on their Likert scales for assessing interest and enthusiasm that his affect is high during the learning activities (Dunlap, 1984). This is most likely because the clinicians focused on his strengths and used child-preferred items and activities. In addition, once Adam begins using two-word combinations, clinicians recast longer utterances. For example, when he requests, "More chips," the adult says, "More chips, please," or "Can I have chips, please?" Whenever possible, he is prompted to repeat the longer sentence, which he generally does without protesting.

Adam's language is progressing nicely, and shortly after his third birthday, the intervention team recommends that he enter preschool. He does not have siblings, and during outings to the park or museum and when the family visits friends or family with children of similar age, he pays little attention to them and prefers to isolate himself and engage in repetitive behaviors. At preschool, an individualized education program (IEP) is developed, and both social and communication goals are the primary targets.

Preschool brings a whole new set of challenges. First, circle time is a disaster. It is highly verbal with stories read, questions asked, and lots of explanations that are far beyond Adam's language comprehension level. Adam often does not pay attention and engages in off-task behaviors during these circle times, including saying words aloud and rolling around on the floor. He will sometimes get up and leave the area to play alone with more interesting toys or engage in repetitive behaviors (e.g., shaking items in front of his eyes). Second, he refuses to play or take turns with other children and regularly gathers an assembly of toys for himself and then yells at any other child that approaches the toys. After Adam yells, his peers leave the area. Thus, functionally, he has his own set of toys and is not engaging in any social interactions.

Clinical problem solving to develop treatment goals to address these areas is threefold. First, clinicians conduct a functional behavior analysis to assess whether any replacement behaviors can be developed. Second, they implement a home-school coordination program. And third, they address social interaction (Koegel & Koegel, 2019). Not surprisingly, the functional behavior assessment indicates that disruptive behavior occurs any time an activity is highly verbal, when Adam has to make a transition from a highly desired activity to a less desired activity, and when another child tries to play with a toy he has taken to a corner of the classroom. Data are collected and indicate that 1) he engages in off-task or challenging behavior throughout the entire circle time; 2) disruptive behavior occurs for 5–10 minutes when he is asked to make a transition; and 3) every time a child approaches him, he exhibits disruptive behavior until the child leaves the area where he is play-ing. These behaviors are being rewarded/maintained by Adam's not having to sit in circle time, his being able to play 5–10 minutes longer before making the transition to a less desired activity, and another child consistently leaving after Adam yells or screams in the child's direction so that he does not have to share the toys he is playing with. Based on this information, a multicomponent intervention program is implemented.

First, for circle time, clinicians implement a priming program (L. K. Koegel et al., 2003). Specifically, every evening his parents read the story that will be read in class the following day. This home–school coordination program familiarizes him with the story. At home, the stories are read in a relaxed and fun manner so that he will enjoy this activity. Priming sessions are not meant to be punitive or punishing in any way, as the child is already avoiding the activity. Priming sessions are pre-sented in an enjoyable, child-friendly manner so as to familiarize the child before-hand with the activity that will be presented the following day (Wilde et al., 1992). Research has shown that priming reduces challenging behaviors and improves on-task engagement (L. K. Koegel et al., 2003). Adam seems to enjoy the priming ses-sions and is certainly engaged when he recognizes the story that has been read to him the night before.

Second, the teacher engages Adam by asking a simple question that matches his language level during her class discussion. This gives him a chance to be involved in the classroom activity at his own appropriate language level. Third, he is taught to say, "I don't understand," when the discussion is too complicated, at which time the teacher will explain the concept in simpler terms. After putting these three inter-ventions in place, Adam's on-task behavior increases to 98% (which was well within the range of his peers), and his challenging behaviors are negligible. On occasion, he begins to engage in some challenging behavior at the very beginning of a story, but once he recognizes the familiar story, he immediately attends to the teacher, suggesting that the priming is effective.

To target transitions from more desired to less desired activities, clinicians give Adam a 5-minute warning, followed by an alert every minute until it is time to make the transition. After a few trials and errors, clinicians determine that when the time is up, it is best to help Adam put away whatever he is working on or to take him away from the playground equipment so that he will not have the reward of playing 5–10 minutes extra while engaging in the challenging behaviors.

Next, to encourage social interaction and to reduce the amount of time he plays alone, clinicians teach Adam to take turns (Koegel & Koegel, 2019). During the first 2 weeks of the intervention, clinicians practice turn taking with an adult to ensure that Adam's play partner takes very short turns to help him learn that he will get another turn rather than lose his favorite toys indefinitely. At first, he is very unhappy when it is not his turn, but by the third week of intervention, he is able to easily take turns with adults. Next, peers are included in the turn taking (Harper et al., 2008). Peers interact and respond differently than adults; therefore, it was important that Adam learn to generalize this skill. In addition to practicing at school, his parents also practice turn taking at home with a neighbor's child. Adam quickly learns that if he calmly waits for another child to take a turn, it will soon be his turn again. During this intervention, he is also taught to make appropriate comments, such as "your turn," "my turn," "good game," and "you won," so that ver-bal social communication can be targeted along with his social interaction. Adam's

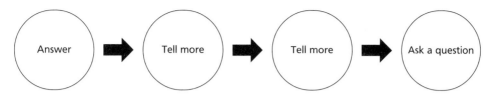

Figure 10.2. Visual framework to describe events.

affect is measured on a Likert scale, indicating that over time, he exhibits positive affect when another child takes a turn. He also smiles when another child encourages him during an activity.

Along with these other intervention programs, language intervention continues, now focusing on more abstract concepts using his favorite activities as well as improving his social conversation. For example, clinicians teach him to use longer utterances to describe events during his favorite activities, using the visual framework shown in Figure 10.2.

Visual cues to accompany verbal instruction can be helpful when teaching social-communication skills (Quill, 1997). During this intervention, the SLP or adult asks, "Do you like the trains?" while Adam is enjoying playing with the trains. Adam is prompted to look at the visual cue and respond, "Yes," then add information, "I like playing with trains," "Percy is my favorite," then ask a question, "Do you like trains?" This practice helps Adam provide more information during social conversation and, by including a question at the end, engage in longer back-and-forth social interactions. Within a few months of regular practice with the schematic, Adam is consistently responding with longer sentences, providing more detail, and asking more questions. As Adam gains mastery, the visual framework is gradually faded.

Adam continues to show steady improvements in preschool, and when he enters elementary school, he continues to be included in a general education classroom. Initially, he is accompanied by a one-to-one paraprofessional who helps him with social interactions and a few inappropriate behaviors. For example, one day he comes home with a half a sheet of his homework page. His mother asks him what happened, and he responds with, "I ate it." After consultation with the paraprofessional, it turns out that not only did Adam eat his homework but he was also regularly engaging in pica, eating small rocks and other nonedible items he picked up off the playground or classroom.

Baseline data shows that Adam is engaging in pica behavior an average of three times a day. To target this potentially dangerous behavior, clinicians implement a self-management program (L. K. Koegel et al., 1999; Koegel & Koegel, 2019). They first assess his baseline to see how frequently he puts inedible items in his mouth. When designing the self-management program, clinicians begin with a period of time that is short enough to have a high likelihood that Adam will experience success. For example, during recess, he usually puts a rock, dirt clod, or other item in his mouth within 5 minutes of the start of recess, so clinicians set a vibrating watch for 3 minutes (Finn et al., 2015). In class, pica is less frequent, usually occurring only once or twice a day, so the time interval clinicians begin with in the classroom is 30 minutes. After the timer vibrates, he monitors whether he has placed anything in his mouth. If he has not put anything inedible in this mouth, he gives himself a point, and those points are accumulated for his self-chosen reward of playing on the computer for a brief period of time at the end of the day.

As he experiences success of completing the short intervals without putting anything in his mouth, the intervals are gradually and systematically lengthened. Within a month, no instances of pica are observed on the playground or in class. In addition, an unanticipated outcome of decreasing the pica is improved social interactions. When he is not spending time searching the playground for small objects to put in his mouth and swallow, he tends to engage more frequently with peers, which provides more opportunities for the paraprofessional (under guidance from the SLP) to prompt prosocial communication.

OUTCOMES

Throughout his elementary school years, Adam continues to improve in many areas, including communication, socialization, academics, and behavior, with support from his paraprofessionals, SLP, teacher, parents, and private in-home therapists. During fifth and sixth grade, the paraprofessional fades support until she helps primarily with socialization during outdoor periods. At one time, Adam reports bullying by classmates in the after-school program that is on the school site, so experienced staff observe in that setting. They notice that when Adam reacts to the bullying (e.g., tells the student to stop, becomes visibly upset), this seems to cause the peers to bully even more, so they work with him on not reacting (Laugeson & Frankel, 2011). In addition, the staff work with the peers to develop some strict antibullying rules and to teach appropriate prosocial behaviors.

Clinicians continue to target social areas with Adam. Providers in his aftercare program help him improve conversations with peers, and his parents provide extra support on his schoolwork. Adam makes steady and consistent progress with his programs, family support, and IEP goals. Outside of school, his parents enroll him in extracurricular activities with his peers to help him form friendships (Laugeson & Frankel, 2011). He becomes an excellent tennis player. Adam enjoys playing competitively and is a good sport when he loses a game.

When Adam enters high school, he participates in a full general education curriculum. However, his parents still spend a significant amount of time after school and on weekends helping him with his homework. As well, he often forgets assignments and homework at school. For the most part, high school students are not completely reliant on their parents to complete homework; therefore, this area needs to be addressed. Further complicating this problem is that Adam reports that he feels uncomfortable asking his teachers for clarification or further explanation of assignments. Therefore, the school collaboratively works with his team to develop an intervention program to address these areas. They designate a specific staff member at the school who will support him and will be responsible for coordinating with the teachers regarding assignments and will assess areas that are challenging for him.

Clinicians begin with one class—a class that has a cooperative teacher and that he is experiencing success in academically. They let Adam know that he is going to be on his own in this class and that his parents will not help him if he forgets his book or assignment, nor will they help him with any homework or projects in the class. His designated staff member prompts him to get the phone number of a fellow student in the class in case he needs some help in the evenings. With support and coordination with the teacher, the staff member carefully teaches him how to use an academic planner and regularly goes over his planner, assesses his understanding of the homework assignments, and monitors homework and project completion. Small adjustments are made in weak areas, such as making sure he has the assignments written down, fully pays attention to homework and project discussions in class, understands what is expected on projects and assignments, and checks the website regularly for assignments. With support in these areas, he quickly becomes independent and completes assignments without needing his parents' help.

Gradually, another course is added after he is completely independent and maintaining a good grade without his parents' assistance. After he is successful in the second course, another is added, and so on, until he is able to succeed in all of his classes without excessive assistance from his parents each day after school and on weekends.

As a high schooler, Adam is now quite independent, receives mostly As and Bs, and only occasionally needs help from his parents. This is a great stress reducer for his parents, as they reported frequent arguments while trying to help him. As well, both parents work full time and were exhausted with the many hours they needed to spend assisting him with homework, emailing teachers about assignments, driving him back to school when he forgot materials in his locker, and checking the school website to make sure he had completed his assignments. Once he learned to complete his projects and homework independently by improving his organizational skills, received peer support, and the school made a few minor modifications to make sure more details were written on the school's website and assignments were carefully explained in class, his independence improved and his reliance on his parents greatly decreased.

Adam is interested in attending college and particularly enjoys math. He plans to attend a junior college while living at home for 2 years, and then he will make the transfer to a 4-year university. Given that he has tremendous family support, responds well to intervention, has several friends, does well in school, engages in leisure activities with peers outside of the school setting, and is becoming self-sufficient and independent, clinicians anticipate that he will do well in college and gain meaningful employment in his area of interest. He may need some monitoring in college to make sure he is able to reach out to peers, engage in social activities, and complete all assignments when the bulk of the day is outside of the classroom, but these are areas that many young college students need to learn. Unfortunately, not all individuals with ASD have such outstanding outcomes, but as research continues and researchers find more and improved methods to help individuals on the autism spectrum succeed, more individuals diagnosed with ASD should have positive outcomes.

Learning Activities

1. Peer-mediated strategies can help support adults with the implementation of goals (Harrower & Dunlap, 2001; Odom & Strain, 1984). For example, a peer could have the remote for accessing a television or game and prompt Adam to say, "Play." Describe a plan to set up peer-mediated intervention for a hypothetical, current, or past client. For that client, would you train siblings, peers, or both? What treatment goals would you target? Within what types of activities would you train the peers? What types of prompts would you teach?

2. Priming is an antecedent strategy that can improve socialization, behavior, and academic performance. When Adam engaged in disruptive behavior during circle time, priming him with the stories before the teacher read them the next day helped to decrease these behaviors. Suppose you are working with a child who you believe would benefit from priming, but there has been little home–school communication and the teacher has been resistant to coordinating with the home team. Using your knowledge of priming and data collected during school observations, write a letter to the teacher requesting priming to be included in the child's program.

3. An additional socialization strategy that can be set up in the classroom and at recess is peer buddy systems (Laushey & Heflin, 2000). Consider setting up a buddy system within a third-grade classroom. What are some age-appropriate questions to prompt buddies to ask? For example, "Find out if your buddy has a pet."

4. Because Adam loved Disney movies and books, Disney was used as the theme of playground activities in order to make it more likely that Adam would want to participate (Baker et al., 1998; R. L. Koegel et al., 2012; L. K. Koegel et al., 2012). What are some other social activities that could be set up that include Adam's interest in Disney? How would these activities need to be organized to ensure that they are mutually reinforcing for peers as well?

REFERENCES

Baker, M. J., Koegel, R. L., & Koegel, L. K. (1998). Increasing the social behavior of young children with autism using their obsessive behaviors. *Journal of the Association of Persons with Severe Handicaps, 23,* 300–308.

Coolican, J., Smith, I. M., & Bryson, S. E. (2010). Brief parent training in pivotal response treatment for preschoolers with autism. *Journal of Child Psychology and Psychiatry, 51*(12), 1321–1330.

Cosden, M., Koegel, L. K., Koegel, R. L., Greenwall, A., & Klein, E. (2006). Strength-based assessment for children with autism spectrum disorders. *Research and Practice for Persons with Severe Disabilities, 31*(2), 134–143.

Dunlap, G. (1984). The influence of task variation and maintenance tasks on the learning and affect of autistic children. *Journal of Experimental Child Psychology, 37*(1), 41–64.

Finn, L., Ramasamy, R., Dukes, C., & Scott, J. (2015). Using WatchMinder to increase the on-task behavior of students with autism spectrum disorder. *Journal of Autism and Developmental Disorders, 45*(5), 1408–1418.

Hardan, A. Y., Gengoux, G. W., Berquist, K. L., Libove, R. A., Ardel, C. M., Phillips, J., Frazier, T. W., & Minjarez, M. B. (2015). A randomized controlled trial of Pivotal Response Treatment group for parents of children with autism. *Journal of Child Psychology and Psychiatry, 56*(8), 884–892.

Harper, C. B., Symon, J. B., & Frea, W. D. (2008). Recess is time-in: Using peers to improve social skills of children with autism. *Journal of Autism and Developmental Disorders, 38*(5), 815–826.

Harrower, J. K., & Dunlap, G. (2001). Including children with autism in general education classrooms: A review of effective strategies. *Behavior Modification, 25*(5), 762–784.

Koegel, L. K., Bryan, K. M., Su, P., Vaida, M., & Camarata, S. (2019). Intervention for nonverbal and minimally-verbal individuals with autism: A systematic review. *International Journal of Pediatric Research, 5*(2), 1–16.

Koegel, L. K., Harrower, J. K., & Koegel, R. L. (1999). Support for children with developmental disabilities in full inclusion classrooms through self-management. *Journal of Positive Behavior Interventions, 1*(1), 26–34.

Koegel, L. K., Koegel, R. L., Frea, W., & Green-Hopkins, I. (2003). Priming as a method of coordinating educational services for students with autism. *Language, Speech, and Hearing Services in Schools, 34*(3), 228–235.

Koegel, L. K., Strong, K., & Ponder, E. (2021). Pivotal Response Treatment. In P. A. Prelock & R. J. McCauley (Eds.), *Treatment of autism spectrum disorder: Evidence-based intervention strategies for communication & social interactions* (2nd ed., pp. 353–380). Paul H. Brookes Publishing Co.

Koegel, L. K., Vernon, T. W., Koegel, R. L., Koegel, B. L., & Paullin, A. W. (2012). Improving social engagement and initiations between children with autism spectrum disorder and their peers in inclusive settings. *Journal of Positive Behavior Interventions, 14*(4), 220–227.

Koegel, R. L., Dyer, K., & Bell, L. K. (1987). The influence of child-preferred activities on autistic children's social behavior. *Journal of Applied Behavior Analysis, 20*(3), 243–252.

Koegel, R. L., Fredeen, R., Kim, S., Danial, J., Rubinstein, D., & Koegel, L. (2012). Using perseverative interests to improve interactions between adolescents with autism and their typical peers in school settings. *Journal of Positive Behavior Interventions, 14*(3), 133–141.

Koegel, R. L., & Koegel, L. K. (Eds.). (2019). *Pivotal Response Treatment for autism spectrum disorders* (2nd ed.). Paul H. Brookes Publishing Co.

Koegel, R. L., O'Dell, M., & Dunlap, G. (1988). Producing speech use in nonverbal autistic children by reinforcing attempts. *Journal of Autism and Developmental Disorders, 18*(4), 525–538.

Koegel, R. L., & Williams, J. (1980). Direct versus indirect response-reinforcer relationships in teaching autistic children. *Journal of Abnormal Child Psychology, 8*(4), 537–547.

Laugeson, E. A., & Frankel, F. (2011). *Social skills for teenagers with developmental and autism spectrum disorders: The PEERS treatment manual.* Routledge.

Laushey, K. M., & Heflin, L. J. (2000). Enhancing social skills of kindergarten children with autism through the training of multiple peers as tutors. *Journal of Autism and Developmental Disorders, 30*(3), 183–193.

Odom, S. L., & Strain, P. S. (1984). Peer-mediated approaches to promoting children's social interaction: A review. *American Journal of Orthopsychiatry, 54*(4), 544.

Quill, K. A. (1997). Instructional considerations for young children with autism: The rationale for visually cued instruction. *Journal of Autism and Developmental Disabilities, 27*(6), 697–714.

Steiner, A. M., Koegel, L. K., Koegel, R. L., & Ence, W. A. (2012). Issues and theoretical constructs regarding parent education for autism spectrum disorders. *Journal of Autism and Developmental Disorders, 41*(1), 1218–1227.

Wilde, L. D., Koegel, L. K., & Koegel, R. L. (1992). *Increasing success in school through priming: A training manual.* University of California.

Facilitating Social Communicative and Social Emotional Competence

A Third Grader With ASD

Amy C. Laurent, Emily Rubin, and Barry M. Prizant

 Jack

 Age 9

 Autism Spectrum Disorder

> **Case 11 engages with the intervention approach and strategies discussed in Chapter 14, The SCERTS® Model: Social Communication, Emotional Regulation, and Transactional Supports (Laurent, Rubin, & Prizant, 2021) in *Treatment of Autism Spectrum Disorder, Second Edition.***

INTRODUCTION

Jack is a 9-year-old boy who was diagnosed with autism spectrum disorder (ASD) at 20 months of age. He and his fraternal twin, John, were carried to full term, pregnancy and had an uncomplicated delivery. According to parent report, Jack and John's family began to notice developmental differences between the boys when they were approximately 14 months of age. Initial concerns included Jack's not using words or babbling when interacting with others; having difficulty shifting his attention away from the TV when others entered the room; crying inconsolably when he experienced certain noises, such as ripping tinfoil; and rarely waving to others or pointing to objects that he wanted. Following his ASD diagnosis, Jack's family pursued early intervention services for him, which he continued until making the transition to the public school system at age 3.

Jack is currently a third-grade student who splits his academic day between an inclusive classroom and a flexible resource room. He accesses the resource room when he is experiencing regulatory challenges and/or when he requires a quieter learning environment. He receives individualized occupational therapy and speech therapy as part of his educational programming. He is a multimodal communicator. When speaking, Jack often uses echolalic scripts from favorite songs to convey his ideas. He is quite effective at doing so, and those who meet him often marvel at his ability to pull out just the right passage for a given event. When not using scripts, he often uses single spoken words to make requests and/or occasionally comment on an object of interest. If picture communication symbols are available to him, he uses them to initiate requests for preferred toys, foods, or activities. In addition, he uses natural gestures (e.g., reaching for things) and facial expressions when interacting with others. He does not currently use a dynamic augmentative and alternative communication (AAC) system.

As noted, most of Jack's communicative initiations are for the purpose of requesting and protesting, resulting in a core vocabulary heavily comprised of nouns. He rarely initiates communication for more socially oriented functions (e.g., greeting, commenting, taking turns). His receptive communicative abilities exceed his expressive abilities, as is demonstrated by his appropriate and timely use of echolalic scripts as well as his ability to respond using contingent actions and so on.

Jack is surrounded by a supportive network of family and friends. Although extended family live at a distance, his neighbors are a tightly knit group of people who look out for one another. See Figure 11.1 for visual representation of Jack's

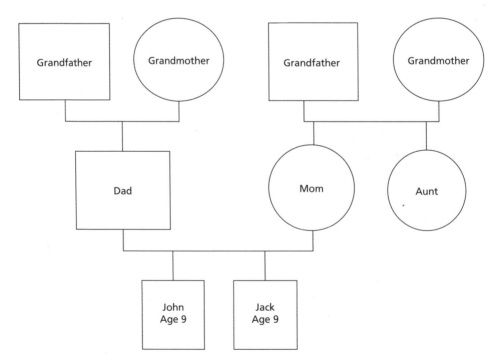

Figure 11.1. Jack's genogram.

immediate family. In fact, the neighbors who live across the street have become honorary grandparents to both Jack and John. Although Jack does not initiate playdates with peers, his brother and his friends often invite Jack to participate in social activities. Jack's participation depends on the nature of the activity and his interest in it. One activity that Jack consistently participates in with great enthusiasm is an inclusive soccer program at a nearby community field. Jack is consistently engaged in this program, and his coach notes he is developing considerable skill in reading the field visually. The high level of physical activity provided by the soccer program is a good fit for Jack, as he is a very active sensory seeker. His family reports that regular and intense movement opportunities help him to regulate his arousal level and attention. He tends to have difficulty doing so otherwise and is easily overwhelmed by environmental factors (e.g., noise, complex visual environments) in sedentary activities. In addition to helping with his attentional challenges, his family notes that intense physical activity is crucial to helping minimize explosive behaviors that he engages in when he experiences significant regulatory challenges.

Given his profile, his family and educational team agree that his most significant needs at this time are his limited communication skills and his challenges maintaining active engagement in ongoing activities. They also acknowledge that although he is surrounded by a supportive social environment, his developmental challenges pose difficulties in accessing a wide range of daily activities in the community. See Figure 11.2 for a visual representation of Jack's social and physical environments.

ASSESSMENTS FOR COMMUNICATION TREATMENT PLANNING

Jack's family and educational team are beginning to implement The SCERTS® (Social Communication, Emotional Regulation, and Transactional Supports) Model as a framework to guide Jack's educational planning. The team has committed to conducting The SCERTS Assessment Process (SAP) for Jack in his home, school, and community (i.e., his soccer program at the park) environments. The SAP is a 10-step procedure that revolves around a criterion-referenced assessment tool (see Table 11.1). It is designed to discern a comprehensive and accurate developmental profile of individuals with respect to their social-communication and emotional regulation abilities and to determine the nature of effective and efficient interpersonal supports and learning supports. See Table 11.2 for a breakdown of the domains and components included in The SCERTS Model.

The team agrees that utilizing the SAP rather than standardized evaluation tools will give them a better understanding of how Jack uses his communicative skills functionally. Specifically, the team considers that assessing Jack during daily activities with his natural partners according to the symbol use curriculum will inform their understanding of his day-to-day functional use of receptive and expressive language (e.g., the how of his communication). They also acknowledge that assessing him according to the joint attention curriculum will provide needed insights into the social aspects of his communicative profile (e.g., the why of his communication). When considering his communication profile, they all agree that the emotional regulation curriculum will also provide insights related to factors influencing his social-communicative competence. In addition to the utility of the symbol use, joint attention, and emotional regulation portions of the SAP curriculum, the team also notes that assessment using the learning support portion of

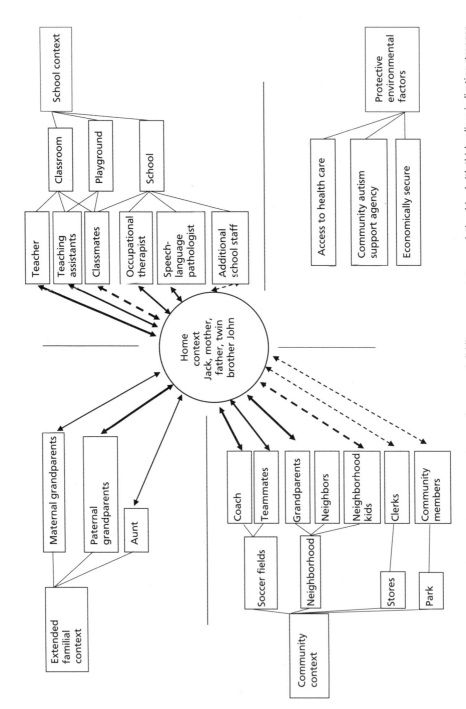

Figure 11.2. Jack's ecomap—personal contexts, connections, and supports. Solid lines represent strong relationships (with thicker lines indicating stronger relationships), dotted lines indicate stressed relationships, and arrows indicate the direction of energy flow and support.

Table 11.1. Ten steps of the SCERTS® Assessment Process

Step 1	Determine communication stage
Step 2	SCERTS Assessment Process–Report (SAP-R) form Gather information from families and teachers or other caregivers using. SAP-R data to be used in planning observation and building profile of student
Step 3	SAP MAP—Identify assessment team members and plan the SAP observation (natural contexts, length of observation, partners, group size, activity variables, transitions): who will observe and take data and when.
Step 4	Team members conduct observations and complete SAP–Observation form at appropriate partners stage Document observed behaviors and consider reported ones via SAP-R form
Step 5	Conduct behavior sampling if needed—that is, if not enough information gleaned from direct observations or parent report to inform scoring of goal areas
Step 6	Compile and integrate information into SAP summary form, summarizing needs and strengths and family perception of SAP-Observation results and priorities
Step 7	Prioritize goals and objectives based on developmental appropriateness, family priority, and functionality
Step 8	Recommend further assessment if needed
Step 9	Design SCERTS educational program
Step 10	Establish ongoing tracking method

Source: Prizant et al. (2006a and b).

Table 11.2. Domains and components of The SCERTS® Model

Domain	Component
Social Communication	Joint attention—the *why* of communication Symbol use—the *how* of communication
Emotional Regulation	Mutual regulation—the capacity to maintain well-regulated state with assistance of another person Self-regulation—the capacity to maintain active engagement without assistance
Transactional Support	Interpersonal support—adjustments in interactive style made by partners Learning support—modifications to activity and physical environment made by partners

Source: Prizant et al. (2006a and b).

the transactional support curriculum will yield important additional information related to Jack's communication modalities.

Using the worksheet for determining stage (Step 1, SAP), Jack's family and team determine that he is a Language Partner within the context of The SCERTS Model. Individuals at this stage of development use both presymbolic and symbolic means to communicate and are developing a repertoire of single words, multiword combinations, and simple sentence structures. They may use echolalia, and their symbolic communication may be spoken or augmented.

Next, his family fills out the SAP–Report form (Step 2, SAP). Jack's special education teacher places a quick phone call to the family to acknowledge receipt of the completed materials and to ask them if they have any further questions. Jack's family is appreciative of the opportunity to provide the school with their perspective related to their son's strengths as well as areas they recognize are ripe for development. The team then meets to plan the observational assessment using The SCERTS Assessment Process–MAP (Step 3, SAP). To ensure a representative sample, the team considers a number of variables in planning the observations. These include, but are not limited to, ensuring that Jack will be observed engaging in activities that vary in their nature (e.g., structured vs. unstructured, motor-based vs. sedentary), engaging in activities that vary in group size (e.g., one-to-one, small group, large group), and during transitions from one activity to the next. Once the observations are agreed on, the team enacts the observation schedule (Step 4, SAP). Activities observed at home include gross motor play, reviewing schoolwork, and preparing and eating a snack. Activities observed at school include an occupational therapy session, a language arts lesson, recess, and lunch. In addition, the team reviews a video-recorded inclusive soccer practice, as they agree this is an important aspect of Jack's life that has the potential to yield information critical to effective educational planning and transactional supports for him.

At the conclusion of the observations, educational team members touch base and determine that they will not need to engage in behavior sampling (Step 5, SAP) as a means to gather further data about Jack's social-communicative and emotional-regulatory abilities. They feel that their thoughtfully planned observations have yielded adequate information to move to Step 6 of the SAP—compiling and summarizing the data. During this process, the team discusses and scores Jack's functional social-communicative and emotional-regulatory abilities according to the language partner curriculum, and they also score his partner's use of interpersonal and learning supports according to the transactional support curriculum.

In the joint attention component, Jack demonstrates a relative strength in his ability to share intentions to regulate the behaviors of others. This is evidenced by his ability to spontaneously request desired objects across partners and social contexts (e.g., snack foods at home and water at school) as well as his fairly consistent ability to request help and other actions (e.g., kicking a soccer ball to his coach in a bid to engage him in a game of pass, handing a portable smart speaker to his mother while saying, "Something different," to request a music station change, requesting to use the bathroom verbally at school). He also consistently demonstrates the ability to protest undesired objects (e.g., attempting to put away schoolwork when brought out in the home environment) and activities (e.g., pushing away a book during a reading activity). In addition to these functions of communication, Jack uses his gaze as well as other natural nonverbal signals, such as gestures and proximity, to secure the attention of his communication partners before he initiates interactions with them (e.g., reaching for cones while looking toward his coach in a bid to help set up a soccer drill). This ability indicates a relatively strong awareness that his social partners are a source not only of assistance but also of social engagement and information sharing.

Within the component of joint attention, Jack presents with several areas of need. These include his challenges in consistently initiating interactions for social functions without considerable structure and support. For example, he generates comments only within the structure of specific visually mediated activities. At home, he initiates a comment when looking at a picture that his mother took with her phone at soccer practice the previous day. The comment, "Shoot it, shoot it Goooaaaal!"—which he pairs with a show gesture—is related to the preferred activity depicted (e.g., practicing penalty kicks). However, he does not comment on other actions or activities that are not preferred or visually supported. Throughout the observations, he often requires assistance to engage in reciprocal conversations, to make comments, and to greet others. He does not participate in any extended reciprocal interactions.

Regarding symbol use, Jack demonstrates a relative strength in his ability to understand nonverbal cues, photographs, and pictures in familiar and unfamiliar activities. During all of the observations, Jack consistently follows situational and gestural cues in familiar activities across partners, contexts, and activities. For example, he responds to school staff without fail when they gesture to indicate items needed to complete activities. In addition, he attends to and uses graphic representations of steps sequentially to move through a new soccer drill when paired with additional gestural cueing from the coaching staff.

Jack is also attentive and responsive to a variety of spoken words and words combinations across contexts and settings. At home, for example, when his twin, John, references a specific book in his room, Jack locates it quickly. In addition, when his mom encourages Jack to find and bite a chewy tube to support his regulation when he is beginning to get frustrated, he does so almost immediately. At school, he participates in a Simon Says game without visual models, and when he is verbally told that a staff member is not available to interact, he responds consistently by shifting his attention away from people. The team also discusses the next steps within the mutual regulation component. These include requesting a partner's assistance to regulate his arousal when his arousal level is mismatched with his environment (e.g., he was amped up and agitated in the library). During this assessment, Jack primarily expresses his emotions through song lyrics and regulates his arousal level through the use of behavioral strategies (e.g., rocking, swinging, biting chews). These predictable presentations provide opportunities for partners to model symbolic emotional expression and/or energy states (e.g., "I am excited" or "I am amped up/fidgety"). The team agrees that Jack's acquisition of these skills will provide quick and easily understandable signals to his partners and will also support his self-regulation. The team also agrees that, in addition to expanding his means for emotional expression, requesting regulatory assistance is an educational priority (e.g., "High five," "Get a drink of water," "Listen to my iPod"). Additional priorities for supporting engagement and self-regulation include supporting his ability to learn to sequence multistep activities independently using visual schedules and supporting his use of self-talk for the purpose of self-regulation.

The team also completes Step 8 of the SAP during this meeting. Step 8 suggests recommending further assessment if needed. Here Jack's team briefly considers whether additional assessment related to cognitive aspects of communication and articulation are needed in order to create an appropriate educational plan to scaffold Jack's communicative development. The team determines at this time that there is no need for further testing.

Based on this discussion, the team selects the following social-communication and emotional regulation objectives for Jack.

- Jack will comment on actions or events within high-interest activities across partners (e.g., family members, school staff, coaches, therapists), contexts (e.g., school, home, community), and in an increasing number of activities per benchmark period (joint attention).

- Jack will engage in extended reciprocal interactions with a variety of partners (e.g., family members, school staff, coaches, therapists), in a variety of contexts (e.g., school, home, community), and in an increasing number of activities per benchmark period (joint attention)

- Jack will use a variety of relational meanings in word combinations, as demonstrated by spontaneous use of agents + actions + objects phrases across partners (e.g., family members school staff, coaches, therapists), contexts (e.g., school, home, community), and an increasing number of activities per benchmark period (symbol use).

- Jack will use language strategies to request a regulating activity or input, as demonstrated by spontaneous use of these strategies across partners (e.g., family members, school staff, coaches, therapists), contexts (e.g., school, home, community), and an increasing number of activities per benchmark period (mutual regulation).

- Jack will use language strategies modeled by partners to regulate his arousal level, as demonstrated by spontaneous use of these strategies across partners (e.g., family members, school staff, coaches, therapists), contexts (e.g., school, home, community), and an increasing number of activities per benchmark period (e.g., emotion cards, regulation strategy choices, visual schedules; mutual regulation).

INTERVENTIONS USED TO ACHIEVE MAJOR GOALS

Once Jack's team determines his goals and objectives, they quickly select transactional support objectives for his communication partners to ensure that his goals are addressed with appropriate supports. His team prioritizes the following interpersonal supports (IS) and learning supports (LS) for use by communication partners:

1. Recognizing signs of dysregulation and offering support (e.g., keying into songs he is singing; IS)

2. Waiting for and encouraging initiations (e.g., giving space and time to process; IS)

3. Responding to communicative bids consistently (e.g., acknowledging them even if they cannot be honored; IS)

4. Adjusting the complexity of language input and social interaction at times of Jack's protests (e.g., decreasing complexity when his arousal level starts to increase; IS)

5. Using augmentative communication support to enhance Jack's communication and expressive language (e.g., increasing use of picture systems; LS)

6. Using augmentative communication support to enhance Jack's emotional regulation (e.g., energy meters; LS)

7. Using support to define steps within a task (e.g., teach Jack to use and navigate schedules independently; LS)

8. Infusing motivating and meaningful materials and topics in activities (LS)

The team then shifts their attention to designing an educational program for Jack that addresses his developmental needs while providing evidence-based support and strategies (Step 9, SAP). They complete SAP activity planning grids for home, school, and community (see Figures 11.3, 11.4, and 11.5).

Activity	Educational goals					Transactional supports
	Jack will participate in extended reciprocal interactions	Jack will comment on actions or events within high-interest activities	Jack will use a variety of relational meanings in word combinations	Jack will use language strategies to request a regulating activity or input	Jack will use language strategies modeled by partners to regulate arousal level	
Transitions				X	X	Provide visuals for smooth transitions to upcoming activities (across-task schedules) and visuals to define steps within each task (within-task schedules). Listen to and respond to Jack's song lyric choices as valid communication. Model language. Provide visuals for emotional expression (Jack is [tired, excited, angry]) with choices of how to cope on the reverse of the visual (e.g., Jack can ask for help, Jack can cuddle).
Physical education	X	X				Structure activities to provide intense movement and resistance. Structure activities for a balance of turns and wait for initiation. Use visuals to define steps of class (e.g., schedule board and video models).
English language arts		X	X			Provide pictures with a range of subject + verb and sentence-building templates to ensure that Jack has a visual to use to comment on books (e.g., "Dragon breathes fire," "Dragon flies in sky"). Provide opportunities for and encourage initiations. Respond consistently to all communicative bids.

Figure 11.3.   School activity planning grid for Jack.

In addition, the team formulates educational and emotional support plans for both family members and professionals comprising Jack's team. Please see Chapter 14 in *Treatment of Autism Spectrum Disorder, Second Edition* for additional information related to plans, which are considered to be critical to comprehensive educational planning within The SCERTS Model.

OUTCOMES

Jack's team monitors his ongoing progress toward his social-communication and emotional-regulation objectives and the fidelity of implementation of transactional supports by the team using data forms provided as part of The SCERTS manuals

Activity	Jack will participate in extended reciprocal interactions	Jack will comment on actions or events within high-interest activities	Jack will use a variety of relational meanings in word combinations	Jack will use language strategies to request a regulating activity or input	Jack will use language strategies modeled by partners to regulate arousal level	Transactional supports
	Educational goals					Transactional supports
Transitions				X	X	Provide visuals for smooth transitions to upcoming activities (across-task schedules). Provide visuals for emotional expression (Jack is [tired, excited, angry]) with choices of how to cope on the reverse of the visual (e.g., Jack can ask for help, Jack can cuddle).
Outside play	X	X				Structure activities to provide intense movement and resistance. Provide visual list of gross motor games for kids to choose from. Provide video models of brother and peers playing less familiar games to watch before play. Structure activities for a balance of turns and wait for initiation.
Snack preparation		X	X			Provide pictures with a range of subject + verb and sentence-building templates to ensure that Jack has a visual to use to comment during snack preparation and to make choices (e.g., "John cut lemon," "Jack squeeze lemon," "Mom pour lemonade"). Include all family member names to encourage sentences about both Jack and those with whom he is interacting.

Figure 11.4.   Home activity planning grid for Jack.

(Step 10, SAP). Throughout this process, the team is particularly concerned with achieving and documenting authentic progress. Authentic progress reflects the acquisition and use of functional skills and abilities in natural contexts for active engagement in roles, relationships, and activities, thereby supporting greater social-communication competence (Prizant et al., 2006b).

Within a 3-month period, Jack makes good progress toward all of his goals. He consistently initiates comments with teammates on the soccer field related to their participation, using developmental word combinations (e.g., "Manuel saved

Activity	Jack will participate in extended reciprocal interactions	Jack will comment on actions or events within high-interest activities	Jack will use a variety of relational meanings in word combinations	Jack will use language strategies to request a regulating activity or input	Jack will use language strategies modeled by partners to regulate arousal level	Transactional supports
	Educational goals					**Transactional supports**
Warm-ups				X	X	Provide visuals to define steps within each task written on wipe-off board. Provide visuals for frequently experienced energy or emotional states (e.g., Jack is amped up) with choices of how to manage that state if needed.
Drills	X	X				Structure activities for a balance of turns and wait for initiation. Use visuals to define steps of drill (e.g., schedule board and video models).
Reflection		X	X			Coach will take one picture with his phone and share with Jack's parents. Show picture to Jack and model comments. Provide visual board of core soccer vocabulary to scaffold comments visually if needed.

Figure 11.5. Soccer activity planning grid for Jack.

the goal kick!"). His spontaneous use of word combinations also increases during academic tasks when he is provided with visual supports. For example, during book discussions, Jack will raise his hand and offer information related to the story, using word banks and sentence templates available to him (e.g., "Dragon breathes fire"). Likewise, his reciprocity and ability to sustain interactions both nonverbally and verbally improve. For example, following the use of video modeling, Jack is able to participate in communication exchanges about soccer activities that had greater than four reciprocal turns. With respect to his regulation objectives, within 3 months, Jack consistently references visual supports provided to him (e.g., regulation strategy choice cards) in home, school, and community environments to select and/or request a regulating activity when his active engagement is diminished. In addition, Jack demonstrates the ability to use those same visual systems to spontaneously convey his emotional state to others. He also demonstrates the ability to independently reference within-task schedules to move through the sequence of a multistep activity and academic block. Overall, family and school staff observe a reduction of explosive behaviors and an increase in active engagement. It should be noted that the team continues to recognize the need to incorporate high levels of physical activity throughout his day as an integral way to support his regulation and therefore also focuses on helping Jack learn how to meet his sensory regulation needs.

Learning Activities _____

1. Jack's team determined that no further testing was required when embarking on his educational planning. Discuss measures that you think may have added valuable information in constructing his educational plan.

2. Write a short memo to school administration to substantiate why the family-centered, transdisciplinary model underlying SCERTS is preferable to individual disciplines being responsible for specific goals or objectives in Jack's individualized education program.

3. Think through the 10-step SAP. Apply these general principles to a student or individual who is currently on your caseload.

4. Considering Jack's educational objectives in light of his inclusive soccer program, what one or two objectives might be able to be addressed in that setting? What transactional supports would you consider putting in place to help him achieve them?

5. Based on your knowledge of Jack and his preferred activities, what types of regulating activities might you, as one of his team members, advocate for to be included in his choice board?

REFERENCES

Laurent, A. C., Rubin, E., & Prizant, B. M. (2021). The SCERTS® Model: Social communication, emotional regulation, and transactional supports. In P. A. Prelock & R. J. McCauley (Eds.), *Treatment of autism spectrum disorder: Evidence-based intervention strategies for communication & social interactions* (2nd ed., pp. 381–412). Paul H. Brookes Publishing Co.

Prizant, B. M., Wetherby, A. M., Rubin, E., Laurent, A. C., & Rydell, P. J. (2006a). *The SCERTS Model: A comprehensive educational approach for children with autism spectrum disorders, Volume 1 Assessment.* Paul H. Brookes Publishing Co.

Prizant, B. M., Wetherby, A. M., Rubin, E., Laurent, A. C., & Rydell, P. J. (2006b). *The SCERTS Model: A comprehensive educational approach for children with autism spectrum disorders, Volume II, Program Planning and Intervention.* Paul H. Brookes Publishing Co.

CASE 12

Making Friends and Maintaining Relationships

A Preteen With ASD

Ashley Brien

 Link

 Age 11

 Autism Spectrum Disorder

Case 12 engages with the intervention approach and strategies discussed in Chapter 15, Social Skills Interventions (Brien & Prelock, 2021) in *Treatment of Autism Spectrum Disorder, Second Edition.*

INTRODUCTION

Link, age 11;9, was diagnosed with autism spectrum disorder (ASD) at the age of 3 years. His birth and medical histories were unremarkable, and he does not have a history of feeding, swallowing, or sleeping difficulties. Developmental milestones for crawling, sitting, standing, and walking were age appropriate. Link began talking at 24 months and was slow to acquire words. By 3 years of age, Link spoke in one-word utterances and had acquired approximately 25 words. These words consisted mainly of nouns and were preferred items, including *mom, dad, car, block, doggy.*

Between the ages of 3 and 7 years, Link received intensive speech-language therapy during which time his receptive and expressive vocabularies improved dramatically. Also, at that time, he began to exhibit aggressive behaviors toward himself and others, including hitting himself or others, spitting, kicking, and running away. These behaviors typically occurred when Link did not get what he wanted, when he was told no, and when his routine was disrupted. He received many school-based services to address these behaviors, including behavioral support from a behavioral consultant, observation and direct support from a neuro-developmental specialist, and pragmatic intervention from a speech-language pathologist (SLP). By second grade, Link's language skills were on par with those with his peers, he was completing academic work that was appropriate for second graders, and his aggression toward others was significantly reduced, although not completely remediated.

Communication Profile

At present, Link communicates through verbal language. His language skills were recently assessed using the Clinical Evaluation of Language Fundamentals–Fifth Edition (CELF-5; Wiig et al., 2013). This is a comprehensive assessment that measures both expressive and receptive language skills. It is designed to assess a student's general language ability as well as specific information regarding receptive and expressive language skills. Seven subtests were administered to Link: Word Classes, Following Directions, Formulated Sentences, Recalling Sentences, Word Definitions, Sentence Assembly, and Semantic Relationships. Of these seven subtests, four were combined to provide information about his Core Language Skills (i.e., Word Classes, Formulated Sentences, Recalling Sentences, Semantic Relationships), three were combined to form an Expressive Language Index (i.e., Formulated Sentences, Recalling Sentences, Sentence Assembly), and three were combined to form a Receptive Language Index (i.e., Word Classes, Following Directions, Semantic Relationships). Link's composite scores for the Core Language Skills, Expressive Language Index, and Receptive Language Index indicate that his language abilities are in the above-average range. Direct observation, coupled with Link's standardized language scores, reveal that he has impressive receptive and expressive vocabularies.

Social Profile

Link is a kind and empathetic child. He is socially aware of when others are sad and often provides them with words of encouragement, frequently empathizing with them by expressing a similar situation during which he was sad. Despite this social awareness of others' feelings of sadness, Link displays many challenges in the social realm, including difficulties in maintaining conversations that are not of interest to him. He often engages in lengthy one-sided conversations about topics that interest him (e.g., a video game character, World War I), and he seems unaware when others are not interested in the conversation. Other social challenges for Link include becoming severely distressed over small problems related to interactions with adults and/or peers that do not go as he expected (e.g., a peer cut him in line or ignored him), when he feels that he is to blame for something (e.g., he didn't get an answer correct), or when he feels someone does not understand him and/or his innermost thoughts. During these instances, he may lash out against others or engage in harmful behaviors toward himself (e.g., hitting self or others, calling others and/or himself names, running away).

Family and Community Context

Link has a supportive family, including his mother, father, and three younger siblings (one sister and two brothers). He has a close connection to his maternal grandmother. Link's mother does not work outside of the home and provides home-schooling to Link's sister and one brother. Link's father owns his own business and is often out of town. Figure 12.1 is a genogram (Goldrick & Gerson, 1985; Prelock et al., 2003; Prelock et al., 1999) of Link's family.

Link attends a public elementary school through which his family has had access to a behavioral consultant and neurodevelopmental specialist; these specialists have provided the family with behavioral and ASD-specific resources since Link first entered preschool, have been advocates for Link's participation in school activities, and continually offer guidance and support outside of the school day as needed. Link receives speech-language therapy services through the school, with a current focus on social-pragmatic communication. Because they live in a rural community, Link and his family experience a general lack of ASD-specific resources outside of the school setting (e.g., lack of extracurricular activities, summer camps, respite, etc.) and limited access to outpatient specialists (e.g., pediatricians, ASD specialists, SLPs, occupational therapists, psychotherapists, behavioral and mental health case workers). The ecomap in Figure 12.2 (Goldrick & Gerson, 1985; Goodluck,

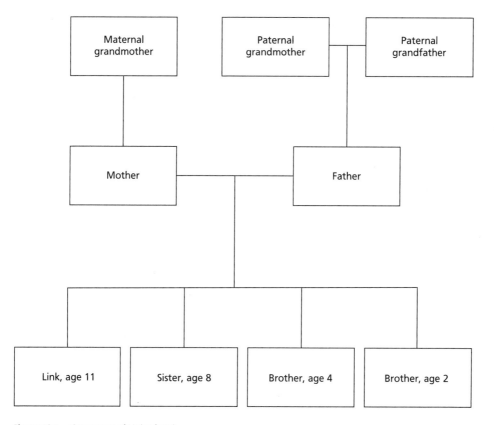

Figure 12.1. Genogram of Link's family.

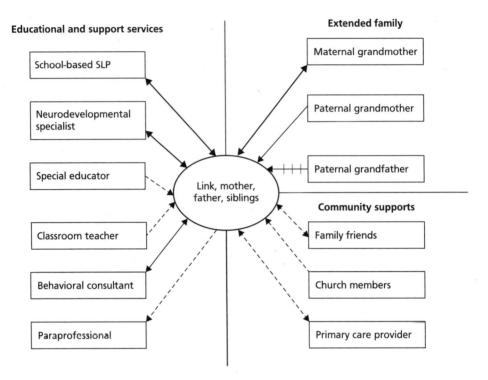

Figure 12.2. Ecomap of Link's personal and professional connections and supports. Solid lines represent strong relationships (with thicker lines indicating stronger relationships), dotted lines indicate stressed relationships, and arrows indicate the direction of energy flow/support.

1990; Prelock et al., 1999; Prelock et al., 2003) shows Link's personal and professional connections and supports.

Broader Profile

Link has significant behavioral challenges, specifically modulating his anger and frustration. He often reacts to small problems with big emotions, becomes anxious easily, engages in physical aggression against himself and others (through name calling, hitting, and spitting). When he gets frustrated, Link sometimes elopes without telling an adult where he is going. Many environmental factors (World Health Organization [WHO], 2007) play a role in Link's behavioral challenges. Specifically, he becomes overwhelmed in crowded environments, and when multiple people try to help him regulate his behavior through discussion of the event, he falls apart. He becomes flustered with the adults, begins talking over them by saying that he does not want to talk about the issue, and eventually runs from the adult to hide (often to the library, where he is usually found sitting on the floor in the corner reading a book). Link's ability to cope when this happens is hindered both when he is at school and at home. He attends a large elementary school. Although there are only 20 other students in his sixth-grade class, the three sixth-grade classes (comprising 65 students and six adults) often meet together, and the entire school often participates in school assemblies and activities. When Link becomes overwhelmed, as he often does in the context of large groups, many adults (e.g., his paraprofessional, special educator, principal, SLP), albeit at separate times, try to process and talk through his behaviors with him. After being approached about an issue by multiple adults, Link's behavior escalates, and he often expresses a defeatist attitude, expressing feelings like, "Everything is all my fault."

Similarly, Link's home environment is often busy. His younger siblings play loudly with one another, run around the house, and often scream with excitement. Because Link is the oldest of the siblings (personal factor; WHO, 2007), he is often given the responsibility of completing chores, specifically loading and unloading the dishwasher and bringing in wood for the woodstove. When Link gets distracted by something of interest to him and his chores do not get completed, his parents become frustrated. Link then becomes increasingly anxious, blames himself, and begins to imagine and describe a better and safer world in which he was never born.

Summary of Most Significant Needs

Link's most significant needs were identified by Link, his parents, and his school team. These areas included managing his anger and frustration as well as participating in reciprocal communication exchanges about topics not of interest to him. Engaging in reciprocal conversations was addressed as a significant need because it affects Link's ability to make new friends and maintain current friendships with other children his age. Link expressed feeling disliked by his peers because he frequently observes his peers talking and laughing with one another and was beginning to notice that this does not happen when he participates in conversations with his peers.

ASSESSMENTS FOR COMMUNICATION TREATMENT PLANNING

In order to develop a treatment plan surrounding Link's most significant areas of need, a number of social-communication assessments were delivered. These tests focused on Link's knowledge of social skills and his ability to use those social skills in real time.

Social aspects of communication were measured directly using the Social Language Development Test–Elementary (SLDT-E; Bowers et al., 2008), Pragmatic Language Skills Inventory (PLSI; Gilliam & Miller, 2006), Theory of Mind Task Battery (ToMTB; Hutchins et al., 2008), and Theory of Mind Inventory–Second Edition (ToMI-2; Hutchins et al., 2008; Hutchins et al., 2012). As described in more detail in the following sections, these four tests were used to gain insight into different levels of Link's social cognition. The SLDT-E and the ToMTB are direct measures of social cognition wherein Link answered questions about the mental states of others. The PLSI and the ToMI-2 are adult informant measures that report on Link's ability to access his social-cognitive knowledge and use it to inform his behaviors throughout the day.

The SLDT-E is a child-informed measure that examines a child's ability to make inferences, take others' perspectives, resolve conflict with peers, support peers, and flexibly interpret social situations. The subtests on this assessment are presented in photograph format in a structured environment. Link scored in the *average* range on this assessment.

The PLSI is a standardized, norm-referenced teacher-rating tool that looks at the pragmatic language skills for children between the ages of 5 and 12 years. The PLSI examines pragmatic language skills using three subscales: Classroom Interaction Skills, Social Interaction Skills, and Personal Interaction Skills. The

Classroom Interaction Skills subtest assesses areas such as the use of topic maintenance, explaining how things work, asking questions when uncertain, and providing enough information to help the listener understand his message. The Social Interaction Skills subtest examines a child's ability to take turns in conversation, follow verbal directions, understand rules, and predict consequences for behavior. The Personal Interaction Skills subtest assesses skills such as initiating conversation, asking for help, negotiating, and using appropriate nonverbal behaviors to communicate.

The PLSI was completed by Link's paraprofessional, SLP, special education teacher, classroom teacher, and neurodevelopmental specialist. An interprofessional approach was taken to glean the best overall picture of Link's pragmatic skills at school. According to this tool, Link's social language skills are *below average* for his age. He demonstrates significant difficulty with personal interaction skills, particularly appropriately expressing feelings of frustration and anger, expressing hurt feelings, asking for help, participating in verbal exchanges with peers, and using appropriate nonverbal behaviors to communicate. Particular challenges in social-interaction skills include knowing when to talk and when to listen, taking turns in conversation, understanding what causes people to not like him, and predicting consequences of behavior. Difficulties in classroom interaction skills include providing sufficient information to help listeners understand what he means, introducing a topic, and maintaining a topic.

The ToMTB consists of 15 questions designed to tap a range of explicit theory or mind (ToM) tasks (i.e., structured tasks measuring ToM competence). The items range in complexity and are presented in the form of static visual stimuli. The initial task tests the ability to identify emotions associated with facial expressions. The second task asks children to infer an emotion associated with desire. The remaining tasks assess advanced ToM abilities, including belief-based emotion, reality-based emotion, second-order belief-based emotion, perception-based beliefs, and false beliefs. Link scored in the *low average* range on this assessment tool. This score indicates that Link has some understanding of ToM competencies in explicit and structured settings.

The ToMI-2 is designed to assess children's applied ToM development (i.e., ToM performance). This tool is a useful supplement to the ToMTB, as it provides the parent's perspective of the child's understanding and effective use of social competencies. This parent-report measure is composed of 60 items assessing a range of empirically based early, basic, and advanced ToM competencies (e.g., "My child recognizes when others are happy," "My child understands the word *know*," "My child understands that people can smile even when they are not happy") and can also be divided into the following rationally based subscales: Emotion Recognition, Mental State Term Comprehension, and Pragmatics (each subscale consists of a mixture of items from the early, basic, and advanced subscales). Link's parents completed the ToMI-2. He scored in the *below average* range, and his specific challenges are presented Table 12.1.

Link's *average* scores on the SLDT-E and the ToMTB indicate that he has a general knowledge of social cognition and social skills. He can identify appropriate social behaviors when presented with structured and explicit tasks. His *below average* scores, however, on the real-world measures of social behavior (i.e., PLSI and ToMI-2) indicate that he has challenges applying his social knowledge to in-the-moment, real-world settings. It is possible that Link is able to hack out solutions to the social problems that are presented in the explicit/structured tasks in a

Table 12.1. Theory of Mind Inventory Subscales and Link's specific challenges as illustrated through his mother's responses

Subscale	Specific challenges	Test items that Link's mother could not endorse, demonstrating areas of challenge
Early	Social referencing: ambiguous situations and reading fear	"If my child saw a strange new object, he would look to me to check my reaction before touching it." "My child understands that when I show fear, the situation is unsafe or dangerous."
Basic	Future thinking	"My child can predict his own emotions to better plan for the future" (e.g., if spending the night away from home, the child knows he will miss Mom, and so he brings his favorite blanket for comfort).
	Cognitive emotion recognition: disgust	"My child recognizes when others are disgusted."
Advanced	Verbal irony	"If it were raining and I said in a sarcastic voice, 'Gee, looks like a really nice day outside,' my child would understand that I didn't actually think it looks like a nice day."
	Complex social judgment	"My child understands the difference between when someone is teasing in a nice way and when a bully is making fun of someone in a mean way." "My child recognizes when a listener is not interested."
	True empathy	"My child is able to put himself in other people's shoes and understand how they feel."
	Interpretive theory of mind: biased cognition	"My child understands that previous ideas and/or opinions of others can influence how we interpret their behavior."
	Common sense: social knowledge	"My child understands that an unfamiliar adult can make guesses about my child's likes and dislikes."
	Situation-based disambiguation of emotion	"My child understands what people think and feel by connecting it to the situation; for example, my child understands that crying because you lost a game is different from crying because you won an award."
Emotion recognition	Cognitive emotion recognition: disgust	"My child recognizes when others are disgusted."
Mental state term comprehension	None	—
Pragmatics	Verbal irony	"If it were raining and I said in a sarcastic voice, 'Gee, looks like a really nice day outside,' my child would understand that I didn't actually think it looks like a nice day."

"non-mentalistic way" (Hutchins et al., 2016, p. 103). That is, Link may demonstrate average skills on measures of explicit social cognition (i.e., SLDT-E and ToMTB) by using a more logical cognitive system (as opposed to a social/mindreading cognitive system) to answer the questions. His performance on the measures of real-world social competence indicate that despite his ability to hack social problems in structured settings, he is unable to use this knowledge to adjust his behaviors.

CLINICAL PROBLEM SOLVING TO
IDENTIFY TREATMENT GOALS AND STRATEGIES

At Link's annual individualized education program (IEP) meeting, his team discussed his scores on the communication assessments described previously and drafted his upcoming treatment plan. Link's interdisciplinary team consisted of Link's parents, the school-based SLP, Link's classroom teacher, his paraprofessional, the school principal, the neurodevelopmental specialist, and the classroom teacher. Including Link's parents in the development of his treatment plan is founded on the evidence of using family-centered care (Beatson, 2006; Prelock et al., 1999). Prior to the IEP meeting, Link completed the Student Skillstreaming Checklist (McGinnis & Goldstein, 1997b) to identify any skills that he would like to work on. One of the skills that Link identified aligned well with the team's identified goals, which was managing anger in ways that do not hurt others or himself. Appropriate team members brought data to the IEP meeting that had been collected for roughly 3 months and were relevant to each professional's content area. The following are qualitative and quantitative data as well as relevant intervention materials each team member gathered:

Speech-language pathologist

- Probe data on the following social cognition areas. These data informed that Link understood the social cognitive concepts in one-to-one, structured settings. Although he demonstrated these skills in this setting with the SLP, he was unable to generalize his understanding to other settings with peers.

  o Social common sense (Hutchins & Prelock, 2018)

  o Verbal irony comprehension (Hutchins & Prelock, 2018)

  o Flexible thinking in social situations (Winner & Murphy, 2016)

  o Identifying thoughts and feelings—big vs. small (Winner & Murphy, 2016)

- A variety of Comic Strip Conversations and Social Stories™ (Gray, 1994, 1998, 2010; Gray & Garand, 1993) developed by Link and the SLP

Neurodevelopmental specialist

- Observational data indicating rates of the following:

  o Challenges modulating emotions according to the size of the problem

  o Missing classwork because of reactions to frustrations

  o Name calling (self and others)

  o Fleeing from classroom and adults

  o Physical aggression to self and paraprofessional

  o Spitting directed at others

  o Increased frustration in unknown settings and/or contexts

  o Dysregulation when he does not get something exactly perfect (e.g., spelling of words, reading of words, math problems)

Classroom teacher

- Incomplete classroom assessments: Many eraser marks and tears in the paper related to Link's frustration with the assignment, his challenges to complete the assignment correctly, or his challenges with spelling

- Classroom assignments: Essays that lack narrative structure and are redundant

Principal

- Number of times sent to the principal's office: 6

- Number of in-school suspensions: 4

- Number of out-of-school suspensions: 1

In addition to this data, Link's family described challenges that are occurring at home. They noted that Link demonstrates difficulty regulating himself and managing his challenging behaviors at home and often reacts to small problems in drastic ways. They indicated that this negatively impacts his ability to move functionally through his day. For example, as one of his chores, Link is responsible for bringing up wood from the basement for the woodstove. Each day, Link's parents have to remind Link to bring up the wood from the basement. Link becomes frustrated that his parents remind him, especially when he is in the middle of playing a video game or reading a book, but he has failed to complete the task when not given a verbal reminder. If, in the process, pieces of wood fall off the pile, Link is required to restack them. As a reminder of this chore, Link's parents placed a picture of the neatly stacked woodpile next to the real woodpile so that Link can see how the wood is supposed to look when it is stacked. In an effort to return to his video game or book, Link often brings up most of the wood required but does not restack the pieces that have fallen. When confronted by his parents about not cleaning up the pieces of wood that fell, Link may become significantly distressed and engage in behaviors that are unsafe to him and worrisome to his parents (e.g., hitting himself in the head, leaving the house without telling an adult, locking himself in the bathroom for hours at a time).

Based on the accumulated data, assessments, observation, and Link's and his family's desires, a treatment plan was developed. It was unanimously decided that the focus of therapy would be social skills intervention, using the program Skillstreaming the Elementary School Child: New Strategies and Perspectives for Teaching Prosocial Skills (McGinnis & Goldstein, 1997a). It should be noted that the Skillstreaming authors have recently published a Skillstreaming intervention guide targeting prosocial skills that are specific to learners with ASD (McGinnis & Simpson, 2017). This version follows the same format as the other Skillstreaming treatment manuals but includes many more prosocial skills that are often challenges in ASD. Despite the version specific to learners with ASD, Skillstreaming the Elementary School Child: New Strategies and Perspectives for Teaching Prosocial Skills was maintained for Link because it addresses skills specific to Link's current challenges. Furthermore, Skillstreaming was chosen because, although it is not yet an evidence-based intervention strategy, the evidence for this program is emerging (Kaat & Lecavalier, 2014). Although a number of social skills intervention packages exist (see Prelock & Brien, 2021), there is limited evidence for these programs. Of these intervention packages, Skillstreaming has more evidence than the others (Kaat & Lecavalier, 2014) and this is why it was chosen for Link's intervention. For children with ASD, learning appropriate social behaviors naturally (i.e., through incidental learning) is a particular challenge. The Skillstreaming intervention program focuses on teaching prosocial behaviors through direct instruction and highlights many behaviors that vary in complexity (e.g., beginning a conversation, dealing with fear, accepting consequences). Skillstreaming is an intervention that is grounded in the principles of modeling, role playing, feedback, and transfer of skills. While the intervention can be delivered to students in one-to-one settings or as a large group, the authors suggest delivering the intervention to a small group of students with similar social challenges.

For Link, treatment goals focused on challenges occurring in school and home that have hindered Link's ability both to make and maintain friendships and to manage his own emotions. The following treatment goals were addressed:

1. **Treatment Goal 1:** Using previously learned social skills intervention strategies, Link will manage his own behaviors to function in multiple environments in safe and appropriate ways by [specified date].

   a. Objective 1: When presented with photographs and video clips of social problems, Link will identify the social problems for 10 situations and generate solutions to the problems (with minimal adult guidance) that maintain the actor's safety by [specified date].

   b. Objective 2: When provided with moderate guidance from an adult (e.g., discussions about behaviors leading to school suspensions), Link will identify five problem areas in his own life (at home, school, in the community) that could potentially affect his or others' safety by [specified date].

   c. Objective 3: In unstructured settings, Link will use strategies to manage his own behaviors (i.e., tell the person why he is angry, walk away for a moment, use relaxation techniques) for five situations that previously would have been challenging in multiple environments by [specified date].

2. **Treatment Goal 2:** In an unstructured environment with minimal adult support, Link will contribute to discussions with peers that are not related to his preferred topics to sustain back-and-forth conversations throughout his day on two occasions by [specified date].

   a. Objective 1: In a structured setting, Link will identify on- and off-topic utterances in static and dynamic scenes with 80% accuracy on two occasions by [specified date].

   b. Objective 2: In a structured setting, when provided with the start of a conversation, Link will provide appropriate on-topic follow-up utterances for two conversational turns on two occasions by [specified date].

   c. Objective 3: In an unstructured environment when having a discussion with peers, Link will independently ask questions and make comments related directly to what the peer is saying for four conversational turns at least three times per day on two occasions by [specified date].

INTERVENTION USED TO ACHIEVE MAJOR GOALS

Per Skillstreaming intervention guidelines (McGinnis & Goldstein, 1997a), the SLP was selected as the group leader, and the neurodevelopmental specialist was selected as the program coordinator. The SLP and neurodevelopmental specialist selected three students to work with Link in a small group. One of the students exhibited social skills challenges similar to Link's, and the other two students were neurotypical and did not require social skills intervention. The neurotypical students were chosen because they were in the same class as Link and identified as having budding friendships with Link.

Prior to the group intervention,

- The SLP and neurodevelopmental specialist offered basic intervention training to Link's team, including prompting Link as appropriate to use the skills he has learned, reassuring and encouraging him during social encounters, and giving social rewards (e.g., praise, compliments). This training was also offered to other adults throughout the school with whom Link interacts (e.g., cafeteria, bus, recess monitors; assistant principal; school guidance counselor).

- The SLP and neurodevelopmental specialist offered Skillstreaming resources and training to Link's parents.

- Link and the SLP determined that the following skills would be addressed during the Skillstreaming sessions: 1) managing anger and 2) engaging in reciprocal conversations.

- The procedures and expectations for the group were described to each student individually.

At the first group intervention session,

- The students, including Link, and the SLP collectively identified group rules:

  o Be kind to one another.

  o Ask questions when one needs help.

  o Do not laugh at one another.

  o Be respectful to everyone in the group.

- All students in the group received a student manual, which included descriptions of the teaching steps, descriptions of the various social skills, and examples of Skillstreaming in action and Skillstreaming homework (McGinnis & Goldstein, 1997b).

At subsequent group sessions, the following teaching steps (adapted from McGinnis & Goldstein, 1997a) were followed:

1. Define the skill

2. Model the skill

3. Establish student skill need

4. Select role player

5. Set up the role play

6.   Conduct the role play

7.   Provide performance feedback

8.   Assign skill homework

9.   Select next role player

In following these steps, each student in the group had equal opportunities to role play. Link did not receive more attention in that role because, during one of the first sessions, he expressed frustration at being singled out among his peers when the SLP suggested he take a second turn role-playing when everyone else had had only one turn.

In the sessions, treatment Goal 1 was addressed first because of the safety concerns regarding Link's behavior to himself and to others. It was also addressed first because Link identified it as a skill that he wanted to learn more about. To address this goal, Link's Skillstreaming group followed the teaching steps outlined previously Skill 31, Dealing with Your Anger, identified in the Skillstreaming manual. Specifically, the students role-played scenarios in which one of the students became angry. The angry student then followed the steps specific to this skill. These included 1) stopping and counting to 10; 2) considering the choices for potential actions: telling the person why you are angry, walking away, practicing a relaxation technique; and 3) acting out the best choice from step 2 (McGinnis & Goldstein, 1997a). Throughout the role-playing activity, the other students in the group offered suggestions and guidance as needed. In addition, the SLP provided input to all children during their role-playing experiences.

Treatment Goal 2 was addressed after initial progress had been made on treatment Goal 1. For this goal, Link's Skillstreaming followed the steps for Skill 7, Contributing to Discussions. The students role-played scenarios during which it is typical for children to engage in peer-to-peer discussion (e.g., recess, lunch, after school). Steps for this skill included 1) deciding if they had something to say to the other role-playing student, 2) asking themselves if what they want to say was related to the discussion that was already happening, and 3) deciding exactly what to say (McGinnis & Goldstein, 1997a). Again, the other students in the group offered guidance as needed, and the SLP provided input as well.

Link was assigned homework to help him generalize these skills. He was asked to try using the skills he learned in the group in other settings, such as in the classroom, on the playground, and at home. After each group session, Link was provided with a Homework Report 1 form (McGinnis & Goldstein, 1997a) on which he identified the skill he was practicing, who he practiced with, and what happened.

The sessions were video-recorded, allowing the students to watch themselves role-play, reflect on their actions, and participate in a discussion about the activity. Several videos from the sessions were sent home to Link's parents to provide them with a better understanding of the intervention as well as Link's participation and progress. This also facilitated their ability to help Link practice the skills and fill out his Homework Report forms.

OUTCOMES

At the beginning of the Skillstreaming intervention, Link had marked challenges differentiating between when other members of the group were acting sincerely and when they were role-playing. Because of this, each member wore a card around his or her neck that said Role-Playing when it was his or her turn to act in the role play. This helped Link to identify when his peers were being sincere and when they were acting. This prompt was faded after three group sessions.

Treatment Goal 1: Managing Anger

Link very quickly met the first objective of this goal. He was able to identify social problems in both static and dynamic scenes and to generate solutions for what the actors could do to maintain safety. It was more difficult for Link to identify problem areas in his own life (Objective 2 of Goal 1), but he was able to do so with guidance from an adult as well as when he was shown concrete evidence for a previous social problem (e.g., torn up assignments). He was then able to generate some possible solutions to these behaviors for future encounters. Link had marked challenges addressing Objective 3 of the first goal and generalizing the strategies learned during Skillstreaming group sessions into other environments. He was able to generalize the skills learned to certain situations (including situations involving his classroom teacher and assignment instructions) but required more prompting from adults when confronted with situations involving peers (e.g., a peer cut him in the lunch line, another student accidentally bumped him in the hall). A prompting card was created and made available to him at all times. With this cue, Link was able to identify the steps in the moment of an incident (i.e., tell the person why he is angry, walk away for a moment, use relaxation techniques) and use at least one of the strategies. Parental report indicated that Link kept a copy of the prompting card on the refrigerator at home and referenced it during appropriate times. They noted that he occasionally referenced the card on his own but frequently required reminders that the card was available when he needed it.

Treatment Goal 2: Reciprocal Conversations

As he did with treatment Goal 1, Link met Objective 1 of Goal 2 very quickly. He was able to identify both on- and off-topic utterances when presented with picture or video scenes. He was also able to provide on-topic responses to conversations when these were contrived in structured settings (e.g., when a character in a story began a conversation and the SLP asked Link, "What would be an on-topic sentence that [the other character] could say now?"; Objective 2). For Objective 3, even after the intense modeling with his Skillstreaming group, Link had challenges generalizing maintaining reciprocal conversations with others throughout his day. He was able to ask questions of his peers about topics that his peers were interested in, as well as provide responses to the peers' utterances for two conversational turns. After two conversational turns, Link usually turned the topic of conversation back to his interests. When reminded that his topic was not the current topic of conversation, Link was able to return to the conversation at hand, but again, was able to do this for only one or two more conversational turns.

Social skills intervention using Skillstreaming proved to be useful for Link's identified treatment goals, with some modifications (i.e., the prompting card). Link's ability to use techniques learned in the intervention regarding managing his anger and frustration increased over the time of the intervention, but Link was unable to independently generalize these skills to all environments. Similarly, Link required reminders to maintain topics of conversation. With continued use of Skillstreaming intervention, it is possible that these areas of deficit could be remediated. It would be useful to include other students in the group session so as to increase the likelihood of generalization across peers.

Learning Activities

1. Link's treatment goals were implemented primarily by his school-based SLP. The SLP trained his paraprofessional in addressing the goals and also sent home videos and additional practice items for Link's family. How could you envision Link's paraprofessional generalizing these goals into the greater school environment? In what school environments might it be best to start generalizing these skills? In which school environments should generalization of these skills wait until Link has a firmer grasp on them in other environments (hint: which environments are significantly overwhelming for Link and thus should not be the first area of treatment? Generalization of treatment should occur when Link is in a calm state and not when he is already overwhelmed).

2. Based on Link's profile, including significant areas of need as identified by his team, what other treatment goals could be addressed? Try to think of interprofessional goals that are primarily addressed by multiple team members. Various team members can address the goals in different ways while still maintaining the same outcome for Link.

3. Because Link is in sixth grade, he will be transitioning to a different school next year for middle school. Based on the information presented in this chapter, write a brief summary (one or two pages) for Link's new school team. Based on your report, the new school team should have a good idea of Link as a person and should be ready to work with Link should he arrive unexpectedly tomorrow. Make sure to include Link's strengths and challenges as well as an abbreviated proposed treatment plan.

REFERENCES

Beatson, J. (2006). Preparing speech-language pathologists as family-centered practitioners in assessment and program planning for children with autism spectrum disorder. *Seminars in Speech and Language, 27*, 1–9.

Bowers, L., Huisingh, R., & LoGiudice, C. (2008). *Social Language Development Test: Elementary.* PRO-ED.

Brien, A., & Prelock, P. A. (2021). Social skills interventions. In P. A. Prelock & R. J. McCauley (Eds.), *Treatment of autism spectrum disorder: Evidence-based intervention strategies for communication & social interactions* (2nd ed., pp. 415–458). Paul H. Brookes Publishing Co.

Gilliam, J., & Miller, L. (2006). *Pragmatic Language Skills Inventory.* PRO-ED.

Goldrick, M., & Gerson, B. (1985). *Genograms in family assessment.* W.W. Norton.

Goodluck, C. (1990). *Utilization of genograms and ecomaps to assess American Indian families who have a member with a disability: Making visible the invisible.* Northern Arizona University.

Gray, C. (1994). *Comic strip conversations.* Future Horizons.

Gray, C. (1998). Social stories and comic strip conversations with students with Asperger syndrome and high-functioning autism. In E. Schopler (Ed.), *Asperger syndrome or high-functioning autism?* (pp.167–194). Plenum Press.

Gray, C. (2010). *The new Social Story book.* Future Horizons.

Gray, C., & Garand, J. (1993). Social stories: Improving responses of students with autism with inaccurate social information. *Focus Autistic Behavior, 8*, 1–10.

Hutchins, T., & Prelock, P. (2018). *Theory of Mind Inventory-2.* https://www.theoryofmind inventory.com/materials-room

Hutchins, T., Prelock, P., & Bonazinga, L. (2012). Psychometric evaluation of the Theory of Mind Inventory (ToMI): A study of typically developing children and children with autism spectrum disorder. *Journal of Autism and Developmental Disorders, 42,* 327–341.

Hutchins, T., Prelock, P., & Chance, W. (2008). Test-retest reliability of theory-of-mind tasks with children with autism spectrum disorders. *Focus on Autism and Other Developmental Disabilities, 23*(4), 195–206.

Hutchins, T., Prelock, P., Morris, H., Benner, J., LaVigne, T., & Hoza, B. (2016). Explicit vs. applied theory of mind competence: A comparison of typically developing males, males with ASD, and males with ADHD. *Research in Autism Spectrum Disorders, 21,* 94–108.

Kaat, A., & Lecavalier, L. (2014). Group-based social skills treatment: A methodological review. *Research in Autism Spectrum Disorders, 8,* 15–24.

McGinnis, E., & Goldstein, A. (1997a). *Skillstreaming the elementary school child- Revised edition. New strategies and perspectives for teaching prosocial skills.* Research Press.

McGinnis, E., & Goldstein, A. (1997b). *Skillstreaming the elementary school child: Student manual.* Research Press.

McGinnis, E., & Simpson, R. L. (2016). *Skillstreaming children and youth with high-functioning autism: A guide for teaching prosocial skills.* Research Press.

Prelock, P. A., Beatson, J., Bitner, B., Broder, C., & Ducker, A. (2003). Interdisciplinary assessment for young children with Autism Spectrum Disorders. *Language, Speech and Hearing Services in Schools, 34,* 194–202.

Prelock, P. A., Beatson, J., Contompasis, S., & Bishop, K. K. (1999). A model for family-centered interdisciplinary practice. *Topics in Language Disorders, 19,* 36–51.

Prelock, P., & Brien, A. (2021). Social skills interventions. In P. Prelock and R. McCauley (Eds.), *Treatment of autism spectrum disorder: Evidence-based intervention strategies for communication and social interactions* (2nd ed., pp. _____). Paul H. Brookes Publishing Co.

Wiig, E., Semel, E., & Secord, W. (2013). *Clinical Evaluation of Language Fundamentals–Fifth Edition (CELF-5).* Pearson.

Winner, M. G., & Murphy, L. K. (2016). *Social thinking and me.* Social Thinking Publishing.

World Health Organization. (2007). *International classification of functioning, disability and health: Children and youth version.* Author.

CASE 13

Understanding the
Causes and Consequences
of One's Own Challenging Behaviors

*An Elementary Schooler With ASD and
Attention-Deficit/Hyperactivity Disorder (ADHD)*

Tiffany Hutchins and Patricia A. Prelock

 Kevin

 Age 8

 Autism Spectrum Disorder and ADHD

> **Case 13 engages with the intervention approach and strategies
> discussed in Chapter 16, Social Stories™ (Hutchins, 2021) in
> *Treatment of Autism Spectrum Disorder, Second Edition*.**

INTRODUCTION

Kevin was diagnosed with attention deficit-hyperactivity disorder (ADHD) at age 6 and with autism spectrum disorder (ASD) at age 8. He has average to low-average language skills, according to formal testing, and is receiving speech and language services in a school that focuses on reading, math, and social skills.

History

According to Kevin's mother, Kevin's birth was unremarkable, as was his social, language and cognitive development in infancy and toddlerhood. In the preschool and school-age years, Kevin's interest in people and friendships has never been questioned, but he is characterized as delayed and unskilled in his ability to initiate and maintain successful social interactions with family members and same-age peers. As noted, Kevin received a diagnosis of ADHD at age 6 years, when his whirlwind activity and inability to focus attention became a concern for his parents. His diagnosis of ASD, which followed 2 years later, had already been suspected by his mother, who had observed his social awkwardness and who was an educator familiar with the presentation of autism in youngsters with good language and intellectual abilities.

Baseline Status

Clinicians conduct a number of formal assessments to gather information about Kevin's cognition, communication, and social strengths and challenges prior to treatment planning.

Communication and Social Profile   At baseline, Kevin demonstrates the following:

- His scores on standardized caregiver reports of autism severity (Social Responsiveness Scale [Constantino, 2005]; Gilliam Autism Rating Scale–Second Edition [Gilliam, 2006]) support his diagnosis of ASD.

- He has average expressive and receptive language (Test for Reception of Language [Bishop, 2003]; Peabody Picture Vocabulary Test–Fourth Edition [Dunn & Dunn, 2007]; Expressive Vocabulary Test–Second Edition [Williams, 2007]).

- His nonverbal intelligence (Test of Nonverbal Intelligence–Fourth Edition [Brown et al., 2010]) is (mostly) in line with his school's previous assessments.

- He has impairments in social skills and significant problem behaviors according to parent report (Social Skills Rating System [Gresham & Elliot, 1990]).

- He has impairments in theory of mind (broadly perspective taking), according to parent report and direct assessment (Theory of Mind Inventory–Second Edition [Hutchins et al., 2012; Theory of Mind Task Battery [Hutchins et al., 2008]).

In summary, Kevin appears to possess relatively strong language abilities, but his performance in the areas of social skills, social communication, and social cognition is weak, as would be expected for a child with a diagnosis of ASD.

Family and Community Context   With regard to the family and community context, Kevin lives with his birth mother, his stepfather, and his two teenage stepsisters. His mother completed college and has a job as a teacher. The stepfather works in construction, and the family lives in a rural area. A family genogram (see Goldrick & Gerson, 1985; Prelock et al., 2003; Prelock et al., 1999) is presented in Figure 13.1, noting Kevin's immediate family with whom he has lived since the age of 2. Kevin knew his birth father, with whom he had lived for the first few years of his life; however, he has had very little contact with him since the time clinicians connected with the family.

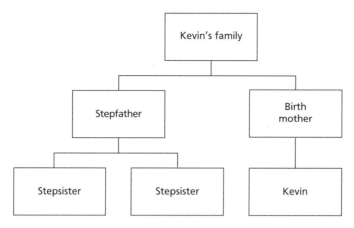

Figure 13.1. Kevin's genogram.

Kevin attends a public elementary school and is in an inclusive classroom with a one-to-one paraeducator to provide academic and behavioral support in the classroom. In addition, he receives pull-out tutoring to support his reading and math skills. He has received speech and language therapy since he was 2 years of age and is currently seeing a speech-language pathologist (SLP) at least once a week with a focus on developing his social thinking skills. In addition, a behavioral interventionist provides consultation on a weekly basis to the educational team, and an occupational therapist (OT) provides monthly consultation. Kevin continues to have developmental follow-up from the local health department that provided the initial diagnosis and ongoing assessment from a developmental pediatrician and a neuropsychologist. Figure 13.2 is an ecomap (see Goldrick & Gerson, 1985; Goodluck, 1990; Prelock et al., 1999; Prelock et al., 2003), which displays professional and personal supports for Kevin and his family; solid lines denote strong relationships, arrows denote direction of energy flow, and dotted lines denote tenuous relationships. Strong relationships and energy flow existed between the school and family and the SLP. Health care professionals at the state's department of health addressed many of the family's diagnostic questions related to Kevin's ASD diagnosis as well as his struggles with inattention and learning. Maintaining friendships has become increasingly difficult because Kevin's pinching, bumping, and touching those around him proved disturbing to his peers and their families. OT consultation is just developing, and goals have not yet been clearly defined.

Broader Profile   Kevin does not have associated medical problems other than his comorbid diagnosis of ASD and ADHD. He is highly active and has difficulty focusing in the classroom, especially if something interesting is occurring in which he wants to participate. Kevin attends to the flickering lights in the classroom and is overly aware of distractions in the hallway and outside the classroom. His self-regulatory ability is challenged when there is too much sensory input on any given day and particularly for those days when he has already arrived tired and unhappy about needing to stop what he is doing to get to school. He does experience anxiety with school transitions throughout the day as well as when there is a substitute teacher or an unexpected event is planned for his class.

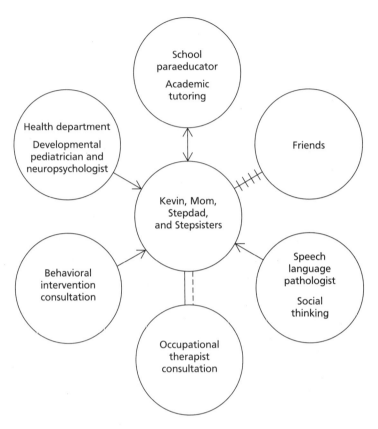

Figure 13.2. Kevin's ecomap.

Summary of Most Significant Needs   Kevin is highly verbal but struggles with
his social communication, theory of mind, attention to academic tasks, and self-
regulation. His self-regulatory challenges, sensory needs, and tendency to respond
impulsivity in unfamiliar situations often lead to challenging behaviors that most
often include pinching but could include touching and bumping into those around
him. These behaviors interfere with his ability to establish and maintain friendships
and lead to calls to his mom at work when an episode results in another student getting hurt.

ASSESSMENTS FOR COMMUNICATION TREATMENT PLANNING

The intervention with Kevin focuses on the challenging behavior of pinching. As
a first step in developing the intervention, clinicians engage in an information-
gathering process that includes child observation and an in-depth interview with
Kevin's mother. They also engage Kevin in a series of Comic Strip Conversations
prior to the development of the Social Stories™ so that they can more fully understand the causes and consequences of the pinching behavior from his perspective.
Through maternal interview, child observation, and their own structured conversations with Kevin, they learn a great deal about the purposes behind and contexts
surrounding his pinching behavior. Kevin pinches family members and children and
adults at school when he is excited, bored, anxious, or angry. As such, pinching

seems to be automatically reinforcing and related to sensory sensitivities and self-dysregulation. Pinching is a daily occurrence, and although Kevin has been told on several occasions that pinching is not acceptable, the pinching persists and even increases in frequency. Kevin is aware of and saddened by the fact that his pinching is often painful to others but reports that he is simply unable to stop.

CLINICAL PROBLEM SOLVING TO IDENTIFY TREATMENT GOALS

The principles that guide intervention include an emphasis on family-centered care (FCC) and evidence-based practice. Employing FCC means that, as researchers and providers, clinicians partner with the family to develop goals relevant to the child, acknowledging the family as the one constant in the child's life (Beatson, 2006; 2008; Beatson & Prelock, 2002; Prelock, 2006). Because an FCC approach to intervention should build on the family's strengths and promote an individual and developmental approach, the clinicians' intervention is designed in collaboration with the family, who are full participants in the assessment and intervention process from completing assessment tools designed to examine Kevin's theory of mind and social communication to helping create the Social Story used in intervention. Further, the family is a critical part of data collection—completing daily diaries on Kevin's recognition of his behavior and its impact on others.

Clinicians also select Social Stories as an intervention because of its evidence for increasing desirable behavior and decreasing undesirable behavior as well as fostering increased awareness of social perspective-taking (Graetz et al., 2009; Kuoch & Mirenda, 2003; Kuttler et al., 1998; Norris & Dattilo, 1999; Ozdemir, 2008; Smith, 2001; Swaggart et al., 1995). To document the fidelity of the intervention, clinicians use fidelity checklists to ensure each story is introduced, read, and discussed in the same manner.

INTERVENTIONS USED TO ACHIEVE MAJOR GOALS

Based on the information gathered, clinicians develop a Social Story to communicate to Kevin what is happening during these pinching events (see Figure 13.3). Their primary goals are to increase his understanding of this challenging behavior and to replace pinching with more adaptive behaviors. Care is taken to ensure that the language level is appropriate and that the words chosen are meaningful and accurate. Clinicians add visual supports in the form of Boardmaker symbols to represent people, places, and behaviors (e.g., pinching), and Kevin's mother and Kevin himself edit the story for vocabulary choices, images, and overall content. Clinicians also develop a plan for Kevin's SLP to share and read the Social Story at school. This helps get various members of the team on the same page while reinforcing key messages across settings and demonstrating to Kevin that different people hold the same social information with regard to the pinching behavior.

OUTCOMES

Data for a 4-week baseline (A) and 6-week Social Story intervention phase (B; total of 11 readings of the Social Story) are presented in Figure 13.4. Subjective data in the form of behavior ratings and maternal daily diaries were collected across AB phases of study. Kevin's mother rated Kevin's ability to resist pinching across settings on a scale of 1 to 10 (higher values indicating more positive outcomes).

What to do when I want to pinch

My name is [pseudonym] Kevin.

I am 9 years old and I go to [name of school].

I know lots of people at home and at school.

Sometimes when I am at home or school or somewhere else, I might pinch someone.

Sometimes I pinch because it makes me feel relaxed, like when I snuggle with my mom. Sometimes I pinch when I get excited, like when I goof around with [Stepsister] and [Dog's name] or wrestle with [Stepfather].

Other times, I pinch when I am bored and tired of waiting.

When I pinch, this can make others think, "I wasn't expecting that," or "I wonder why Kevin pinched me."

They might also think, "Ouch! That hurts!" or "I wish he wouldn't do that."

I have worked hard with [interventionist] to learn about other things I can do when I feel like pinching.

When I want to pinch at home, I can talk to my mom about it.

I can also hug my mom or squeeze her hand.

I might also do a thumb-war or a hand massage to help me stop pinching.

When I want to pinch at school, I can snap my fingers.

I can also tell [school speech language pathologist's name] that I feel like pinching, and she can try to help me to stop.

I am still learning how not to pinch, and that is okay.

It makes my mom happy when I try to find things to do instead of pinching.

Figure 13.3. Kevin's Social Story.

Data from this preexperimental design reveals that maternal subjective ratings of positive behaviors increased from 4.0 during baseline to 8.2 during intervention, including many days with no pinching. Several of the mother's reports support the quantitative data and suggest qualitative shifts in Kevin's understanding of and ability to engage in discussions about pinching. For example, one report reads, "No pinching all day. He began to ask questions about when he first started pinching. We talked about other behaviors that he used to have (biting, scratching, pushing) that he's learned not to do. Kevin agrees that the [social] story is very true to what he does and how he feels." Other comments during this period reveal how Kevin was using strategies provided in the Social Story, including, "He did not pinch me today. Instead, he buried his face into my chest and began to squeeze me. He wanted to

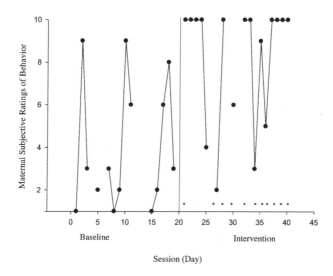

Figure 13.4. Maternal behavior ratings of Kevin's ability to resist pinching across settings on a scale of 1 to 10 (higher values indicating more positive outcomes). Asterisks appearing during the B phase indicate when the Social Story was read.

pinch me during homework this evening, but he snapped his fingers instead (on his own, no prompt!)."

Intervention using Social Stories appears to be immediately effective, and although pinching was not totally eliminated during intervention (see Figure 13.4), Kevin's mother is nevertheless enthusiastic about the therapeutic changes she has seen in Kevin's behavior and understanding. This is exemplified in her comment, "If you would have told me a year ago that we would be able to go a full day without pinching, I would have said that was crazy. We have many days now of no pinching at all!"

This example highlights some important considerations for using Social Stories to address challenging behaviors in ASD. First, it illustrates the use of a family-centered approach for creating meaning-making in socially and culturally relevant ways. Second, it underscores the importance of the information-gathering process and the collection of meaningful and accurate information. Third, it illustrates the importance of adopting an attitude of genuine respect for the individual, one that recognizes the unique perspective of the individual and uses this as a framework to developing a personalized treatment plan. Finally, Kevin's story exemplifies the power of communication and social learning for facilitating introspection and analysis to support more optimal outcomes. Indeed, this mother's reports support that Social Stories can help children think through a challenging situation so that they may make more adaptive behavioral decisions.

Learning Activities

1. How might you use a Comic Strip Conversation to support Kevin's challenges in regulating his sensory needs while increasing his awareness of how his behavior affects others and influences his ability to make and keep friends?

2. Develop a parent training for parents of children with ASD on how to develop and use Social Stories to support their social communication and social interaction. Consider multimedia approaches such as a video training, examples of Social Stories, fidelity checklists, and data sheets.

3. How might you use telepractice to support parents of children with ASD who live in rural communities or for practical reasons find it difficult to access clinical services and wish to implement Social Stories as an intervention for their child with ASD?

4. Create a single-subject design for assessing the effectiveness of a Social Stories intervention for a child with ASD. Identify the child's social-communication needs in consultation with the family. Establish the outcome measures you will use to assess the child's pre- and postintervention performance on measures of theory of mind and social communication. Determine the role of the parent in the collection of performance data.

5. Develop a plan for implementing Social Stories in an inclusive educational setting for a child with ASD. Consider what providers would be involved in the intervention; determine appropriate targets for the Social Story based on the child's needs and what is known about the available research related to likely targets; create a Social Story with an educational team to facilitate increased social understanding for the identified child; and establish a plan for implementation, data collection, and treatment modifications as needed.

REFERENCES

Beatson, J. E. (2006). Preparing speech-language pathologists as family-centered practitioners in assessment and program planning for children with autism spectrum disorder. *Seminars in Speech and Language, 27*, 1–9.

Beatson, J. E. (2008). Walk a mile in their shoes: Implementing family-centered care in serving children and families affected by autism spectrum disorder. *Topics in Language Disorders, 28*, 307–320.

Beatson, J. E., & Prelock, P. A. (2002). The Vermont Rural Autism Project: Sharing experiences, shifting attitudes. *Focus on Autism & Other Developmental Disabilities, 17*(1), 48–54.

Bishop, D. (2003). *Test for Reception of Grammar: Version 2: TROG-2*. Psychological Corporation.

Brown, L., Sherbenou, R., & Johnsen, S. (2010). *Test of Nonverbal Intelligence–Fourth edition* (TONI-4). PRO-ED.

Constantino, J. (2005). *The Social Responsiveness Scale (SRS)*. Western Psychological Services.

Dunn, L., & Dunn, D. (2007). *PPVT-4: Peabody Picture Vocabulary Test–Fourth edition*. Pearson.

Gilliam, J. (2006). *The Gilliam Autism Rating Scale–Second edition (GARS-2)*. PRO-ED.

Goldrick, M., & Gerson, B. (1985). *Genograms in family assessment*. W.W. Norton.

Goodluck, C., (1990). *Utilization of genograms and ecomaps to assess American Indian families who have a member with a disability: Making visible the invisible*. Northern Arizona University.

Graetz, J. E., Mastropieri, M. A., & Scruggs, T. E. (2009). Decreasing inappropriate behaviors for adolescents with autism spectrum disorders using modified social stories. *Education and Training in Developmental Disabilities, 44*(1), 91–104.

Gresham, F., & Elliot, S. (1990). *The Social Skills Rating System (SSRS)*. Pearson.

Hutchins, T. L. (2021). Social Stories. In P. A. Prelock & R. J. McCauley (Eds.), *Treatment of autism spectrum disorder: Evidence-based intervention strategies for communication & social interactions* (2nd ed., pp. 459–490). Paul H. Brookes Publishing Co.

Hutchins, T. L., Prelock, P., & Bonazinga, L. (2012). Psychometric evaluation of the Theory of Mind Inventory (ToMI): A study of typically developing children and children with autism spectrum disorder. *Journal of Autism and Developmental Disorders, 42*, 327–341.

Hutchins, T. L., Prelock, P., & Chace, W. (2008). Test-retest reliability of a Theory of Mind Task Battery for children with autism spectrum disorder. *Focus on Autism and Other Developmental Disabilities, 23*(4), 195–206.

Kuoch, H., & Mirenda, P. (2003). Social story interventions for young children with autism spectrum disorders. *Focus on Autism and Other Developmental Disabilities, 18*(4), 219–227.

Kuttler, S., Myles, B. S., & Carlson, J. K. (1998). The use of social stories to reduce precursors to tantrum behavior in a student with autism. *Focus on Autism and Other Developmental Disabilities, 13*(3), 176–182.

Norris, C., & Dattilo, J. (1999). Evaluating effects of a social story on a young girl with autism. *Focus on Autism and Other Developmental Disabilities, 14*, 180–186.

Ozdemir, S. (2008). The effectiveness of social stories on decreasing disruptive behaviors of children with autism: Three case studies. *Journal of Autism and Developmental Disorders, 38*, 1689–1696.

Prelock, P. A. (2006). *Communication assessment and intervention in autism spectrum disorders*. PRO-ED.

Prelock, P. A., Beatson, J., Bitner, B., Broder, C., & Ducker, A. (2003). Interdisciplinary assessment for young children with Autism Spectrum Disorders. *Language, Speech and Hearing Services in Schools, 34*, 194–202.

Prelock, P. A., Beatson, J., Contompasis, S., & Bishop, K. K. (1999). A model for family-centered interdisciplinary practice. *Topics in Language Disorders, 19*, 36–51.

Smith, C. (2001). Using social stories to enhance behaviour in children with autistic spectrum difficulties. *Educational Psychology in Practice, 17*(4), 337–345.

Swaggart, B. L., Gagnon, E., Bock, S. J., Earles, T. L., Quinn, C., Myles, B. S., & Simpson, R. L. (1995). Using social stories to teach social and behavioral skills to children with autism. *Focus on Autistic Behavior, 10*(1), 1–16.

Williams, K. (2007). *Expressive Vocabulary Test–Second edition*. Pearson.

Learning to Approach and Vocalize With Peers During Playground Time Using Self-Modeling

A Preschooler With Moderate to Severe Autism

Tom Buggey

 Rosa

 Age 4

 Autism Spectrum Disorder

Case 14 engages with the intervention approach and strategies discussed in Chapter 17, Video Modeling for Persons With ASD (Buggey, 2021) in *Treatment of Autism Spectrum Disorder, Second Edition*.

INTRODUCTION

Rosa had a normal birth without noticeable trauma. She began walking at 14 months, at which time her parents, both educators, became concerned because Rosa was not vocalizing and had difficulty attending. Their pediatrician was reluctant to refer Rosa for further assessment because of her young age; however, she was referred to early intervention services when she turned 2. At that time, she was still not using words, her fine motor skills were significantly delayed, and she exhibited social skills that were typical of autism. At 28 months, she received a diagnosis of moderate to

155

severe autism spectrum disorder (ASD) and began to receive speech and occupational therapy services at home. At 3 years, she was enrolled in the Siskin Children's
Institute, a private preschool that served children from birth to age 5 years, with
children with disabilities making up 50% of the enrollment. She was placed in an
inclusive classroom with 3- to 4-year-old children and continued to receive support
services in both speech and occupational therapy that were conducted partially in
and partially out of the classroom. Rosa is now 4 years old and continues to be in
this inclusive classroom.

Areas of Need

Areas of need can be areas of developmental delay obtained from assessments or
identified by caregivers. Rosa has several needs identified by parents and staff that
are reflected in her individualized family service plan (IFSP). The two major concerns are socialization with peers and use of language, both verbal and nonverbal.

Baseline Status

Rosa's abilities prior to the beginning of instruction related to the behaviors being
addressed in treatment.

Communication Profile   Rosa is able to use five basic signs: BATHROOM, HUNGRY,
MORE, HELP, and PLEASE. BATHROOM and MORE are the only signs she uses without prompting. She also recognizes and uses picture symbols as part of her daily schedule. None
of the school staff observe Rosa using words vocally. Rosa's mother reports occasional
use of one-word utterances at home, including "Mom," "Dad," and her sister's name.

Social Profile   Socially, Rosa engages mainly in solitary play. On the playground,
she consistently moves to the periphery, playing with leaves from bushes, where she
will strip them down to the veins or hold blades of grass and stare at them for long
periods. She will move away when anyone comes into her proximity. There is one
other child, Tara, who has a mild physical disability and tremor whom Rosa permits
to get close. Rosa exhibits empathy when others are in distress. Any time she hears
crying on the playground, she stops what she is doing and approaches the individual
with a concerned face.

Family and Community Context   Rosa and her family live in a small southern
city. Access to medical care and early intervention is convenient without long waiting lists. The only exception is that there are no developmental pediatricians (DP) in
residence. However, a DP from a larger urban center visits once per week. This is the
professional who completed an examination and confirmed Rosa's diagnosis of ASD.

The family has one other daughter, Gretchen, who is 7 years old. Rosa's father
is a professor in the music department at the university in town, and her mother is a
former elementary educator who began working as an aide in the same school that
Rosa attends. Both parents are from out of state and have no family connections in
the region. They have a limited network of friends made up of fellow employees at
the university and Rosa's school along with connections made through autism support organizations within the community. The two main support organizations are
the local branch of the Autism Society and a privately funded nonprofit called the
City Autism Center that provides birth to death services for persons with autism

and their families. The Autism Center provides support and services to the family and other community agencies. Figure 14.1 displays the family's community connections, with solid lines to the family representing strong direct connections and dashed lines representing more indirect relationships among community agencies.

Broader Profile (Behavioral, Sensory, Medical Needs)   Rosa has no major medical issues other than seasonal allergies. She is generally healthy and rarely misses school. Rosa is potty-trained but still has occasional accidents, often related to having difficulty communicating her needs. She also has difficulty sleeping. Rosa is not very compliant or responsive to requests to complete tasks, often ignoring them. She will sometimes clean her room, wash her hands, and put toys away without prompting. When pressured, Rosa will move away and engage in self-stimulation (usually rocking). Occasionally, she will have tantrums, especially when pressured to comply with requests.

The only persons who can play with (or near) her at home are her sister, Gretchen, and a neighbor boy who sometimes visits her when she is playing in her yard. Her play is proximal rather than interactive. She will accept objects handed to her, but she quickly discards them. Social-pragmatic rules are a mystery to Rosa when interacting with her sister or the neighbor. She will not directly interact with them, although she will exhibit parallel play. If one goes to the swings, she will follow and also swing. She even tolerates being pushed on the swing. There are no

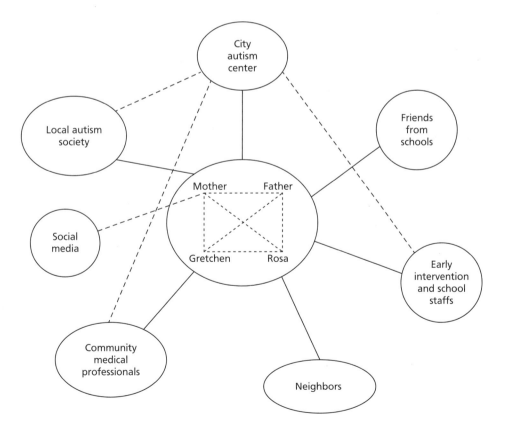

Figure 14.1.   Family and community connections for Rosa.

environmental issues that restrict her movement or ability to participate in tasks at home or within her school.

Auditory assessment is problematic; however, her hearing appears to be normal based on her occasional responses to voices and sounds. She loves listening to music and watching kids' shows on TV. Rosa likes to watch TV with her family and will participate in simple learning games on a video console. She had a magnetic resonance imaging (MRI) brain scan shortly after turning 3 that did not identify any abnormalities of brain or auditory physiology. Nonetheless, Rosa does cover her ears when there are loud sounds like thunder or someone screaming, suggesting possible auditory processing issues.

Major Complicating Issues   Difficulties with communication and engagement with others provide the major challenges for Rosa's participation in family and school activities. She is beginning her second year in an inclusive preschool with a strong emphasis on play and discovery learning. Although she is compliant with requests regarding school routines like lining up and sitting and eating at lunch (using picture symbols to communicate schedule transitions), her first year went by with very limited interactions with others, averted eye gaze, and no verbalizations. Several weeks prior to intervention, clinicians replaced the picture symbols in her visual schedule with actual images of her in the environment. The teachers report improvement in her interest in and use of the picture symbols. For example, clinicians took a photo of her standing next to the toilet for potty time. The typically developing children at the school are comfortable with most children with disabilities who are attending. However, children with autism do present challenges, because their disability is invisible, and peers receive little or no positive feedback when approaching them in play situations. When approaching a peer in distress, Rosa will typically stand about 6 feet in front of the person and look at him or her with concern. When a child is seated on a bench, Rosa will occasionally sit at the far end of the bench with a peer; however, she looks down while seated.

The school has disability awareness training for all children; however, it is difficult for 3 and 4 year olds to understand the silence and perceived rejection that Rosa exhibits. Also, her occasional tantrum or meltdown frightens some children.

Summary of Most Significant Needs

Information and planning are done in a series of individualized education program (IEP) meetings related to adding an amendment to Rosa's plan to allow the use of video self-modeling. Parents and staff at the school, including therapists, a representative of the public schools, and a researcher at the local university housed at the school, participate in determining Rosa's most significant needs and specific behaviors to target. They determine that social play, including initiations and verbalization, are critical needs.

ASSESSMENTS FOR COMMUNICATION TREATMENT PLANNING

Formal assessment of Rosa's speech, hearing, and language development is difficult because of her overall language delay and unwillingness to cooperate. Much of her present level of functioning was derived from direct observation and reports from parents, teachers, and therapists.

Rosa experiences difficulty with articulation and fluency. Her parents and teachers report that Rosa has an unusually low, deep voice that is described as gravelly. She uses several words at home, including "Mommy," "Gettin" (for Gretchen), and "dog." Teachers and therapists in her first year of school do not hear her use any words.

The only formal measure that Rosa participates in is the Peabody Picture Vocabulary Test–Revised (PPVT-R; Dunn, 1981), although she stops cooperating after her first error. A true score is not obtained, but her performance to that point indicates a moderate delay in receptive vocabulary. Parents and staff corroborate that her receptive skills are more advanced than expressive skills, although both are delayed.

As described previously, MRI results indicate normal physiology in the ear. Direct observation of her reactions to sounds show that she is not deaf, but a valid measure of acuity is not available. In addition, Rosa had no observable problems with swallowing.

Aside from the PPVT-R results, the only other assessments are parent and teacher reports using the Childhood Autism Rating Scales (CARS-2, Schopler & Van Bourgondien, 2010). The scores obtained show that her parents rated Rosa slightly higher across the range of areas measured, but both are in line with moderate to severe autism with an overall score of 38 out of 60, with 38 being the lowest score denoting severe autism. Areas with the lowest scores were Emotional Response/Emotional Expression and Regulation of Emotions, Verbal Communication, and Relating to People.

In addition to areas of need revealed by the CARS-2, Rosa exhibits averted eye gaze, moves away when approached by peers or adults, and positions herself away from others on the playground. She communicates only with the teacher and classroom aide, almost entirely through the use signs, gestures, or picture symbols.

Rosa's speech-language pathologist (SLP) and parents agree to focus on signing and picture symbols as the first steps in improving communication. The SLP works together with the parents in assessing needs, determining goals and objectives, implementing interventions, and evaluating progress.

CLINICAL PROBLEM SOLVING TO IDENTIFY TREATMENT GOALS

Rosa's preschool uses Routines-Based Interviews (McWilliam, 2010) completed by school personnel in conjunction with the parents to determine needs of the family and child. The school prides itself in being family centered and uses routines-based early intervention for children from birth through age 5. Interdisciplinary team meetings are held every 6 months, although this is not typically required for children with special needs beyond age 3. All members of the interdisciplinary team provide input into evaluation, goals development, intervention implementation, and outcome assessment.

Rosa is in a supportive environment for implementation of her treatment plan. The home is rich in toys and books. The family is very motivated, and Gretchen provides a source for peer interaction. Likewise, the school offers center-based play areas with ample materials and an almost 50:50 ratio of children with and without disabilities. The school is also staffed with a nurse and physical and occupational therapists. The classroom has a lead teacher, two aides, and a program utilizing senior-citizen volunteers. Complicating situations relate to Rosa's autism behaviors.

INTERVENTIONS USED TO ACHIEVE MAJOR GOALS

Video self-modeling (VSM; refer to the section on VSM in Chapter 17 of the accompanying text) is used with Rosa because of her slow progress with traditional methods being used in the classroom and therapies. Rosa's parents are interested in trying something new.

Overall Plans for Support

In school, one intervention that is successful is initiation of a buddy system, wherein all children have a partner with whom they hold hands during transitions out of the classroom to another activity and location. Rosa complies with this system. Rosa's mother knows of the research being conducted at the school regarding VSM with children with ASD and approaches the researcher about including Rosa in the research. Research on VSM had been carried out only with children with ASD who were 5 years old and older prior to this request (e.g., Buggey, 2005; Wert & Neisworth, 2003), although Buggey (1995) used VSM to teach 4 year olds with language delays new morpheme use. Two other children on the autism spectrum who are Rosa's age are also recruited for the study.

Communication- or Social-Interaction–Related Intervention(s)—VSM

VSM (refer to the VSM section in Chapter 17 of the accompanying text) requires a video of the child demonstrating desired behaviors in a process called feed-forward (Dowrick, 1983). Feed-forward allows viewers to see themselves engaged in advanced, appropriate behaviors. For example, mean length of utterance (MLU) can be expanded by allowing a child to watch him- or herself talking in longer sentences that are repeated after a therapist's prompting. The video will have the scenes of the prompting removed, showing only the child using longer utterances. Because Rosa will not comply with requests or cooperate in the making of the video, researchers have to improvise a movie to make it appear that she is interacting with peers. The plan is to take videos on the playground and choose clips that approximate the desired behaviors. Also, Rosa is given additional play time on the playground with handpicked peers who are asked to interact with her. On another day, only Rosa and a classmate, Tara, are taken out to the playground to play. It is during playtime with Tara that the researchers hear Rosa call Tara by her name.

    The researcher and a graduate assistant observe Rosa's behavior on the playground and then begin collecting baseline data (refer to the section Assessment for Treatment Planning and Progress Monitoring in Chapter 17 of the accompanying text) regarding social initiation, which is defined as moving near a peer to engage in activity, touching a peer, and vocalizing to a peer appropriately (getting their attention rather than screaming). Time is allowed between baseline and the viewing of the video to ensure that the filming has not caused changes in her behavior. Clips from the video footage are chosen on the basis of relevance to the desired outcomes. When she is on the playground with the two peers, the peers are asked to provide Rosa with tools while playing in the sand. Occasionally, she will take the tools and the peer will stay in her proximity, creating the appearance of parallel play. The clip with Rosa vocalizing to Tara is featured along with more footage of Tara trying to keep up with Rosa, making it appear that they are playing together. In one short clip, Tara goes down a slide, followed by Rosa. Tara is waiting at the bottom with arms outstretched, and she said "Rosa, hug." Rosa walks to her with arms outstretched but veers away at the last second. There is another clip where her buddy is asked to step in to push Rosa on the swing.

The video is edited using a Mac laptop and the editor iMovie, which is provided free in every Mac computer. MovieMaker is likewise available on most PC platforms. These programs are very user friendly, making them ideal for parents and professionals. The completed video begins with a picture of Rosa holding hands with her buddy as they move to the playground. A title appears with narration stating, "This is Rosa's video! Let's watch Rosa playing with her friends." The title is included just to make it appear more TV-like. Then the carefully edited clips are added along with a soundtrack of soft music to cover up background noise and prompts from adults. The actual sound from the video is left in when Rosa is laughing on the swing while being pushed and when she says Tara's name. The closing is a still frame of the almost-hug with Tara and a voice overlay of "Nice job playing with your friends, Rosa!" followed by children cheering. Rosa views her video nine times over 5 days. She is taught the sign for MOVIE and requests to watch it four times. Thereafter, the video is withdrawn.

OUTCOMES

The results of the videos are presented in Figures 14.2 and 14.3. The first solid black set of points indicates Rosa's baseline performance. The second light gray set of points indicates observations periods that included or followed VSM viewing, and the final gray set is Rosa's maintenance data without the video. All interactions during baseline were her approaching individuals who she thought had taken something she was playing with. During and following viewing of her movie, the interactions change considerably in quality. Most notably, Rosa's initiations result in prolonged engagement and include appropriate verbalizations while playing. Similar results are observed by teachers in the classroom and by parents in the home.

The emergence of language on the playground is a shock to all, given that there was only one word ("Tara") and laughing in her intervention video. She uses the names of classroom peers and speaks mostly in one-, two-, and three-word utterances. Thus, all goals are achieved. There are still days when Rosa seeks isolation on the playground and does not interact, but these are rare and seem to be related to external factors.

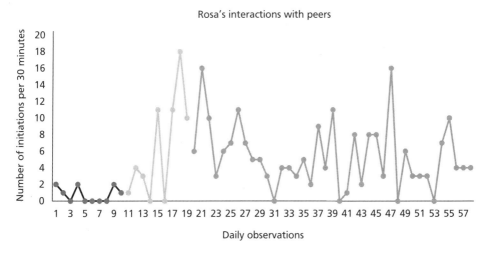

Figure 14.2.   Rosa's number of initiations to peers.

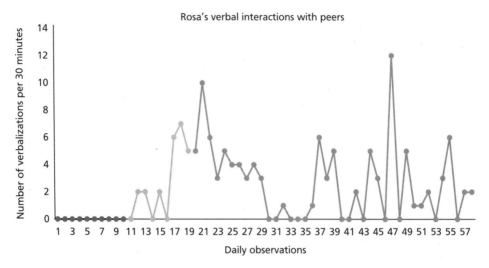

Figure 14.3. Rosa's number of verbal initiations and responses to peers.

For example, during the period of observation from day 29 to day 35, Rosa experiences significant spring allergies and is very subdued. Maintenance observations are carried out for almost the entire spring semester of school, and although there is variation, she still plays and talks to peers. It should be noted that the data represent only initiations or positive responses to initiations by others (thus, her engagement time is not shown) and that the playground time was 30 minutes.

The researchers never asked why VSM seemed to be so effective. They were interested only in behavior change. However, it would seem that the videos did provide a feed-forward effect in that Rosa could see herself as she could be. Watching the video may have allayed her anxiety or fear of social interactions, or it may have provided a sort of visual template for appropriate interactions. This could explain why generalized effects of VSM are seen in many studies (e.g., Catania et al., 2013; Decker & Buggey, 2014; Jones et al., 2013). For example, Decker and Buggey allowed middle school students to view themselves reading fluently. Their reading fluency improved, and teachers also reported positive changes in hygiene, friendliness, willingness to read orally, and overall attitude.

Rosa's teachers and therapists are thrilled with the results and note that her peers no longer are put off by Rosa's behaviors and are initiating much more frequently. Toward the end of the year, Rosa's mother approaches the researcher and jokingly asks if they can do another video of her "not talking to everyone in the grocery store."

Learning Activities

1. Propose alternative measures that might have been used in Rosa's early evaluation that may have provided more insight into her condition and prognosis.

2. Use your knowledge of language development to demonstrate how morpheme use, MLU, pragmatics, or another language skill could be taught in sequence using VSM.

3. Discuss how VSM might be implemented by parents under the guidance of an SLP.

4. Consider ethical problems raised in the use of videos and how the ASHA Code of Ethics or Roles and Responsibilities documents might prove helpful to resolving them.

5. Reflect on the solutions identified in the particular case and whether those same solutions might work for individuals of different developmental levels, diagnoses, and/or cultural backgrounds.

REFERENCES

Buggey, T. (1995). An examination of the effectiveness of videotaped self-modeling in teaching specific linguistic structures to preschoolers. *Topics in Early Childhood Special Education, 15*, 434–458.

Buggey, T. (2005). Applications of video self-modeling with children with autism in a small private school. *Focus on Autism and Other Developmental Disabilities, 20*, 180–204.

Buggey, T. (2021). Video modeling for persons with ASD. In P. A. Prelock & R. J. McCauley (Eds.), *Treatment of autism spectrum disorder: Evidence-based intervention strategies for communication & social interactions* (2nd ed., pp. 491–522). Paul H. Brookes Publishing Co.

Catania, C. N., Almeida, D., Liu-Constant, Reed, F. D. D. (2013). Video modeling to train staff to implement discrete-trial instruction. *Journal of Applied Behavior Analysis, 42*, 387–392.

Decker, M. M., & Buggey, T. (2014). Using video self-and peer modeling to facilitate reading fluency in children with learning disabilities. *Journal of Learning Disabilities, 47*(2), 167–177.

Dowrick, P. W. (1983). Self-modeling. In P. W. Dowrick & J. Biggs (Eds.), *Using video: Psychological and social applications* (pp. 105–124). Wiley.

Dunn, L. M. (1981). *Peabody Picture Vocabulary Test–Revised (PPVT-R)*. American Guidance Service.

Jones, J., Lerman, D. C., & Dechago, S. (2014). Assessing stimulus control and promoting generalization via video modeling when teaching social responses to children with autism. *Journal of Applied Behavior Analysis, 47*(1), 37–50.

McWilliam, R. (2010). *Routines-based early intervention: Supporting young children and their families*. Paul H. Brookes Publishing Co.

Schopler, E., & Van Bourgondien, M. E. (2010). *The Childhood Autism Rating Scale–Second edition* (CARS™-2). Western Psychological Services.

Wert, B. W., & Neisworth, J. T. (2003). Effects of video self-modeling on spontaneous requesting in children with autism. *Journal of Positive Behavior Interventions, 5*, 300–305.

Index

Tables and figures are indicated by *t* and *f* respectively.

Notes